Legally Yours

PRAISE FOR *LEGALLY YOURS*

'To know your rights—to avoid legal trouble, to protect yourself against harassment, to negotiate your property rights as a woman—is to empower yourself. This book will help you do that and live a stress-free legal life.'

**—Indira Jaising, senior advocate,
Supreme Court of India**

'*Legally Yours* is a timely resource that raises awareness on women's legal rights in India. Using real-world examples, it simplifies complex legal concepts on workplace rights, property laws and family matters, empowering readers from diverse backgrounds to navigate the legal landscape with confidence and better understand frameworks affecting women's lives.'

**—Susan Jane Ferguson, Country Representative,
UN Women India**

'What I love most about this book is how inclusive it is. Whether you're a teenager dealing with cyberbullying or a woman in her sixties looking to understand inheritance laws, there's something for everyone. It's like a handbook you didn't know you needed—but once you've read it, you won't be able to live without it.'

—Navya Naveli Nanda, entrepreneur

'This book is like having a legal best friend who gives you clarity, confidence and the knowledge to make empowered decisions.'
—**Masoom Minawala, entrepreneur and content creator**

'A valuable resource for women to empower themselves. Legal nuances have been captured in simple and accessible language.'
—**Saurabh Kirpal, senior advocate, Supreme Court of India**

'A must-read! From workplace rights to personal relationships and legal remedies, it's a comprehensive toolkit for today's woman to own her voice and her rights.'
—**Malini Agarwal, entrepreneur and digital influencer**

'Manasi is one of the rare legal minds in this country whose vast and thoughtful work around women's rights is straightforward, accessible and valuable. Where complicated laws leave you with several questions, Manasi's book provides simple answers.'
—**Nikhil Taneja, co-founder and chief, Yuvaa**

'*Legally Yours* is a must-read. Manasi's clear explanations make understanding legal rights easy and accessible for women of all ages.'
—**Ramya Krishna, actor**

Legally Yours

Every Woman's Guide to Her Legal Rights

Manasi Chaudhari

HARPER
NON-FICTION

First published in India by Harper Non-Fiction 2025
An imprint of HarperCollins *Publishers* India
HarperCollins *Publishers* India, Cyber City, Building 10-A, Gurugram,
Haryana-122002, India
www.harpercollins.co.in

2 4 6 8 10 9 7 5 3 1

Copyright © Manasi Chaudhari, 2025

P-ISBN: 978-93-6569-790-2
E-ISBN: 978-93-6569-786-5

The views and opinions expressed in this book are the author's own and
the facts are as reported by her, and the publishers are not in any way
liable for the same.

Manasi Chaudhari asserts the moral right
to be identified as the author of this work.

All rights reserved. No part of this publication may be reproduced,
stored in a retrieval system, or transmitted, in any form or by any means,
electronic, mechanical, photocopying, recording or otherwise,
without the prior permission of the publishers.

Without limiting the exclusive rights of any author, contributor or
the publisher of this publication, any unauthorized use of this publication
to train generative artificial intelligence (AI) technologies is expressly
prohibited. HarperCollins also exercise their rights under Article 4(3) of
the Digital Single Market Directive 2019/790 and expressly reserve this
publication from the text and data-mining exception.

Typeset in 11/15 Adobe Caslon Pro at
HarperCollins *Publishers* India

Printed and bound at
Thomson Press (India) Ltd

This book is produced from independently certified FSC® paper
to ensure responsible forest management.

HarperCollins *Publishers*, Macken House, 39/40 Mayor Street Upper,
Dublin 1, D01 C9W8, Ireland

To my parents, partner and puppy

The detailed notes pertaining to this book are available on the *HarperCollins Publishers* India website. Scan this QR code to access the same.

Contents

A Special Note by Navya Naveli Nanda	xiii
Foreword by Mrunalini Deshmukh	xv
Introduction	xvii

1. **Never Asked for It: The Legal Guide to Sexual Harassment** — 1
   - What Counts as Sexual Harassment? — 2
   - Eve-teasing — 10
   - Molestation — 13
   - Stalking — 19
   - Flashing — 24
   - Rape — 31

2. **Cyberbullying: The Unseen Threat** — 39
   - Who Are Trolls? — 41
   - Voyeurism — 44

Sextortion	47
Cyberflashing	53
Identity Theft	58
Death and Rape Threats	62

3. Work, Work, Work: Your Rights in the Workplace — 68

What Counts as the Workplace?	70
The POSH Act	73
Equal Pay for Equal Work	94
Maternity Benefits at Work	96

4. Behind Closed Doors: Domestic Violence — 106

What Is Domestic Violence?	107
Action to Take against Domestic Violence	120

5. All about Marriage: How to Safeguard Yourself — 131

Marriage Law and Religion	132
How Do I Register My Marriage?	142
Prenuptial Agreements	156
Forced Marriage	160
Marrying an NRI or Foreigner	165
Dowry	173

Contents

6. Divorce: The Exit Option — 178
- Contested Divorce — 181
- Mutual Consent Divorce — 187
- Alimony and Maintenance — 201
- Custody and Visitation — 205
- Divorce, Separation and Annulment — 214
- Remarriage — 219

7. Live-in Relationships: To Tie the Knot or Not? — 223
- Are Live-in Relationships Legal? — 225
- Rights in a Live-in Relationship — 229

8. Money Matters: Better Plan Than Be Sorry — 238
- Inheritance — 241
- Stridhan — 243
- Succession Planning — 258
- Wills — 266
- Trust Funds — 271
- Gifts — 275

9. Reproductive Rights: Your Body, Your Choice — 278
- Abortion — 279
- Adoption — 289
- Surrogacy — 303

10. Legal Remedies: Knocking on the Doors of Justice — 317

    Police Complaints — 319
    Filing a Court Case — 329
    Rights against Arrest — 338
    Getting Bail — 341

Conclusion — 345
Quiz Time! — 347
Acknowledgements — 351
Notes — 353

A Special Note

Legally Yours is not just a book—it's a game-changer. It takes the complexities of the law and translates them into something we can all understand and use. With real-life cases and easy references, it makes serious, often daunting topics accessible and even interesting. This is not a book that lectures; it speaks to you like a friend who's got your back.

I've known Manasi for a while now and I can say this with confidence: her passion for empowering women and her gift for making legal rights easy to understand are truly inspiring. As the founder of Pink Legal, a platform that went viral for empowering women with knowledge about their rights, Manasi has been a relentless advocate for change. She's not just someone who knows the law—she understands how it affects our everyday lives and cares deeply about helping women navigate it.

What I love most about this book is how inclusive it is. Whether you're a teenager dealing with cyberbullying or a woman in her sixties looking to understand inheritance laws, there's something for everyone. It's like a handbook you didn't know you needed—but once you've read it, you won't be able to live without it.

Reading *Legally Yours* feels like having a conversation with someone who genuinely wants to help. It's empowering, eye-opening and, above all, actionable. You're not just learning about your rights—you're learning how to stand up for them.

So, here's my advice: read this book. Share it with your friends, sisters, mothers and daughters. Let it be the start of something bigger—a world where every woman knows her worth and her rights, and isn't afraid to demand both.

This book has the power to change lives. And I couldn't be prouder to introduce it to you.

Mumbai   **Navya Naveli Nanda**
February 2025

Foreword

As a family lawyer with decades of experience, I've heard countless stories of women who feel trapped, unaware of their rights or how to assert them. Whether it's property battles, personal safety or navigating the minefield of marital laws, several women suffer due to a lack of legal knowledge.

Legally Yours: Every Woman's Guide to Her Legal Rights is a significant contribution to the landscape of legal literature in India. Written by Manasi Chaudhari, an award-winning lawyer and the brain behind Pink Legal—an innovative platform for women's rights—this book serves as a comprehensive legal toolkit.

As a family advocate, I believe that knowledge is power. Only when a woman understands her rights can she make informed decisions that shape her future. This book equips women with the tools they need to protect themselves, safeguard their futures and assert their rights.

Manasi has a knack for demystifying the law. She doesn't overwhelm readers with legal jargon—instead, she explains it in accessible language, using relatable examples and actionable steps that make complex concepts easy to digest. Whether you're battling harassment, seeking clarity on inheritance, or navigating the delicate waters of marriage and divorce, this book is a go-to guide.

Manasi has poured her heart and expertise into creating a resource that's practical, insightful and, most importantly, transformative. India is at a turning point. Women are no longer confined to the margins; they're driving change in every sector. Today, women form a significant portion of the workforce—challenging norms, breaking barriers and forging their own paths. But empowerment doesn't end at the office—it must extend into every facet of life, especially when it comes to legal rights. *Legally Yours* bridges this critical gap, ensuring that women can stand confidently, make informed choices and safeguard their futures. I have no doubt that it will become a trusted companion for women across India.

Mumbai   **Mrunalini Deshmukh**
January 2025

Introduction

Let's Simplify Your Legal Rights

Why should you read this book? Well, let me start by saying that I am not going to answer this question just yet. In fact, you will be able to answer it yourself in less than a minute!

So, are you ready to take on this challenge?

Let us start with a quiz. Consider these scenarios. Will you know what to do if:

1. You are in a public place and someone catcalls you?
2. Your ex-boyfriend (or partner) threatens to leak your private photos?
3. Someone stalks you?
4. Your friend is going through a nasty divorce and her husband refuses to pay alimony?
5. Your friend wants to protect her children's rights in a divorce?
6. Your colleague sexually harasses you at work?
7. Someone you know is being abused in a live-in relationship?

Introduction

8. Your cousin is being forced into marriage by her parents?
9. You want to file a police complaint against someone?
10. You want to inherit property from your family?
11. Your office is planning to fire a colleague who just had a baby?
12. You need to file a court case and appoint a lawyer?
13. Someone you know wants to opt for an abortion?

If you don't know the answers to most (or any) of these questions, then this book is a *must* for you!

Let me tell you something personal. One night around 10 p.m., I was driving home from work in my hometown Hyderabad when I got into a small accident with another car. Our bumpers 'bumped' at a signal. Out came two men, shouting and screaming. They blocked my car and tried to open the door. I was alone; no one came to help. When I tried to drive away, they broke my side-view mirrors.

I was furious, but I was more worried for my safety. I didn't know what to do. The people around did not intervene. Luckily, I had the presence of mind to quickly pull out my phone and take a picture of the other car's number plate. As a lawyer, I knew that this picture could serve as evidence.

The next day, I decided to file a police complaint against the two men. I wanted to ensure that they learnt the lesson that they could not simply get away with abusive behaviour without consequences.

Going to a police station for the first time was intimidating. I was not sure if the police would take my complaint seriously.

I could recall scenes from movies where the police are not friendly. That day, I experienced first-hand how scary it is for women to stand up for themselves in India, especially if they don't know the law.

The only thing that gave me the strength to walk into that police station by myself was the fact that I knew my legal rights. This experience pushed me to launch Pink Legal, India's first digital platform that explains to women their rights in a simplified manner. And here I am, four years after starting Pink Legal, writing a book that will hopefully empower every woman in India to stand up for herself.

Think of this book as a lawyer friend you always wanted but never had. Someone whom you can ask all your random 'legal' questions, no matter how silly they sound. Or someone who will patiently explain your rights to you, of course, minus the legal jargon!

Now, you may very well say that I am not fighting a legal case. Why do I need to know my rights?

Consider this. Have you taken out a health insurance policy? (If you haven't, you should!) Why does one take a health insurance policy? Not because they are unwell or anticipating falling sick in the next one year. We do it as a protective measure, to be prepared in case something goes wrong in the future.

Knowing your legal rights is the same. You shouldn't wait for something to go wrong and then frantically google half-baked information or run to the nearest lawyer's office. Instead, you should be able to sit back and understand your rights in that situation, and what you should do next. In short, be cool about your rights!

Remember, awareness is cool. Awareness is empowering.

Is This Book for YOU?

Yes, yes and yes! Whether you are sixteen or sixty years old, or having a mid-life crisis; and whether you come from a city that never sleeps or from heartland India, this friend will give you true legal enlightenment! Also, no matter which faith you follow—whether you are a Hindu, Muslim, Christian or non-religious person—this book has you covered.

Is this friend only for women? Absolutely not! Although it is about women's rights, it is for everyone, irrespective of gender. After all, everyone needs a lawyer best friend to help make sense of their rights and to empower others around them.

This book is an A-to-Z guide about women's legal rights in India. Be it cyberbullying, trouble at the workplace, domestic violence, marriage and divorce, understanding your inheritance rights, navigating a live-in relationship, sexual harassment or dealing with the police and courtrooms—THERE IS SOMETHING FOR EVERYONE!

How to Navigate This Book?

The language used in this book is extremely simple, devoid of intimidating jargon, to make you feel like it is a friend talking to you. There are also plenty of chai–coffee breaks where you can take fun quizzes, learn through examples from movies and get a glimpse into real-life cases.

I have divided this book in a way that you can pick whichever topic you want, independent of the others, and start with that. Once you are done with your subject of choice, feel free to browse through the others, so that you have a comprehensive understanding of all your rights.

In Part I, you can read about all your legal rights in different spheres of life. In Part II, you will understand how to file a police complaint, the court processes, etc.

Keep the index handy so that you can switch between sections, if you need to, to understand a topic in further depth. For example, while reading the Domestic Violence chapter you may want to flip to the Police Complaint section in Chapter 10 to understand how to take action.

So, get your chai or coffee ready (What is your preference? I am usually a coffee person, but rainy days call for garam masala chai!), pick a nice spot and let us have some fun (and get empowered in the process). Pinky promise, you will not be able to put this book down without feeling like you have learned something new. Here's to a more confident and self-assured you!

Interesting Facts about the Indian Legal Landscape

What is our legal system like? Is it anything like what they show in the movies? How long does it take to fight a court case? More importantly, is going to court always the best solution?

As someone who has had experience in the Supreme Court, high courts and lower courts, I can tell you that our legal system is extremely complex. If I were to draw an analogy, I would compare it to the human body. We know how elaborate the body is, with its numerous organs, systems, glands, muscles, bones, nerves, etc. No wonder medicine is one of the toughest subjects to master. The legal system is similar. It takes lawyers years of training and experience to be completely well-versed with all the laws and procedures. But we will try to understand the important laws through this book, in a quick and fun way.

Here are three interesting facts about the Indian legal system:

1. India follows what is called the 'common law system'.

This means that in addition to legal statutes, judgments given in courts (high courts and Supreme Court) are also considered law. For example, the Supreme Court passed a landmark judgment in 2018 decriminalizing homosexuality in India. This judgment led to the decriminalization of homosexuality in India.

A Supreme Court judgment is applicable to the entire country. A high court judgment, however, is applicable only to the state concerned. Therefore, if the Madhya Pradesh High Court gives a ruling, it will be considered a law only in Madhya Pradesh, not in Andhra Pradesh! The moment you cross a state's boundary, the laws may change. Sounds bizarre? Well, this is how the system functions.

The other type of legal system is the civil law system, which only considers codified statutes (and not judgments) as law. The common law system is followed by most former British colonies, or what are known as Commonwealth countries, such as Canada, Australia, Hong Kong, Ireland, the UK, etc. The civil law system is mainly followed by European countries (such as France, Germany, Spain and others), their former colonies and East Asian countries like China and Japan.

2. India has more laws than you can count in a lifetime!

As of March 2024, India had close to **900 central laws** alone![1] Apart from central laws, each state has its own set of laws. We have twenty-eight states, so do the math if you want! Add to this the numerous judgments that courts pass on a daily basis, which also have the same value as codified laws (as explained above). I would imagine the Indian laws as a spider web, with numerous lines, all separate yet interconnected, coming together to form a special pattern.

3. Many laws in India still reek of a colonial hangover.

Some of our laws are so ancient that they have been around since the 1800s, even before our great-great-great-grandparents were born! While we have abolished a few of them, many are still around. For example, the main criminal code of the country, the Indian Penal Code (IPC), was passed by the British in 1860. This statute has now been renamed as the Bharatiya Nyaya Sanhita (BNS), 2023, with a few changes. However, majority of it is still the same. In the era of electric cars (and research on flying cars), think of the Indian legal system as a vintage Ambassador car being passed down for generations with fresh coats of paint!

POINTS TO REMEMBER

1. Personal laws, i.e. laws for marriage, divorce, adoption of children and inheritance of property, are based on religion and may vary based on your religion.
2. Sexual harassment laws are not gender-neutral, at least not yet. They are drafted in a way that the victim is female and the perpetrator is male.
3. In all real-life examples in the book, the names of the persons have been changed. Fictional names are used to protect identities.
4. The main criminal code of the country, which lays down a list of crimes and their description is the Bharatiya Nyaya Sanhita, 2023 (formerly known as the Indian Penal Code). In addition to this, you also have criminal penalties in other statutes. For example, the Information Technology Act of 2000 makes hacking a crime.
5. Civil laws are spread across hundreds of different laws, which are specific to the topic they deal with. For example, the Protection of Women from Domestic Violence Act, 2005, seeks to protect women from domestic violence; the Dowry Prohibition Act of 1961 looks to ban giving and receiving of dowry.

1
Never Asked for It: The Legal Guide to Sexual Harassment

In this chapter, we will bust common myths about sexual harassment, understand the law around molestation, stalking, eve-teasing, etc., and outline the first steps you must take against any kind of sexual harassment.

What Counts as Sexual Harassment?

What is sexual harassment? What action can I take? Which law protects me? I am sure your mind must be teeming with a hoard of questions! Before we get into our legal rights, let us do a quick exercise to understand *why* we need to know the law.

Hold up the fingers of your hands. As you read each of the statements below, put a finger down if you, or a woman you know, has experienced that situation.

Put a finger down if:
1. You've ever faced catcalls or been whistled at in public.
2. You've ever felt unsafe walking alone at night.
3. You've ever been touched inappropriately without your consent.
4. You've ever received unwanted sexual comments about your body or appearance.
5. You've ever been made to feel uncomfortable or objectified by someone's gaze.
6. You've ever been pressured or coerced into engaging in sexual activities against your will (even if it was a hug or a touch that was sexual in nature).
7. You've ever been denied opportunities or promotions because of your gender.
8. You've ever felt hesitant to speak up about facing sexual harassment because you fear backlash.

How many fingers did you put down? If you put even five fingers down, you surely understand why you need to know your rights about sexual harassment.

Do this exercise with your friends and family and see how different each gender's experience is. You will notice that women put their fingers down more compared to men. Do it with your mother, grandmother and aunts. See if there is a difference in experiences across generations. If anything, this exercise will help you drive home the importance of women's legal rights and help men build empathy towards the sexual harassment that women around them face.

Is Sexual Harassment Only Physical?

Simply put, sexual harassment refers to any unwelcome behaviour/attention of a sexual nature. While it is a serious issue that needs to be handled with care, we will try to understand our rights concerning it without making it feel heavy.

When we think of sexual harassment, we typically imagine some form of physical harassment. This is a common myth that needs to be busted. The reality is that sexual harassment can be physical, verbal and non-verbal.

Forms of sexual harassment

Physical   Verbal   Non-verbal

Let us unpack each of these one by one.

1. Physical Sexual Harassment

Physical harassment is an act where someone touches you sexually against your will. It is not limited to aggressive or violent acts. It includes subtle actions, unwelcome touches and non-aggressive sexual behaviour like inappropriate gestures or lingering touches.

Note: Physical harassment *need not be aggressive or violent*. Any kind of unwelcome touch (even a tap on the shoulder or a graze against the thigh) amounts to sexual harassment when it is *without your consent*.

Common examples of physical harassment include:

i. Groping: Touching or squeezing body parts like breasts, buttocks, thighs, etc. This usually happens in public transport/crowded places.

ii. Touching anywhere on the body: This includes someone touching your face, lips, holding your hand(s), putting their arm(s) around your waist or shoulder, inside your clothes, or anywhere that makes you uncomfortable.

iii. Inappropriate brushing or rubbing: Making deliberate and unwelcome physical contact in a sexual or intimate manner, such as brushing against someone's body or rubbing up against them. This is common in public transport, where the harasser tries to pass it off as a 'mistake' because of the crowds.

iv. Unwanted advances during physical proximity: Making unwelcome sexual advances, such as grinding, rubbing or pressing against someone's body without their consent, often in crowded spaces.

v. Touching or removing clothing without permission: Touching, adjusting, or attempting to remove a person's clothing without their consent, such as undoing buttons, lifting straps, or pulling at zippers.

>
> **Food for thought**
>
> In the Bollywood movie *Kabir Singh*, the protagonist (Kabir) kisses a girl whom he fancies (Preeti) the very first time they meet, without her consent. Do you think this was an act of physical sexual harassment?

2. Verbal Sexual Harassment

Verbal sexual harassment means sexually inappropriate comments and statements. It includes any kind of sexual harassment through words.

Common examples of verbal sexual harassment include:

i. Objectification and lewd comments: This includes anyone making sexually suggestive remarks or objectifying women based on their appearance or body parts. For example, commenting on a woman's figure, making explicit remarks about her body, or using derogatory language.

ii. Double entendre: This includes the use of double-meaning statements or dialogues that have sexual connotations disguised as humour. These statements or dialogues often rely on innuendos, wordplay, or cleverly veiled references to sexual acts.

iii. Inappropriate propositions: Propositioning or suggesting sexual favours in exchange for professional opportunities, promotions or personal benefits. This can create a hostile and uncomfortable environment for the person being targeted.
iv. Calling someone sexually suggestive names: These include 'item', 'bomb', 'mirchi', 'pataka', 'sexy' and 'maal', among others. It is easy to identify these words when you hear them, especially when you consider the tone in which they are said.
v. Telling adult (sexual) jokes: This includes cracking jokes that make you uncomfortable. What is important is the impact that such a joke has on the listener (for example, making them feel objectified), rather than the intent of the person telling the joke ('I was just joking').
vi. Passing comments about your body: This includes comments about your looks, like 'you have a beautiful body', 'you have great lips', 'you have a sexy butt', 'I like the shape of your body', 'you look sexy', 'your legs are looking sexy', etc.
vii. Singing songs with the intent of teasing/troubling: Examples of this include eve-teasing on the streets, slowing a car down to match your speed while playing suggestive songs, etc.

3. Non-verbal Sexual Harassment

Non-verbal sexual harassment means any kind of harassment through gestures or actions, without involving oral communication or physical contact.

Common examples include:
i. Staring: This includes looking at someone in a way that makes them uncomfortable. How many times have you travelled in public transport and felt uneasy because of someone's stare? Now that you know that this is a form of non-verbal sexual harassment, you don't need to let it go or suffer in silence the next time it happens.
ii. Unwelcome sexual gestures: Examples include perpetrators making unwelcome motions or signs with their hands or through other body movements.
iii. Facial expressions: This includes winking, blowing kisses, licking or smacking the lips, which make the receiver of such attention feel objectified.

All of the above are simply illustrations to help you understand that sexual harassment can take place in any form, not just physical. We will delve into specific types of sexual harassment in the coming sections of the book.

The 3 'A's of Sexual Harassment

1. ANYONE can be a sexual harasser. It is not always a stranger. Often, harassers are people you know, like a colleague or an uncle.
2. Sexual harassment can happen ANYWHERE. It can be in a public space, at the workplace or at home.
3. Sexual harassment can happen ANYHOW. It need not be physical. Even non-physical acts like words, gestures and actions, which have sexual implications, amount to harassment.

What Counts as Consent?

Now that we have understood what comes under the purview of sexual harassment, let us focus on the nuances of consent. What is consent? It is a conscious, unambiguous and affirmative agreement to engage in a sexual activity. Simply put, consent is a yes, a thumbs-up!

As per Section 375 of the Indian Penal Code (IPC), now Section 63 of the Bharatiya Nyaya Sanhita (BNS), consent has been defined as: '... an unequivocal voluntary agreement when the woman, by words, gestures or any form of verbal or non-verbal communication, communicates willingness to participate in the specific sexual act; provided that a woman who does not physically resist to the act of penetration shall not by the reason only of that fact, be regarded as consenting to the sexual activity'.

Phew! That sounds complicated, but let us break it down:
1. An unequivocal voluntary agreement: Consent must be unambiguous (without any room for doubt) and voluntary (out of free will). This means that if you are doubtful, or saying yes out of pressure, it is not consent.
2. By words, gestures, or any form of verbal or non-verbal communication: Consent can be expressed in any form. It can be through words, gestures, actions and body language. For example, if you are physically resisting (without saying the word 'no'), your resistance will be considered as lack of consent.
3. Communicates willingness to participate: Through verbal or non-verbal cues, you should communicate

agreement or willingness to participate in sexual activity.
4. In the *specific* sexual act: Any sexual activity comprises multiple acts. Consent for one part of a sexual activity does not imply consent for any other part. For example, if you agree to a kiss, that does not mean you are okay with your partner touching your private parts. Consent is necessary for each and every step of the sexual act.

This also implies that consent granted on one occasion does not mean a life-long agreement. For example, agreeing to a kiss once does not mean saying yes to kisses at any point in the future.

Note: Colloquially speaking, consent must be enthusiastic. As the word 'enthusiastic' suggests, it means a definitive YES rather than simply an absence of a NO.

Do not mistake the following for consent:
1. Absence of a 'no': Just because you did not say no does not mean you said yes. You could be confused or unsure in the moment.
2. Lack of resistance: If you are in a position where you are not able to resist, be it because of safety concerns, if you feel overwhelmed, or if you are unable to comprehend what is happening, your lack of resistance (also known as 'submission' in law) is not equal to consent.
3. Consent given under the influence of a substance: If you are under the influence of any substance, such as alcohol or drugs, rendering you incapable of truly understanding what is happening, then it is not considered consent.

4. Consent granted out of pressure: If the only reason you agree is because your partner is pressuring you to say yes, then it is not considered consent.

To put it simply, if consent were a feedback form with 'Yes', 'No' and 'Maybe' as options, the only correct answer is YES, which must come from within you, without any shadow of doubt or confusion.

Now you may wonder, what does asking for consent sound like? Consider these options.

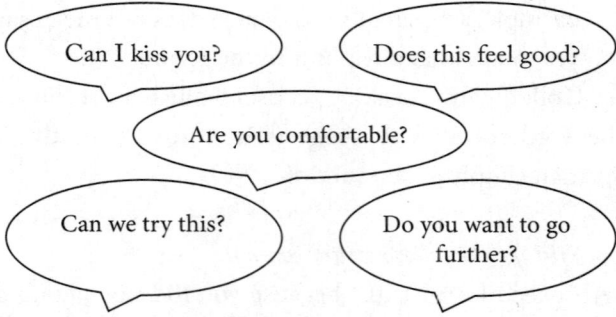

What if Someone Eve-teases Me?

How often have you encountered sexual harassment while strolling down a street? Public spaces—markets, public transportation, streets and parks—are common settings where women endure harassment. While we may lack precise statistics to substantiate this claim, it is reasonable to assert that nearly every woman in India has encountered sexual harassment in a public place at least once in her life.

The ubiquity of day-to-day harassment is evident during routine tasks like commuting to work or college, visiting the local grocery store, or a simple walk in the park. The unwelcome stares, catcalls and inappropriate advances seem to accompany us everywhere. Regardless of whether God is omnipresent or not, sexual harassers certainly appear to be omnipresent!

Dealing with sexual harassment, on a daily basis, can be incredibly frustrating and exhausting. But what if we were to empower ourselves with knowledge about our legal rights and, thereby, efficiently handle such situations? By understanding how to respond appropriately, we can avoid suffering in silence. This section aims to provide you that insight.

Verbal and non-verbal sexual harassment in public places is commonly referred to as eve-teasing. Here are a few examples:

1. Saying obscene or vulgar words
2. Singing obscene songs
3. Doing any obscene act
4. Cat-calling a woman
5. Passing sexual remarks against a woman
6. Whistling suggestively at a woman
7. Making vulgar faces or gestures at a woman

Which Laws Protect You against Eve-teasing?

The good news is that you have not one but three legal provisions under the BNS[1] that can serve as protection against eve-teasing:

1. Section 296: This section pertains to the offense of obscenity in public, including acts, songs or words that are obscene or indecent.

2. Section 75: If a man makes sexually coloured remarks against a woman, it is a punishable offence.
3. Section 79: This section makes saying vulgar words or gestures, intended to outrage the modesty of a woman, punishable.

The above provisions make eve-teasing not just illegal but also criminal. The law is on our side! However, what is not on our side is the poor implementation of such laws. Therefore, even though we have rights on paper, they don't always materialize effectively in real life.

The 3 'C's to Take Action against Eve-teasing

1. Call it out: If you are in a crowded public space, call out the act and the attention of others around you. Often, you will be surprised at the impact this can have. Most sexual harassers operate with the belief that their victims will keep quiet. The moment you draw attention to their actions, it not only embarrasses them but also serves as a reminder in case they try to do something like that again.

   However, always remember to keep your safety as priority. Assess your situation carefully and call out the harasser only if you feel safe. For example, if it is a crowded bus, your daily route to work or college, or if you know that your friends or family are a call away, you are in a better position to draw attention than if you are in a lonely area, in an unfamiliar place, or away from the safety net of friends or family.

2. Collect evidence: Collect whatever evidence you can against the harasser, like audio/video recordings, witnesses and CCTV footage. These will come in handy if you choose to file a police complaint. They will also provide a starting point for the police to investigate.
3. Complaint: You can file a police complaint against the harasser, using the legal provisions explained above. If you see any police officers around, reach out to them immediately as they may be able to take swift action then and there.

What to Expect When You File a Police Complaint against Eve-teasing?

Police response may vary from issuing a warning to the harasser(s), summoning them to the police station or, in more severe cases, detaining the harasser(s) for a few hours. The extent of police action depends on how seriously they take your complaint and the gravity of the sexual harassment.

It can be frustrating if the police refuse to treat your complaint seriously or do not act upon it, but don't lose hope. By confronting the harasser or by gathering evidence, you will have taken the initial step to signal that such acts will no longer be tolerated in silence. This may serve as a deterrent, discouraging the harasser from committing further acts.

What Is Molestation?

Groping or molestation is a form of physical sexual harassment that consists of intentionally touching someone, in a sexual manner, without their consent. Have you ever been in a crowded bus, or a music concert, where a man purposely falls on you, or touches your body, blaming it on the crowd? This is not an 'oops moment'; it is groping.

Although colloquially both terms are used interchangeably, molestation refers to more severe forms of groping. For instance, touching someone's breasts, buttocks or any other private part, usually with force. That is not to say that groping or molestation is always aggressive or violent, but as long as it is non-consensual, it is sexual harassment.

In this chapter, for the sake of convenience, we will use the terms interchangeably.

Who Are These 'Hidden' Sexual Predators?

We always imagine a scenario of molestation to involve a lonely place, a stranger and an aggressive act. However, this is far from the truth. Did you know that research shows that most sexual predators are known to the victims?
Many of them are family members of the victim, which makes it even harder to identify and take action.[2]

#TrueStory (Trigger Warning)

We, at Pink Legal, once came across a disturbing case, where Riya (name changed), a young teenager, was molested by someone she considered a grandfather figure. Let us call this man 'X'. Riya had gone to visit X and

> his wife, who were relatives of her grandparents. When X and Riya were alone in a room, X started putting his hand between her thighs. Initially, Riya thought that X was being affectionate. Soon, she realized that the touch felt wrong. She tried to leave the room, but X caught her hand, pulled her back and started rubbing his body against hers. Riya had to struggle to free herself from his grip. For a man in his seventies, he was certainly strong when it came to molesting a young girl. All this happened in broad daylight, with the whole family (including X's wife) in the house.

The reason I am sharing this story (even though it is disturbing) is because this is not a one-off case. What this young girl went through is, unfortunately, not uncommon. We never know where these predators may be. More often than not, they are a part of our circle. What makes matters worse is that when the molester is a known person, we often give them the benefit of the doubt. In fact, we start questioning and second-guessing ourselves for overthinking. In such scenarios, it becomes more difficult to listen to our gut and identify the sexual harassment.

Which Laws Protect You against Molestation?

There are four sections of the BNS that you can consider in cases of molestation.

1. Section 74: This section makes using physical force against a woman, with the intention to outrage her modesty, a punishable offence.
2. Section 75: This section makes physical contact and advances, involving unwelcome and explicit sexual overtures, by a man against a woman a punishable offence.
3. Section 76: This section comes into play if the molestation also involves taking off or removing any part of the clothing.
4. Section 133: This section makes assault or criminal force illegal in general.

What Action Can You Take against Molestation?

In most cases of molestation or groping, we don't take action because we are clueless about what to do. The biggest fear and question is, 'What is the proof?'

Take Riya's case as an example. When she told her family about what had happened, they felt sorry for her and had an internal discussion, but they did nothing. There was neither a police complaint nor even a reprimand for X's disgusting behaviour.

What do you think the family should have done? At the very least they should have called out X and taken him to task as a family. Next, they should have informed all the family members so that the others could keep their girls safe. Also, they should have ideally filed a police complaint against him.

Sexual Harassment

>
> **Food for thought**
>
> In our society and families, there is often a hushed silence when it comes to protecting the feelings and identity of sexual predators like X. The family members care more about the damage it will cause to X's reputation, than what really matters, like safeguarding their girls from sexual assault. The same silent family members will leave no stone unturned to gossip about the girls in their family, be it the daughters, daughters-in-law or nieces. They will question everything from her choice of clothes to the gender of her friends, forgetting that their idle gossip not only harms the reputation of the girl, but can damage her emotionally.
>
> Unfortunately, as a society, we are more comfortable pointing fingers at a girl's conduct than condemning those who assault her.

What Are the 3 'C's against Molestation/Groping?

1. Call out: As explained in the eve-teasing section, call out the harasser then and there. Calling out is good in cases where the molestation happens in a crowded place (like public transport or a music concert). It will help you gather public support and embarrass the harasser. It can also help you catch the eye of security guards, who can move the harasser away from you. If the molestation happens in a private place, where there is no one around

to call out to, focus on getting out first. Prioritize your safety before you regroup and take action.
2. Confide: Getting groped or molested can be traumatic, not just physically but also emotionally and mentally. If you are dealing with sexual harassment, don't make it harder for yourself by trying to handle it alone. If possible, confide in a trusted friend or family member. Having support can make it easier for you. You can also consider getting professional help, such as seeing a psychologist.
3. Complaint: If you wish to take the legal route, you can file a police complaint. I am not expressly mentioning collection of evidence as a separate point of action, because molestation often happens behind closed doors and without witnesses. This makes it difficult to collect evidence. Don't worry about this though. You can still go ahead and file a complaint; your word is evidence enough.

The book will touch upon the basics of filing a police complaint in a later section.

When Should You File a Complaint?

You should file a complaint as early as possible. If you have any evidence, such as marks on the body, torn clothes, or recordings, you can submit these too. If you don't have evidence, don't worry, it does not mean you shouldn't file a complaint.

A word of caution here. Not all police complaints lead to criminal cases. This can be due to various factors like external influence (if you know what I mean) or lack of evidence. Having said that, it is not always necessary to have a criminal case to get justice or teach your harasser a lesson. Sometimes, just the fact that the accused is called to the police station for questioning is lesson enough. It serves as a strong warning!

What if Someone Is Stalking Me?

Stalking is a form of sexual harassment where a person repeatedly tries to contact or gives unwanted attention to another person, *against their will*. For example, you are going home from college and someone follows you. Stalking can assume a physical form—like following someone—or be evident through other ways of communication, like phone calls, messages, social media, etc.

#TrueStory

One of my friends, Nisha (name changed), was stalked for two years when she was in high school. The stalker would follow her everywhere—school, colony, on Facebook and to after-school tuitions. He even got hold of her number and would call and text her continuously. Nisha was terrified. She didn't know what to do. She was scared for her safety. At the same time, she was afraid to tell her parents because she feared that they would put a stop to all her activities. She would end up paying the price for the stalker's harassment. She continued living with this fear for two years, until one day her brother noticed that she looked visibly shaken. She finally confided in her brother who called up the stalker and threatened to report him to the police. Luckily, after that phone call, the stalker stopped following Nisha around.

Nisha's case is not uncommon. According to statistics, one case of stalking is reported every fifty-five minutes in India.[3] And these are just the reported numbers. It is common knowledge that most cases go unreported, maybe because stalking is not considered a very serious crime, or girls are scared to report it fearing social stigma and being forbidden to step out of their houses.

> #### #ReelToReal
>
> Bollywood movies are known to glorify stalking as romance, creating generations of men who think it is the right way to get the girl of their dreams. For instance, in *Raanjhanaa*, a school-going girl (played by Sonam Kapoor) is stalked by a boy (played by Dhanush) in their hometown. When she refuses to acknowledge him, he slashes his wrists as an 'act of love'.
>
> In 2015, an Indian man was accused of stalking two women in Australia. In a bizarre turn of events, the stalker's lawyer successfully argued that pursuing a woman, hoping she would fall in love with him, was quite normal behaviour for an Indian man given the cultural influence of Bollywood movies![4]

How Do You Recognize Stalking?

Do you see a familiar face everywhere you go? Do you feel like you are being followed? Do you think someone is monitoring your activities? Is someone trying to make contact despite you making your lack of interest clear? If your answer to any of these questions is yes, then you are probably being stalked.

Stalking may include:
1. Persistent following or surveillance of the victim.
2. Unwanted and intrusive communication, such as excessive calls, texts or emails.
3. Sending unsolicited gifts or letters.
4. Showing up at the victim's home, workplace or other frequented locations, without their consent.
5. Spreading rumours or false information about the victim.
6. Monitoring the victim's online activities or hacking into their personal accounts.
7. Threatening (verbal, written or implied) the victim or their loved ones.

If you find yourself confused, always listen to your gut. We, as women, are conditioned to second-guess ourselves and give people the benefit of the doubt more than necessary. Remind yourself that you don't find every interaction uncomfortable and conclude every overture to be stalking, right? Then why this one? It must be for a reason (even if you can't explain it).

Which Laws Protect You against Stalking?

You are protected against stalking under the following sections of the BNS:
1. Section 78: This section makes stalking a criminal offence in the following ways:
    i. Physical stalking: Following a woman and contacting her, or trying to contact her, despite her clear indication of disinterest.

    ii. Online stalking: Monitoring a woman's internet use, such as emails, social media handles, etc. We will discuss this in detail in the section on cyberbullying.
2. Section 351(1): This is to do with criminal intimidation if your stalker is threatening you or trying to intimidate you in any way. This provision makes it a criminal offence for anyone to threaten another person with injury to their body, property, reputation, or to a loved one.
3. Section 329(1): This section covers criminal trespassing if the stalker enters your private premises, like your house. This provision makes entering someone's private property, with the intent of committing a crime, threatening them, or creating nuisance, a criminal offence.

What Should You Do if You Are Being Stalked?

As we saw in Nisha's case, taking action is not always easy, especially in our society where we have to strike a delicate balance between safety and freedom. It can sometimes take victims months to report stalking, but until then, you should make sure you protect yourself. The 4 'C's against stalking, which are in a slightly different order from other scenarios, can come in handy.

What Are the 4 'C's against Stalking?

1. Confide: Stalking often persists over long periods of time. It is not a one-time act. The stalker starts tracking the movements of his victim and gathers information about her whereabouts—where she lives, works, goes to

school, who she meets, etc. This puts the victim's safety at risk. Therefore, if you feel like you are being stalked, always confide in someone. Ensure another person is aware of the situation, so that they can protect you if needed.

Note: If you feel like you are being stalked, especially for a long time, avoid lonely and dark places, at least till you take action against your stalker. If you can't avoid it, share your live location with someone who can help you if needed.

2. Collect evidence: Gather as much evidence as possible against the stalker. It could be their vehicle number, a photo of them, their social media profile(s), screenshots of any calls/messages, etc. All this evidence will be extremely useful if you file a police complaint.
3. Call-out: Like Nisha's brother, if you have someone in your circle who can sternly warn the stalker, try it. It is not advisable that you speak to him directly, as he may not take it seriously. He might even take it as a form of encouragement, that you noticed and acknowledged his unwanted advances. As unfortunate as it is, if a man warns the stalker, it is more likely that he will back off, as he will think you have someone to protect you.
4. Complaint: If the stalking does not stop, and all measures fail, file a police complaint. Take as much evidence with you as possible as it will help the police have a starting point to track the stalker. The police will first issue him a warning. Usually, such a warning is sufficient to scare the stalker away. If he still does not stop, then the police

may take stricter action like placing him in lock-up. The level of police action can vary based on the gravity of the stalking and how seriously they take your case.

What Is Flashing?

Flashing, or indecent exposure, is the act of exposing one's private parts to others without their consent. This is usually done to harass the other person and sexually gratify oneself. For instance, if a man flashes his penis at a woman, or masturbates in front of her, without her consent, it amounts to flashing. As disgusting as it sounds, flashing is sadly a common form of sexual harassment.

One of the common means men use to flash women is by pretending to ask for directions. When the woman responds, he flashes his penis at her. Another common form of flashing happens on public transport, where men get into relatively empty buses or trains and start masturbating in ways that the victims can see what they are doing.

Sexual harassers who flash women derive pleasure from the shock and fear they create. By exposing their private parts, they send the message that it is not they who are vulnerable but the victims. For this reason, school girls are often targets of flashing; they are likely to be more vulnerable and fearful.

Unfortunately, most victims do not report cases of flashing because either they are not aware that it is a criminal offence, or they fear lack of support from their family or the police. Some even worry that telling their parents will limit their freedom. All these concerns are legitimate.

However, all hope is not lost. Things are changing slowly but positively. There have been many cases in India where victims of flashing have complained against the harassers and got them arrested.

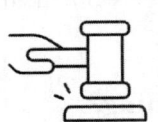

Woman Gets Driver, Who Flashed Her, Arrested

A twenty-one-year-old woman (let's call her Sara) was travelling in a taxi in Mumbai with her mother. Sara was sitting in the front passenger seat. Barely ten minutes into the ride, the driver started flashing her (exposing his penis). Shocked and horrified, she told him repeatedly to stop the vehicle, which he refused to do. Finally, she took out her phone and started filming him till they reached their destination. Sara immediately went to the nearest police station. Based on the video clip and the taxi's registration number, the police tracked the vehicle and arrested the driver.[5]

ATM Flasher Gets Arrested

In another incident, a thirty-eight-year-old man flashed a twenty-three-year-old woman (let's call her Jessica) and touched her inappropriately inside an ATM. He got into the ATM on the pretext of helping her, but then started flashing her. Jessica immediately started filming him, seeing which the harasser fled. Luckily, there were police constables nearby and Jessica showed them the clip. The harasser was caught and an FIR was registered against him.[6]

While what happened to the victims is unfortunate, these cases are important wins because:
- The harassers will hopefully have learnt a lesson and will think multiple times before harassing women again.
- Prompt police action gives hope to other women and encourages them to report such incidents.

Which Laws Protect You against Flashing?

There is no specific law in India against public indecency or flashing. However, legal remedies are available under other broad provisions of the BNS like:

1. Section 79: This is to do with outraging the modesty of a woman. It makes any word, act or gesture, which is intended to outrage the modesty of a woman, a criminal offence. Therefore, public masturbation would be covered under this.
2. Section 75: This is to do with sexual harassment. It makes physical contact and advances, involving unwelcome and explicit sexual overtures, by a man against a woman a punishable offence.
3. All sections of the BNS pertaining to molestation: If the harasser touches the victim in any way, molestation charges will come into the picture. You can refer to the previous section on molestation for the legal provisions.
4. Section 270: This criminalizes any kind of public nuisance. Public masturbation or flashing in a public place can attract this section.

Note: Here, specific legal provisions have been listed for your benefit, so that if you have to file a police complaint, you have a basic idea of your legal rights. However, sometimes the police note down complaints under different sections, based on the general practice of that police station/jurisdiction. Make sure that, even if the police list additional sections, the ones listed above are included.

What Are the 3 'C's of Flashing?

1. Call out: Most flashers thrive on shocking the victims and operate with the belief that there will be no consequences. If you are in a safe public place, you can call out his action and embarrass the harasser.
2. Collect evidence: As evident in the real-life examples of Sara and Jessica, recording the incident promptly and noting down other details, like the vehicle number, can help get the harasser arrested. Collect any evidence you can. If you have your phone, make sure to take recordings/photographs (whatever is possible).
3. Complaint: Again, as in the cases of Sara and Jessica, file a police complaint *as soon as possible*. Give the police a copy of all the evidence you have. It can be a difficult step to take, especially if you anticipate that the police will not take action. However, it is always worth a try, more so if you have evidence. Sara and Jessica's cases also show us that the police do take action and things are changing for the better.

>  **Food for thought**
>
> Do you think flashers should be publicly named and shamed (such as putting up their photo/video on social media)? After all, they seem only too eager to do everything in public!

Should I Call Out a Sexual Harasser on Social Media?

Have you thought of putting up evidence, or calling out a sexual harasser on social media? The answer to whether you should use social media is both yes and no. After all, social media is like a double-edged sword.

On the one hand, it can help you get some relief. Due to the lack of legal recourse, many of us turn to social media to call out our harassers and amplify our concerns. In such cases, social media can help you gather support, speak up from the safety of your phone and publicly shame the harasser.

On the other hand, posting on social media can come back to bite you. The harasser may use underhand tactics to get back at victims, like creating fake profiles or starting a counter-campaign. Posting on social media can also give your harasser an opportunity to point a 'legal' finger back at you, in the form of defamation. They can claim that your post brought them disrepute. Of course, defamation cases are difficult to pursue and prove, but they can have a chilling effect on the victim, scaring her into withdrawing the complaint.

Pro tip: If you choose to call out your harasser on social media, don't share personal details like their phone number, address, identity card, etc., as that will put you in the wrong. Why give them a chance to point fingers at you when you are the victim in the first place!

Social media is an important tool to speak up and have your voice heard. Unfortunately, the same tool can also be used by your harasser. The intention here is not to scare you, but to make you aware of both sides of the coin. Use social media for your benefit, but don't get caught up in a dark web.

POINTS TO REMEMBER

1. Sexual harassment can be physical, verbal or non-verbal.
2. Most acts of sexual harassment are punishable under criminal law.
3. Collect as much evidence as you can, like a recording, screenshot, or even noting the appearance of the harasser.
4. In some cases, publicly calling out your harasser can be a good-enough response. But always remember, your safety comes first.
5. If you choose to file a police complaint, do so as soon as possible, so that evidence is not lost.

> **EXERCISE TIME**
>
> ### The Harassment Scramble
>
> Unscramble the letters to form terms related to sexual harassment:
>
> 1. CTNOESN:
> 2. TKINSGAL:
> 3. TOAELNMSOTI:
> 4. BRVLAE:
> 5. CPYHISAL:

Answer key:
1. Consent 2. Stalking 3. Molestation 4. Verbal 5. Physical

Rape

It is a myth that rape is simply violent, forceful sexual intercourse against a woman's wish. While that, of course, amounts to rape, the law covers several other aspects.

Let us begin by understanding what constitutes as rape under the Indian law. Rape means any of the following sexual acts without the woman's consent:

1. Sexual intercourse: Inserting the penis into the vagina/anus/mouth/urethra.
2. Oral sex: Applying the mouth to the vagina/anus/mouth/urethra.
3. Using any other body part (such as a finger) to penetrate the vagina/anus/mouth/urethra.
4. Inserting any object into the vagina/anus/mouth/urethra.
5. Forcing the woman for sexual intercourse, or oral sex, with any person.

From the above breakdown, it is clear that penetration or 'penetrative' sexual intercourse is not the only criteria to constitute rape. Non-consensual oral sex is also considered rape.

The act of rape is defined in Section 63 of the BNS. The punishment for rape, and the acts of rape which attract higher punishment, are outlined in Section 64 of the BNS.

Does rape have to be violent or forceful?
No. If any sexual act given in the definition of 'rape' is done without the woman's consent, it will count as rape. There is a subtle difference between violent and forceful acts and acts

without consent. We all understand what force and violence are. We see examples of these in movies that portray a rape scene. 'Without consent' simply means the woman did not agree, even if she did not put up a fight.

What is the punishment for rape?
The punishment for rape is jail for a minimum of ten years, which may extend to life imprisonment, along with a fine. In extreme (or rarest of rare) cases, such as the Nirbhaya case of 2012, the punishment can be death penalty (as per Section 64 of the BNS).

In case rape is committed by a woman's relative, guardian, teacher, or anyone else in a position of trust or authority, the punishment is more stringent.

What Is Marital Rape?

Marital rape is when a woman's husband forces her into any kind of sexual activity, like sexual intercourse or oral sex. Rape is rape; it should not matter whether the rapist is the husband or a stranger. Sadly, marital rape is not a punishable offence in India. The definition of rape  under the law specifically excludes marital rape as a crime.

Why so? We can blame it on our patriarchal society, which believes that it is a wife's duty to sexually please her husband, and partly on colonial hangover. The law regarding rape was laid down by the British, under the IPC that has now been replaced by the BNS. The BNS was an opportunity for our lawmakers to change the law, but they did nothing.

Around thirty-two countries in the world do not criminalize marital rape, and India is one of them.[7] It is time we realize that marriage is not a licence to rape. It is not a ticket to have sex without consent. It is high time that the law reflects this as well.

The only exception where marital rape is considered rape by the law is if the husband and wife are separated, i.e., not living together, or if the wife is under eighteen years of age.

What Is Date Rape?

Date rape refers to a specific type of rape where the woman is intoxicated or drugged without her knowledge, such that she might have temporary memory loss. It usually happens at social events and parties where the rapist adds a tasteless, odourless substance to a woman's drink without her knowledge.

Date rape is punishable as rape in India, as it falls under the category of 'lack of consent due to intoxication'. Usually, the biggest hurdle in a date rape case is proving that the woman did not give consent or that the substance was added to her drink.

How Can One Prove Date Rape?

1. Collect as much evidence as you can.
2. If you can, retain samples of the drink for a lab test.
3. If you wake up the next morning with a suspicion of date rape, get a blood test done for traces of alcohol or drugs.

> 4. Collect all photos and videos of the event/party. You never know what may prove to be helpful.
> 5. Speak to others who attended the party to gather as much information as you can about the event.
> 6. Anyone who witnessed either the spiking of your drink or your behaviour afterwards (such as being confused, out-of-control, not being yourself or feeling your head spin) can be part of the witness testimony.

Tips to keep in mind at a party

1. Always get your drink yourself, directly from the source.
2. Never leave your drink out of sight or unattended.
3. Be extremely cautious who you share a drink with.
4. Trust your instinct. If something suddenly feels off with your drink, stop drinking it.

How to understand if your drink has been tampered with

1. **Unexpected taste or smell:** Even though most substances are odourless and tasteless, some may impart a slight bitterness or a strange chemical taste. If your drink suddenly tastes different, stop drinking it.
2. **Change in colour or appearance:** Some substances might cause a drink to look cloudy or slightly altered, though this isn't always the case.
3. **Unusual fogginess or bubbles:** If you notice bubbles or excessive fizz in a drink that shouldn't have it, it might be a sign of tampering.
4. **Excessive drowsiness or sudden dizziness:** If you start feeling extremely sleepy, dizzy, confused or disoriented

after consuming a drink, especially more than what would be expected based on how much you've had, it could be a sign that your drink was spiked.
5. **Impaired memory or coordination:** A drugged drink can make it difficult for you to walk, stay focused or even recall what happened shortly after drinking.
6. **Unconsciousness or blacking out:** If you or someone with you suddenly loses consciousness after consuming a drink, it could be a red flag.

I know and understand that it is not a girl's job to alter herself to ensure that she is not 'date-raped'. Date rape should not happen, no matter what. Unfortunately, we live in a society that largely holds only a woman responsible for her conduct. These tips are mentioned here as words of caution.

> ### Is Oral Sex Rape, if There's No Resistance?
>
> Let's consider a real-life case.[8] A Bollywood director was accused of rape through oral sex. In her testimony, the victim said that the director kissed her. She said no and pushed him away. He then started pulling her underwear down and forcefully performed oral sex. The victim objected and tried to pull up her underwear, but he was much stronger. She said that she remembered the words of Nirbhaya's rapist from a documentary, according to which Nirbhaya would have been alive had she not fought back. The victim wanted to get out of the situation quickly, so she faked an orgasm to end the act. Now, this is not the typical violent rape that we usually imagine.

In this case, the act of rape was neither penetrative nor violent. But it still amounts to rape because the victim said 'no'. Always remember, no means no, and consent is key.

What happened in the above case? The trial court found the director guilty of rape. This ruling was later overturned by the Delhi High Court, a decision upheld by the Supreme Court. However, the Delhi High Court's judgment has been criticized by sections of the public,[9] questioning if there is a 'right way to resist' for a woman to prove rape. Just because she did not scream and shout, does it mean that she granted consent? Of course not!

The high court's judgment could be a reflection of other factors, such as the bias of the judge, the patriarchal society we live in and the general mindset that 'the woman must be lying'. Guess the gender of the judges who gave the judgment at the high court and Supreme Court? I am sure you can guess the answer without having to google it!

What are the first steps to take if you, or someone you know, has been a victim of rape?
1. Go for a medical examination: Do this at the earliest, especially if you are injured in any way. If you can, avoid taking a bath before the examination. This is to make sure that any evidence on your body, like DNA samples or body fluids, are not washed off and get recorded in the medical examination.
2. Save all evidence: This includes clothes, hair samples and body fluids that are collected on any object that you may have come in contact with (like a bedsheet).

3. Keep your clothes in a separate bag: Avoid any contact, or tampering with the clothes worn by the survivor at the time of the crime. They may contain the DNA of the accused.
4. Make a note of important details: These include the date, time and place of the crime, details of the accused (like birthmarks or tattoos, which can be used to identify the accused), any witnesses, what you did before and after the crime, and any other details you may recollect. This will help you at the time of filing a police complaint and also be useful when the case goes to court. Do this even if you are unsure about going to the police, because it will help in case you decide to file a complaint later.
5. File a police complaint as soon as possible: Filing a complaint early has two main advantages. You will remember all the important and pertinent details as your memory is still fresh, and the police will be able to start their investigation and prevent loss of time.

Survivors of rape often go through immense physical and mental trauma. Understandably, they can take time to file a complaint. Sometimes, complaints are filed after years. Remember, there is NO TIME BAR on when you can file a complaint against a crime. You can do so whenever you are ready. However, it is highly recommended that you file it at the earliest, so that evidence is not lost due to passage of time.

POINTS TO REMEMBER

1. It is NOT your fault.
2. Rape is not always forceful or violent. Even oral sex without consent counts as rape.
3. No means no. You can show your consent (or lack of it) through words, actions or gestures. You do not need to say the word 'no'.
4. Retain all evidence. Get a medical check-up done as soon as possible.
5. You can file a police complaint whenever you are ready. There is no time limit.

2

Cyberbullying: The Unseen Threat

This chapter will help you understand how to deal with various types of cyberbullying, along with listing the legal provisions that can protect you against each of these. At the end, there is a page on how you should deal with cyberbullying in general.

Introduction

How many times do you unlock your phone in a day? My score is roughly forty times. Our phones have almost become a part of our bodies, and social media is an extension of our minds and hearts. While we all enjoy watching funny videos, sharing information and catching up with friends virtually, our increased online activity has made us susceptible to the dark side of the internet—cyberbullying.

According to the 2020–21 annual report of the National Commission for Women (NCW), cases of online harassment against women have increased by five times since the outbreak of the Covid-19 pandemic.[1] These figures are scary. Does that mean we should stop using the internet and social media all together to protect ourselves? That would be like saying we should stop walking on the road for fear of getting into an accident.

The internet is here to stay, grow and become an even more integral part of our lives. Therefore, it is important for us to understand how to protect ourselves. This chapter will explain the laws that protect you and suggest a course of action against each form of cyberbullying.

A few basics to know:
1. We have only one law for everything related to the internet, called the Information Technology (IT) Act, 2000. This law is more than two decades old and has not caught up with developments in technology.
2. You can file a complaint against cyberbullying with the cyber crime cell of your city. Most metro cities have one. The process is similar to filing a regular police complaint. If your city does not have one, file a complaint at a regular police station.

> **Activity Time:** Does your city have a cyber crime cell? If you are not sure, do a simple online search to find out!

Who Are Trolls? How Do I Deal with Them?

If you are familiar with the digital world, then you have definitely heard of trolling. Trolling is a form of cyberbullying where trolls deliberately say nasty and hurtful things about someone online. Trolls can either be real people hiding behind the anonymity of a keyboard, or they can be cyberbots (a robot that acts like a human).

While trolling affects everyone, irrespective of gender, age or profession, it makes women particularly vulnerable online. For example, journalist Rana Ayyub has been the target of brutal trolling for her tweets. Apart from receiving death threats, her personal information was leaked all over the internet, and she has been called all sorts of distasteful names like 'Islamist', 'Jehadi Jane', 'didi' and what not.[2]

What Should You Do if You Are Trolled?

1. Block and ignore: Most trolls are faceless, useless keyboard warriors frustrated with their own lives. Sometimes the best solution is to ignore and block them. A troll's only objective is to trouble you, but if they realize that you simply don't care, it is no longer fun for them.
2. Change your settings: Some platforms, like Instagram, allow you to change your settings so that only your friends or people who you follow back can comment on your photos. If that is not possible for you, set up a filter that will 'restrict' or automatically block certain types of comments.

3. Call out and shame: Sometimes naming and shaming the troll can also help. If the troll is a real person, they are sure to feel embarrassed for being called out as a bully (do remember to attach screenshots as proof).
4. Should you complain? Filing a police complaint may not be the most effective solution for trolling, simply because the police do not have the resources to deal with the large number of trolling cases. They may not take your complaint seriously unless you are an influential person.
5. Defamation suit: If you know who the troll is or if it is a specific person, then you can file a defamation suit against them. A defamation suit is filed when someone 'defames' another person, i.e., says things that can tarnish a person's name and reputation. Trolling is included in this category. While most defamation suits don't really result in conclusive judgments, filing a suit itself can serve as a strong warning and deterrent. You should take a lawyer's help for this.

Which Laws Protect You against Trolling?

Trolling is nothing short of a hate crime committed online and should ideally be dealt with strictly. We had a dedicated provision, Section 66A of the Information Technology Act, which criminalized sending offensive messages to anyone through any means of virtual communication. However, in 2015, the Supreme Court struck this section down for being vague and unconstitutional, given its misuse by the government to silence dissent.

Let us see which laws can protect us. Only keywords are stated here.
1. Bharatiya Nyaya Sanhita
    i. Section 78: Cyberstalking
    ii. Section 351(4): Criminal intimidation by anonymous communication
    iii. Section 79: Outraging the modesty of a woman
    iv. Section 356: Criminal defamation
2. Information Technology Act, 2000
    To be honest, the IT Act does not have a provision any more to directly attack trolling. All we can do is try and fit it into other legal provisions like:
    i. Section 66C: identity theft
    ii. Section 66E: violation of privacy
    iii. Section 67, 67A, 67B: transmitting or publishing obscene material in electronic form

Note: In addition to all the laws discussed above, if the victim is below the age of eighteen, they will have additional protection under POCSO (Protection of Children from Sexual Offences) Act of 2012.

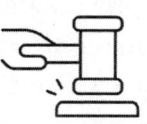

What about My Right to Privacy?

In 2017, the Supreme Court recognized the 'right to privacy' as a fundamental right (under the Right to Life in Article 21 of our Constitution) thanks to the landmark case of *Justice K.S. Puttaswamy vs Union of India*. Any form of cyberbullying that compromises the victim's privacy, such as voyeurism, trolling, identity theft, etc., will also

> be protected under the fundamental right to privacy. However, constitutional rights operate at a very macro level and it is difficult to take direct action under them. For example, you cannot go to a police station and file a complaint citing violation of your privacy.
>
> It is good to know that we have a right to privacy, but as of now, we cannot do much with it!

What Is Voyeurism? What if Someone Is Spying on My Private Moments?

Do you remember, when we would peep into our classmate's notebook or try to copy someone's notes, our teachers would say, 'Don't be a Peeping Tom!'? Voyeurism is basically the technical term for 'Peeping Tom' behaviour. It means secretly watching someone engage in a private (sometimes sexual) act, without their knowledge or consent. For example, secretly watching someone taking a shower, spying on a woman in a changing room or watching someone engage in sexual intercourse. If you have heard of changing room scams, where the owners/workers of small shops place hidden cameras and record women changing their clothes, they fall under the purview of voyeurism.

Voyeurs derive pleasure from secretly watching others. An example of this was portrayed in Netflix's *Lust Stories 2*. One of the stories in this collection depicts voyeurism in its most basic form. A working woman who lives alone comes home one day to find her house help having sex on her bed. She is initially shocked, but later finds herself drawn to watching them. When she realizes that this is an everyday affair, she starts coming home at the same time to secretly watch her maid in the act. Her act of spying, without the maid's knowledge or consent, is voyeurism.

Can Voyeurism Lead to Blackmail?

In many cases, voyeurs don't just stop at watching the woman. They go on to capture private moments and then threaten to leak them. Sharing a woman's private photos or videos (which are sexual in nature) without her consent is also voyeurism. We will return to this in the section on 'sextortion' below.

#MovieTime

Recall the movie *Drishyam* (a Tamil movie with Telugu and Hindi remakes)? Do you remember what set off the amazing twists and turns of this film? In the movie, a teenage boy hid a cell phone to record his classmate removing her clothes and showering in the bathroom. He later blackmailed her for sexual favours and threatened to upload the video on social media if she resisted. This was a clear case of cyberbullying involving voyeurism and sextortion.

What Are the 3 'C's against Voyeurism?

1. Close the hole: If you know that someone is spying on you through a particular spot (like a keyhole), close it immediately so that the voyeur does not get a chance to do it again.

2. Call out: If it feels right and safe, call out the voyeur publicly. It is *they* who should be ashamed, not you. Most voyeurs operate with the mindset that they will either not get caught or the victim will be too embarrassed to say anything.
3. Complaint: If the voyeurism is also accompanied by extortion, or is part of a larger activity (like a changing room scam), you should definitely file a police complaint. If it is a case like the Netflix example from above, or someone privately watching you, you can still file a police complaint. Try to gather evidence to support your complaint. For example, if you know that the voyeur spies on you at a certain time from a certain place, set up a secret camera to catch him in the act.

Which Laws Protect You against Voyeurism?

We know that spying on someone, especially their private moments, is not okay (even on a moral level). The law agrees and, believe it or not, there is a dedicated section in the BNS that criminalizes voyeurism.

1. Section 77 of BNS: According to this section, voyeurism includes doing any of the following acts without a woman's consent:
    i. Watching a woman in a private act (such as sexual activity, using the lavatory or bathing, etc.), where she is in her undergarments or her private parts are exposed.
    ii. Capturing or sharing images/videos of a woman engaged in a private act.

2. Section 66E of the IT Act: This section says the same thing, but in the digital context. It punishes whoever captures, publishes or shares images/videos of a private area of any person without their consent, thus violating their privacy.

What Is Sextortion?

Picture this. Sameer and Leela (both fictional characters) are in a relationship. They agree to record themselves in a sexual act, for their personal viewing. However, after a few months, they break up and Sameer starts threatening Leela that he will leak their private video. Leela panics and does not know what to do. She is worried about how this will impact her family and what people will say about her. She will do anything to stop Sameer from leaking the video, which Sameer takes advantage of to extract a huge amount of money from her. Leela has to break her bank account and secretly sell jewellery to pay Sameer. Sounds familiar? Such incidents are extremely common in our country.

This is sextortion. Simply put, sextortion is demanding money/sexual favours from someone by threatening to release sexual content about them. The harasser typically blackmails the victim to extract money, or to make the victim perform sexual acts.

Sextortion is not always through a stranger secretly capturing you. In most cases, the harasser is someone close to the victim, someone who has access to private moments (for example, an ex-boyfriend or a jilted lover). It can also be a case where the victim agreed to capture or share her private photos/videos with the harasser, like in Sameer and Leela's example. The bottom line is that consent to capture *is not equal to* consent to share. Just because Leela agreed to record their private moments for private viewing does not mean she agreed for Sameer to share them with a third person or blackmail her.

Note: It is important to mention that it *does not matter* whether the private images/videos were captured without the victim's consent, or if she had shared them with the harasser herself. If the woman *did not consent to sharing the images/videos with a third person*, he does not have the right to share them.

A close cousin of sextortion is revenge porn, which involves sharing explicit, or intimate, photos or videos of a person (mostly online), without their consent. As the name suggests, revenge porn is usually done to take revenge from the victim (example, if a relationship goes sour), or to humiliate or threaten the victim.

What Should You Do if You Are a Victim of Sextortion?

1. **Keep calm:** I know this sounds like the last thing you can do in such a situation. However, if you panic, you will not be able to think straight and end up giving in to your blackmailer's demands. Try to assess the best possible course of action to minimize the damage.
2. **Get support:** Telling your family or well-wishers about the situation can be difficult; you don't know how they

might react. If you can't get your family's support, turn to your friends. This is important because sextortion puts the victim under tremendous mental pressure, which is impossible to deal with alone.
3. **Collect evidence:** Quickly collect all the evidence you can—screenshots of chats, phone calls or emails. Also make a note of the phone number or social media profile the harasser is using to contact you. This will be useful when filing a police complaint.
4. **File a police complaint:** This is an important step in cases of sextortion because the police will be able to trace the harasser using the IP address of his device. They can even confiscate his devices and make him delete all the content. Here, it is important that you tell the police if you fear that the harasser may leak your content if they call him. In such a case, the police can use other means to catch the harasser off-guard.

Note: You can file a complaint with a women's police station or cyber cell, if your city has one. If not, head to a regular police station. If possible, take a lawyer with you, as this will make the police take your case more seriously.

How can you protect yourself when sharing nudes with your boyfriend or anyone?
Again, I know it is not a woman's job to alter her behaviour so that a criminal doesn't attack her. But given the society we live in, it won't hurt to exercise some caution. In some cases, prevention truly is better than cure.

Here are some tips on sharing nudes (even if you are in a relationship):

1. Only share your pictures with someone you trust. A partner who truly cares about you will never force you to share private content if you are not comfortable.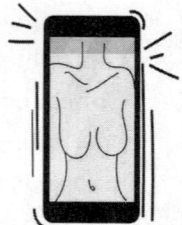
2. Use apps that allow the receiver to open the image only once. Do not allow screenshots without your knowledge. For example, Snapchat, WhatsApp, Instagram and most other social apps have this feature.
3. While sharing, cut out your face and remove identifiable marks, such as a birthmark or tattoo.
4. If you are storing your private pictures on your phone, laptop or other personal devices, keep them extremely secure.
5. If you use any cloud backup, like Google photos, make sure you use a secure email id, which only you have access to.

I want to stress on the 'even if you are in a relationship' part, because in most cases of voyeurism and sextortion, the harassers are people close to the victim, someone the victim trusted. Once the relationship is over, or if things get rocky, the same trusted ex-boyfriend can blackmail the victim. We worry way too much about an imaginary stranger harassing us, without realizing that it could be someone who has already won our trust. I don't mean to make you mistrustful of all relationships.

I just want to urge you to be careful. As they say, wear your seatbelt at all times, even if you are with the best driver.

Which Legal Provisions Protect against Sextortion and Revenge Porn?

We have multiple laws that protect us against sextortion and revenge porn. Only keywords are stated here:

1. Bharatiya Nyaya Sanhita
    i. Section 74: Outraging modesty through assault/criminal force.
    ii. Section 75: Sexual harassment in general.
    iii. Section 77: Voyeurism.
    iv. Section 79: Insulting modesty/infringing privacy.
    v. Section 351(1): Criminal intimidation, threatening a person with injury to cause the person to do/not do an act.
    vi. Section 308(1): Putting a person in fear of injury to induce delivery of anything valuable (like money).
    vii. Section 356: Defamation, which includes words or signs, spoken or published, intending to harm someone's reputation.
    viii. Section 294: Sale, rental, distribution, public display, or any other means of distributing or placing into circulation obscene publications.
2. Information Technology Act
    i. Section 66E: Capturing, publishing or transmitting image(s) of private area without consent (equivalent of voyeurism).

ii. Section 67: Publishing or transmitting lascivious material (images).
iii. Section 67A: Publishing or transmitting sexually explicit acts (videos).
iv. Section 67B: Publication, distribution, facilitation or consumption of sexually explicit material containing children.
v. Section 72: Confidentiality and privacy violations.
3. Section 4, Indecent Representation of Women Act: Distributing material representing women in an indecent form.

The good news is that Indian courts are getting strict about cyberbullying cases.

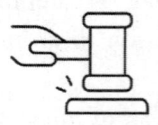

Revenge Porn: Harasser Gets Jailed

In a 2017 case from West Bengal, the accused took advantage of his relationship with the victim to access her nude videos from her mobile phone. When the victim ended the relationship, the accused started blackmailing her and uploaded the videos on various porn sites, along with the victim's private information. A court in West Bengal convicted the accused under a gamut of sections from the IPC (now BNS) and IT Act, and sentenced him to five years in jail, along with a fine.

The judgment in the case *(State of West Bengal vs Animesh Boxi*[3]*)* was historic because it was the first conviction for revenge porn in India. The sequence of events in this case is a classic example of revenge porn and sextortion cases.

> ### Harasser Denied Bail in Sextortion Case
>
> In a case from Odisha in 2020, the harasser and the victim were involved in a romantic relationship. The harasser assaulted the victim and filmed it on his mobile phone. He then threatened to leak the videos. Later, he posted the videos on Facebook nonetheless. After the victim and her parents complained to the police, the content was taken off Facebook.
>
> In this case, *Subhranshu Rout vs State of Odisha*, the high court refused bail to the harasser. It also noted that the leaked videos violated the 'right to privacy' of the victim.[4]

What Is Cyberflashing?

Do you recall flashing from a previous section? Cyberflashing is the online version. We have all heard the cringeworthy and horrific story of opening your inbox on a dating app or social media to discover an unwanted guest—an unsolicited 'dick pic'.

Essentially, cyberflashing is when someone sends explicit or offensive images of genitalia without consent (like dick pics). This invasive and disrespectful behaviour can leave victims feeling violated, unsafe and deeply uncomfortable. Although cyberflashing predominantly targets females, any gender can fall victim to such harassment.

What Should You Do if You Become a Victim of Cyberflashing?

1. Block the harasser: Block all accounts and numbers of the harasser. Remember to take screenshots, in case you need evidence later.

2. Change your settings: Many social media apps have the option of allowing only people you know to send you messages, or to even censor content that may be explicit. This will help prevent future cases.
3. Call out and shame: If possible and safe for you, call out the person on social media. Ask multiple people to report the account as spam. In many cases this works, because the harassers send offensive pictures thinking the victims will be too embarrassed to say anything (like flashing in person, if you recall). It is not the victim but the harasser who should be embarrassed!
4. Should you file a complaint? You can file a complaint. However, the extent of police action could vary based on the seriousness of the case and the proactiveness of the police. In fact, I was having a conversation with my friend and renowned influencer Malini Agarwal about this the other day. Sometimes even celebrities and influencers find it difficult to draw police action for cyberflashing complaints. Therefore, I would say it depends on your luck. But don't let this stop you from complaining, because the more we ask for our rights, the higher our chances to make the system take our concerns seriously.

Which Laws Protect You against Cyberflashing?

Again, there is no specific law for cyberflashing, so we pick and choose sections from a whole list of laws. These are more or less the same as listed under the previous section on sextortion, minus the sections related to threatening and blackmail.

Among the laws applicable to cyberflashing are sections 75, 79 and 294 of the BNS and sections 67 and 67A of the IT Act. You can refer to the descriptions in the previous section.

What Is Cyberstalking?

By now we understand what stalking is. When the same thing happens online (someone keeping tabs on all your activities without your consent), it is called cyberstalking. Examples include:

1. Online surveillance: This includes constantly monitoring a person's online activities, such as tracking their location and check-ins, or knowing their online presence status.
2. Unwanted messages: This includes repeatedly sending unsolicited (and often threatening or explicit) messages through email, social media or messaging apps.
3. Tracking the victim through various apps.
4. Syncing devices with the victim to monitor their activity.

In a nutshell, cyberstalking includes any online activity done to contact or monitor a victim without their consent. Sometimes, it can be accompanied by physical stalking.

What Should You Do if You Are a Victim of Cyberstalking?

1. Block: Try to identify the means that the stalker is using to keep tabs on you. For instance, is it constant messaging, or has he hacked into your profile or computer? Once you identify this, you should immediately block the stalker from everywhere, change your password and reformat your device, if necessary.
2. File a complaint: If the online stalking is accompanied by physical stalking, then you must file a police complaint

because it gets dangerous. For more on this, please read the section on stalking in the previous chapter. If it is only online stalking, the police may not take the complaint seriously, so your best bet would be to remove all access points between you and the stalker.

Which Laws Protect You against Cyberstalking?

Unlike other instances of cyberbullying, online stalking has a dedicated section in our legal system!

1. Bharatiya Nyaya Sanhita
    i. Section 78: This states that 'any man who monitors the use by a woman of the internet, email or any other form of electronic communication, commits the offence of stalking'. This section includes all the examples discussed above.

    Often, stalking is also accompanied by other related crimes such as blackmail, leaking private content, etc. Based on the nature of stalking, the following sections can also be brought in:

    ii. Section 351 (4): This mentions criminal intimidation by anonymous means. For example: if the stalker hides behind an anonymous identity and threatens the woman with consequences if she does not listen to him.
    iii. Section 79: If the stalker violates a woman's privacy by persistently sending her offensive mails or messages on social media platforms.
2. Information Technology Act
    i. Section 67/67A: This pertains to the stalker publishing or transmitting any obscene content about the victim online.

ii. Section 66E: This involves online voyeurism and the consequent violation of privacy (for details, see the section on voyeurism).

The good news is that cases of online stalking are being taken seriously.

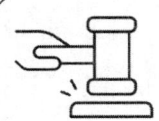

Online Stalker and 'Loverboy' Arrested

One Rizwan Ansari,[5] based in New Delhi, was repeatedly messaging a woman who had accepted his friend request on Facebook. He threatened to kill her if she did not talk to him. The woman and her husband filed a complaint through the National Cybercrime Reporting Portal (NCRP). The Delhi Police used technical surveillance and informers to trace Rizwan's IP address. He was then arrested for cyberstalking and other related offences.

Tips to Protect Yourself against Cyberstalking

1. If you have a public profile, don't post your live location on social media. If you want to share on Instagram that you went to the most happening restaurant in your city, wait till you leave before tagging any location.
2. Avoid sharing sensitive personal information, such as your address or phone number, online. Use private messages for such communication.
3. Regularly google yourself to see what information is available about you online. Address any incorrect or invasive information as needed.

What Is Identity Theft?

The internet is flooded with fake profiles. Almost every day I see someone on social media post a story asking people to block and report a fake profile. In many cases, fake profiles are used by scamsters to commit financial fraud by luring the victim's friends to send money. Fake accounts are also used to bully women by sending false messages to people on her friend's list, putting up fake/morphed images, or even sharing private contact information.

Nowadays, identity theft has become more advanced. With artificial intelligence progressing faster than we can keep up, deepfakes have become the latest tool of cyberbullies. In a study conducted in 2019 by AI company DeepTrace, an astonishing 96 per cent of deepfakes were identified as pornographic, with 99 per cent of these instances featuring women.[6]

#ReelToReal

Actress Rashmika Mandanna's viral deepfake video drew much-needed light to this new form of cyberbullying. In this video, Rashmika's face was imposed on the body of another woman who was shown entering an elevator in a bodysuit. The deepfake looked so real that if it hadn't been called out, most of us would have believed that it was Rashmika herself. The Delhi Police's Special Cell reportedly registered an FIR against unknown persons in this case.[7]

What Should You Do if You Become a Victim of Identity Theft?

1. Alert everyone: Let everyone know that the said profile is 'fake' and they should not engage with it. Also ask everyone to block it and report it.
2. Complaint: If the fake profile is being used to blackmail you, to put up real or morphed sexual photos of you, or to leak your private details, file a police complaint immediately. There are real-life cases listed below, where the police arrested the person who created a fake profile.

However, if it is yet another fake profile being used by scamsters, or say your college frenemy, then filing a complaint may not help much. It won't be 'serious enough' for the police to take action. Your best bet would be to either ignore and block it (if it is an impersonal fake for financial fraud) or to call it out in public/social media.

Which Laws Protect You against Identity Theft?

The law is yet to catch up with online identity thefts, which is why we have to fit the crime into other laws and sections.

1. Information Technology Act
    i. Sections 66C and 66D: These deal with identity theft and apply to stealing someone's identity using personal credentials or impersonation to commit fraud.
    ii. Section 66E: This section is applicable in cases of deepfakes that involve the capture, publication

or transmission of a person's images using mass media, thereby violating their privacy.
   iii. Sections 67, 67A and 67B: These sections can be used to prosecute individuals for publishing or transmitting deepfakes that are obscene or contain sexually explicit acts.
2. Bharatiya Nyaya Sanhita
   i. Section 319(1): This section applies to cheating by impersonation, i.e., when a person is pretending to be someone else. This is applicable for cases of fake profiles.
   ii. Section 79: This is our universally applicable section, which makes words, gestures or acts intended to insult the modesty of a woman a crime.
   iii. Section 356: These sections address criminal defamation, which apply here because deepfakes and fake profiles cause damage to the reputation of the victim.
   iv. Sections 336: These sections are applicable to cases of forgery. Identity theft, being a virtual form of forgery, falls under these provisions as well.

Note: The sections of the Indian Penal Code, now renamed as the Bharatiya Nyaya Sanhita, were originally meant for real-world crimes. However, due to the lack of an alternative law for online crimes, we extend the same sections to cyber crimes as well.

Bail Application Rejected for Creator of Fake Profile

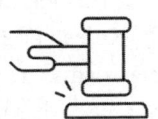

In *Jitender Singh Grewal vs State of West Bengal*,[8] the accused created a fake Facebook account of the victim and uploaded her obscene pictures to this account. The police lodged an FIR against him under various sections of the Indian Penal Code and Information Technology Act. The accused filed a bail application to prevent arrest, but the trial court rejected his application, a decision that was upheld by the Calcutta High Court. The rejection of bail by both courts is significant, as otherwise the accused would have been free to continue with his life despite his acts of cyber bullying.

Anticipatory Bail Rejected for Oversmart Cyberbully!

In the case of *Hareesh vs State of Kerala*,[9] the accused created a fake Facebook profile of the victim, posted morphed obscene photographs of her online and then mentioned her mobile number under the said post, allowing strangers to contact her.

Thereafter, he filed an anticipatory bail application. An anticipatory bail application is made when you expect to be arrested. The Kerala High Court rightfully rejected his application, on the grounds that the materials on record affirmed his involvement in the offence and that it would not be proper for the court to interfere with the investigation.

Further, the Information Technology (Intermediary Guidelines and Digital Media Ethics Code) Rules, 2021, 3(1)(b) and 3(2)(b)[10] also prohibit digital platforms from hosting any content that impersonates another person and require them to take down 'artificially morphed images' of individuals, once alerted. In case they fail to take down such content, they risk losing 'safe harbour' protection—a provision that protects social media companies from regulatory liability for third-party content shared by users on their platforms.

What about Death and Rape Threats?

Giving women death or rape threats on social media has become the latest fad in cyberbullying. The trolls are so out of control that, back in 2021, even Virat Kohli and Anushka Sharma's ten-month-old daughter was not spared. A man sent her a rape threat on Twitter after the Kohli-led Indian team did not perform well in the T20 Men's Cricket World Cup. Even prominent female journalists like Barkha Dutt, Rana Ayyub and Nidhi Razdan have time and again received rape threats, especially if they reported against the ruling party. In fact, Razdan went on record on Twitter, asking Instagram to take action against such bullies.

While we don't know what happened about Razdan's FIR, let us understand what you should do if someone tries this on you.

1. Block and report: Block the trolls and report them on the social media platform concerned. I know this sounds like nothing, but it is the first step, especially for your mental peace.
2. Record all evidence: Screenshot all evidence of the threat(s) and save it in one place that is handy.
3. Report it to the police: File a police complaint with the cyber police/regular police, whichever is available to you. Death and rape threats are serious; they are literally open calls to commit a crime. We must file a complaint against them.

Which Laws Protect You against Death or Rape Threats?

Believe it or not, there is no law that criminalizes death and rape threats in India. We have to collect different provisions from multiple laws, much like other forms of cyberbullying.

1. Bharatiya Nyaya Sanhita: Under the BNS, the laws that offer protection are sections 75 (sexual harassment), 79 (outraging the modesty of a woman) and 351 (punishment for criminal intimidation).
2. Information Technology Act: Under the IT Act, the laws that offer protection are sections 67 and 67A, which deal with digitally transmitting obscene material.

It is important to note that the above sections are indicative, i.e., we can fit death and rape threats under these. However, each police station may tweak this list and add or delete sections. Just make sure that the ones listed above are covered, even if other sections are added.

> 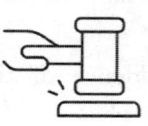 **Case in Point**
>
> In 2020, a man named Shubham Mishra posted a two-minute graphic rape threat against a female comedian, Agrima Joshua, because he was offended by one of her jokes(!) This man was traced to Vadodara and the local police lodged an FIR against him.[11]
>
> Sometimes, an FIR itself is enough because it teaches the troll a lesson, that he could go to jail for his online threats. It also sends a message to other bullies, that they stand to meet the same fate if they do something like that.

Social Media Platforms Need to Do More to Protect Their Female Users

In conclusion, I want to ask you something. Do you think internet companies like Meta, which owns Facebook, Instagram and WhatsApp, should also be made responsible for making the internet a safe space for women? To think about it, if cyberbullying is an earthquake, social media platforms are its epicentre. However, these platforms have done little or nothing to prevent cyberbullying.

With the amount of money and resources that Meta has access to, and pumps into research and development on how to keep users on their platform for longer, it is hard to believe that they have not been able to devise a system that can detect nuanced forms of cyberbullying. The same Meta, however, has come up with an extremely efficient mechanism where it automatically detects the sound in any video you upload. And if there is a copyrighted song in the background, it will not let you upload your video.

How do you explain something like this? The answer is simple. Platforms like Meta and Google earn revenue from copyright owners (like music labels, production houses, etc.), but not from women who become victims on their platform. Isn't it high time that our laws and policymakers ensure that these platforms put in equally stringent checks (like their copyright checks) to protect the safety and dignity of their users?

File That Complaint!

In most cases of cyberbullying, victims hesitate to approach the police, either due to social stigma or because they feel that the police will not help. Most offenders also operate with the belief that they will never get caught. However, as evident in the cases above, the police *do* take action in many cases. In fact, the police have the power to trace the device of the offender through the IP address and seize it. Even a warning from the police sometimes serves as a deterrent.

POINTS TO REMEMBER

1. Cyberbullying can happen in various forms, like online stalking, sextortion, voyeurism, trolling, creating fake profiles, etc.
2. For most cases of cyberbullying, there is no dedicated law (at least not yet). You need to fit a concoction of different sections to every case.
3. Many forms of cyberbullying, like sextortion, death and rape threats, and voyeurism also attract criminal law provisions.
4. For serious cases of cyberbullying (like sextortion), you must file a police complaint. For issues like trolls, you can consider other options.
5. You can file a complaint with the cyber crime cell or a regular police station.

EXERCISE TIME!

Cyberbully Buster

Match the terms on the left with the correct meaning on the right.

Term	Definition
A. Sextortion	1. The act of gaining sexual gratification by observing someone in a private situation
B. Voyeurism	2. A manipulated video or audio recording that appears to be real but is fake
C. Trolling	3. The act of making derogatory comments to provoke responses
D. Deepfake	4. A threat of sexual assault used to intimidate someone
E. Rape Threat	5. Extorting money or favours by threatening to reveal private information

Answer key:
A-5; B-1; C-3; D-2; E-4

3

Work, Work, Work: Your Rights in the Workplace

In this chapter, we will explore your rights at the workplace—right from sexual harassment to equal pay for equal work and maternity benefits.

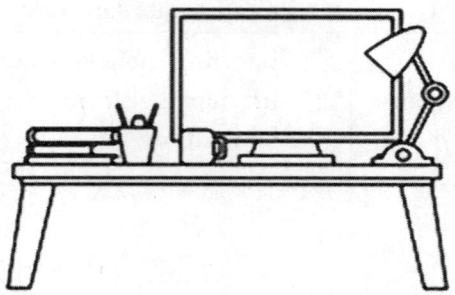

Introduction

Thanks to the popular #MeToo movement, all of us have a fair idea about sexual harassment at the workplace. For the uninitiated, the #MeToo movement is a global social campaign that gained momentum in 2017. It aimed to raise awareness about, and combat, sexual harassment and assault, particularly in the workplace, by encouraging victims to share their experiences and holding the perpetrators accountable.

In India, the movement led to the exposure and resignation of prominent individuals in the film, media and entertainment industries, sparking conversations about consent, power dynamics and the urgent need for change in societal attitudes and legal frameworks surrounding sexual misconduct. For example, the director of *Queen*, Vikas Bahl, was accused of sexually harassing a female colleague. The incident was made public by the victim and resulted in Bahl's dissolution of partnership in a production company.[1] A former union minister of state, M.J. Akbar, was also accused by several women (including prominent journalists) of sexual misconduct during his tenure as a celebrated editor, which led to his resignation as a Union minister.

These cases, among others, played a crucial role in exposing the magnitude of sexual harassment issues in India, prompting a broader dialogue on the need for systemic change, improved workplace safety and accountability for perpetrators of misconduct.

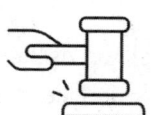

#MeToo: Justice against an Oppressive Defamation Case

At the peak of the #MeToo movement, journalist Priya Ramani tweeted about the sexual harassment she faced from M.J. Akbar. After Ramani's tweet, around twenty other women accused Akbar of sexual harassment. As public criticism against him mounted, he was forced to resign as a Union minister.

However, in a typical turn of events, Akbar denied all the allegations and filed a defamation suit against Ramani for damaging his reputation and demanded a ridiculous amount as compensation (amounting to crores).

Ramani fought back. After two and a half years of legal battle, the Delhi High Court held that Ramani was not guilty of defamation. This judgment was not only a personal win for Ramani, but also a collective victory for all survivors of sexual harassment, who are often threatened and silenced in a similar manner.[2]

What Counts as the Workplace?

The POSH Act or the Sexual Harassment of Women at Workplace (Prevention, Prohibition and Redressal) Act, 2013, defines a workplace as 'any place visited by the employee, arising out of or during the course of employment, including transportation provided by the employer for undertaking such a journey'. The definition has been deliberately kept open-ended to allow for a liberal interpretation.

Therefore, a workplace is not just your office desk. It includes:

1. **Your entire office space:** All the space your organization covers is included under this, not just the desk, cubicle, cabin or floor you work on. For example, if you work for an IT company that has many buildings, a lawn, etc., in its office space, the entire area (and not just your office building) is the workplace.

2. **Office transport:** If your office provides transport, like a bus or a cab, this also becomes part of the workplace. Private/public transport will not count, as it is not provided by your employer.

3. **Eating and recreation spaces:** Office canteens, mess, lounges or any recreation areas in the office are also a part of the workplace.

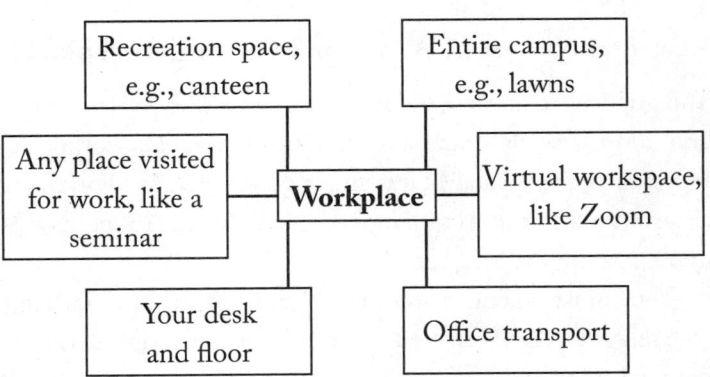

Since the definition uses the terms 'any place visited ... arising out of or during the course of employment', a workplace can, by extension, be said to include the following:

1. Your office sends you to a client's workplace for a meeting. The client's office, and the transport to and from the office (if provided by your employer), becomes a part of the workplace.
2. You go out for fieldwork as part of your job. Every place you visit (and transport to and from that place, if provided by the office) becomes the workplace.
3. You are sent on a work trip. The hotel where your office puts you up and the places you visit for meetings are part of the workplace.

Technically, as per the broad definition, the above scenarios should be included in the official definition of 'workplace'. However, since the Act does not specifically mention them, this extended concept is subject to interpretation by the courts.

Law against Sexual Harassment at the Workplace

The good news is that India has a law dedicated to prevent and address sexual harassment of women at the workplace. It is called the Sexual Harassment of Women at Workplace (Prevention, Prohibition and Redressal) Act, 2013, popularly known as the POSH Act.[3]

You must spend some time and effort familiarizing yourself with the Act, to ensure you know your rights. Let us now delve into it.

What Led to the POSH Act?

Before we get into the provisions of POSH, let me tell you a story, about a woman named Bhanwari Devi, to whom we owe the POSH Act.

Bhanwari Devi was a social worker from Bhateri, Rajasthan. She worked as a *saathin* (friend) with the government to address grassroots-level issues within the community. In 1992, as part of her social work, she tried to prevent the marriage of a nine-month-old baby within a Gujar family (the so-called dominant upper caste) in her village. Bhanwari Devi belonged to the Kumhar caste (the lower caste).

Her attempt at stopping the child marriage angered the Gujars who lashed out at Bhanwari Devi and her husband. They not only boycotted the family but also beat up her husband and made Bhanwari's employer fire her. One day, when Bhanwari and her husband were working in their field, five men from the Gujar caste attacked her husband with sticks, leaving him unconscious. They then took turns to gang rape her. Imagine Bhanwari's unbreakable spirit, especially considering the social context, she still went ahead and filed a police complaint against them. The five accused were arrested but acquitted by the Rajasthan High Court, thanks to the local influence of the accused.

Bhanwari's fight for justice was picked up by local newspapers and women's organizations. It garnered widespread attention and sparked public outrage, leading to an outcry for legal protection against sexual harassment at work. Several women's rights organizations, led by an NGO called Vishaka, filed a case in the Supreme Court of India, seeking justice for Bhanwari Devi and the protection of women's fundamental rights.

In 1997, the Supreme Court passed a landmark decision called *Vishaka and Others vs State of Rajasthan*, issuing strict guidelines against sexual harassment of women at the workplace. These guidelines are popularly called the Vishaka Guidelines. Until the POSH Act was enacted in 2013, we only had the Vishaka Guidelines to protect women at work.

Basics of the Posh Act

1. Who does the Act protect?
   The POSH Act protects any aggrieved woman against sexual harassment by a male. Who is an aggrieved woman? It includes every woman who is working in a workplace, in any capacity.
   i. It does not matter whether she is employed on a permanent, contractual, temporary or daily-wage basis.
   ii. It does not matter whether she is getting paid or if she is a volunteer/trainee/intern. It also covers women who are not 'employed' but work in a consultant's capacity (for example, in professional services like medicine and law, companies don't bring on everyone as employees on their rolls. Instead, they hire them as consultants).

Technically, the Act also protects women who visit a workplace, even if they are not employed there (for example, if you go to an office for an interview or meeting).

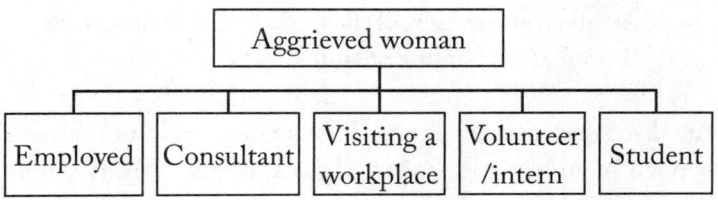

Note: The POSH Act only protects women against sexual harassment by men. It does not protect men against sexual harassment, nor does it protect women against sexual harassment by other women.

2. What counts as sexual harassment at the workplace?
   The POSH Act covers three forms of sexual harassment: physical, verbal and non-verbal (as mentioned in Chapter 1). This includes any kind of:
   i. Unwelcome physical contact and advances.
   ii. A demand or request for sexual favours.
   iii. Making sexually coloured remarks.
   iv. Showing pornography.
   v. Verbal or non-verbal conduct of a sexual nature.

Apart from the above-mentioned generic forms of sexual harassment, the POSH Act also includes specific scenarios like:
1. Quid pro quo: Promise of special treatment at work (like a promotion) in exchange for sexual favours, or threatening to stop promotions or terminations if you refuse sexual demands.
2. Hostile environment: Creating a hostile or uncomfortable work environment for the woman

if she refuses sexual favours, such as insulting or humiliating her out of spite.

As discussed earlier, sexual harassment need not always happen in an obvious 'violent physical assault' way. It can be the smallest things, which we as women are often taught to brush off as casual.

Here are a few everyday examples of what can count as harassment at the workplace:

1. Any non-consensual touching, such as inappropriate hugs, unwelcome touching of the body or brushing against someone in a sexual manner.
2. Making sexually explicit remarks.
3. Sharing adult/sexual jokes.
4. Engaging in explicit conversations about someone's personal life, body or appearance.
5. Repeatedly asking a colleague out on dates, despite their refusal or discomfort.
6. Persistently flirting with a co-worker, sending unsolicited romantic or explicit messages or gifts, or creating an uncomfortable and intrusive atmosphere.
7. Sharing sexually explicit images, videos or written content through electronic means, or displaying them within the workplace.
8. Sending unwanted sexual messages or explicit content through emails, chat platforms, or social media channels related to work.

> **Activity Time:** If you work in an office, how many of these have you experienced or seen around you?

What if My Colleague Was Just Being Friendly or Playful?

I am sure we ask ourselves this question each time we are in an uncomfortable situation. Should I give him the benefit of the doubt? What if he was just being friendly? Maybe I am being too sensitive? Here's the thing. There is a clear difference between being friendly or complimenting someone, and being sexually inappropriate.

Let us break down a few common dialogues:

Friendly comment/ Compliment	Inappropriate/ Sexual comment
You have a great smile.	Your lips are sexy. I love your lips.
You look fit.	You have a great/sexy body. You have a great figure.
I could drop you home, if you are okay with it, or I can call you a cab.	I will drop you home, I insist. (Or any other remark disregarding your comfort.)
How are things at home?	How is your sex life? How's your physical life with your husband?
You are great at your job, but you can be better (or other professional advice).	You are good at your job, but you can do better if you give me some favours (or any hint at sexual favours).

Friendly comment/ Compliment	Inappropriate/ Sexual comment
Feel free to ask for help if you need it.	I can help you get to the top, but you must be willing to 'compromise' (hinting at a sexual favour in return for a promotion).

The context and your comfort are paramount in such scenarios. For example, if a group of friends share an adult joke and have a good laugh, it will not amount to sexual harassment because they share a level of comfort and understanding as a group. However, if a random male colleague or boss shares an adult joke with his female colleague, it may make her feel uncomfortable or objectified. It is essentially the same situation, but in a different context, which makes it sexual harassment and not 'just a joke'.

A commonly used defence by sexual harassers is: 'I didn't mean to harass her. I was just joking!' Or they may play the righteous and offended card: 'I was being nice by asking her out or sending gifts. How can she take that as harassment? *Achai ka zamana nahi raha* (There's no point doing good)!'

The courts understand this trick, which is why it is clearly stated that the law will look at what the victim felt and not whether the accused had the intention to harass. If the victim felt uncomfortable or violated, it will amount to sexual harassment.

Pro tip: When in doubt, trust your gut. If you feel confused about a particular act being sexual harassment or not, ask yourself if it made you feel uncomfortable. If the answer is yes, then you know that it is harassment. Remember, you don't feel uncomfortable all the time or around all men. If a particular man or situation is making you uncomfortable, then there is something wrong. We must learn to trust our instincts.

Casual Sexism

Casual sexism is subtle or seemingly harmless actions, comments, or behaviour that perpetuate gender stereotypes or discriminate against women. It exists all around, right from backhanded compliments between friends like, 'You drive quite well, for a girl,' to excluding women from social gatherings among co-workers at the workplace.

While casual sexism can be extremely frustrating to deal with, legally, there is a difference between sexism and sexual harassment. If the sexism becomes sexual in nature, then it amounts to sexual harassment. For example, commenting sexually about a female colleague's appearance, body parts, clothing, etc., or cracking adult jokes to create a hostile work environment.

Sexism is covered under other laws, too. For instance, if you receive unequal pay for equal work, or you face discrimination for taking maternity leave, you can seek recourse under those specific laws. This is discussed later in this chapter.

> **#ReelNotReal**
>
> In the popular Netflix show *Never Have I Ever*, Kamala, a smart and talented engineer, is made to clean beakers in her laboratory by a male supervisor. She is also made to bring coffee for her male colleagues and excluded from after-work social gatherings. One day, Kamala puts her foot down and breaks a bunch of test tubes on purpose to make her sexist supervisor clean up after her! Of course, in real life, we don't break test tubes. There are other ways of teaching sexist colleagues a lesson.

While you can't always file a complaint under the POSH Act for casual sexism, there are other ways to tackle it.

1. Assertive communication: Clearly tell people your boundaries, opinions and ideas. For example, 'I am not comfortable with what you said. It seems to be sexist. I would prefer if you don't speak to me like that in the future.'
2. Build allies and support networks: Collective voices are always more effective than a lone voice. Connect with other colleagues, both women and men, who share similar values regarding gender equality and create a support system. By working together, you can challenge casual sexism, amplify each other's voices and create a united front against discriminatory behaviour.
3. Document incidents: Keep a record of specific instances of casual sexism, including dates, times, individuals involved

and what actually happened. You can use this as evidence if you need to file a formal complaint. Documentation helps to establish a pattern and strengthens your case.
4. Seek guidance from HR or senior management: If your workplace has clear policies for a positive and equal work environment, you can approach the HR or senior management to report incidents of casual sexism. This will depend on the support that your company's organizational structure provides.

Sexual Harassment in the Remote Working Model

In the times of work from home, the POSH Act must go beyond the office. Now, your desk at home, sometimes even your bed, becomes the place from where you work, right? Does that mean your bed is your workplace? No. But the POSH Act *will* extend to all interactions done for the purpose of work, such as emails, WhatsApp, phone calls and Zoom calls.

Here are a few everyday examples:
1. Sending inappropriate messages (with sexual innuendos) late at night or beyond working hours.
2. Forcing female employees to be on video calls, in one-on-one settings, when they are not comfortable.
3. Asking female employees to adjust the camera to reveal more than their faces.
4. Sending sexual images, links, jokes or messages via any communication medium (WhatsApp, email, SMS, etc.). This applies to forwarded messages and those sent on a group chat.

Again, context and comfort are the key elements. Two colleagues who are friends and share a sexual joke or picture with no objection from either, is different from a male boss sending a sexually suggestive joke to female colleagues.

How Do I Take Action under the POSH Act?

The most important part of the POSH Act is the 'how'. How do you take action against workplace sexual harassment?

1. Collect evidence: Record on your phone, take screenshots, look for CCTV footage (make note of the time and date) and look for witnesses. Collect all the evidence you can, as and when the harassment happens. Save this evidence securely on your personal (and not your office) device/email.
2. Gather support: If you know anyone else who has gone through something similar in your office, or if there are other female/male colleagues who will be willing to stand up for you, gather them around. You don't have to fight this battle alone.
3. Complaint: File a complaint using the POSH Act against the harasser.
    i. How to file: Your complaint should be in writing and submitted to the Internal Complaints Committee (ICC) of your organization. If your organization doesn't have such a committee, file a complaint with the HR (Human Resources). It can be a hand-written or typed letter, or an email. Always check if your organization has a procedure in this regard.

ii. **When to file:** You should file the complaint as soon as possible. This is to ensure that the evidence gets preserved, you set the ball rolling early and the harasser doesn't get away with the abuse for too long. According to the POSH Act, the time limit to file a complaint is three months from the incident. If it is a series of incidents, then file a complaint within three months from the latest incident. You can also file after three months, but there should be a good justification for the delay.

#TrueStory

Remember the series of #MeToo allegations in Bollywood? While most of them were Twitter or social media accusations, in a couple of cases (such as Tanushree Dutta's accusation against Nana Patekar) a formal complaint was registered by the Mumbai Police. However, later in 2019, the police gave Nana Patekar a clean chit due to lack of evidence. The allegations in question were from 2008, almost a decade ago. Passage of time makes it difficult to prove the allegations, making the battle even tougher for the victim. Therefore, always collect evidence and file a complaint ASAP (as soon as possible).

Note: Apart from filing a complaint under the POSH Act, you can also file a regular police complaint for sexual harassment under the Bharatiya Nyaya Sanhita (already discussed in Chapter 1). The remedies under POSH and the BNS run parallel, and one does not exclude the other.

I recommend that if your organization has an ICC or internal mechanism, approach it first, simply considering that the police may not be very responsive to POSH complaints and ask you to go to the ICC first. However, if it is a serious case of harassment (whether physical or non-physical) and you feel that your organization will not help you, then gather all the evidence and go straight to the police.

Be mindful of your rights as a complainant:
1. Confidentiality: The complaint itself and the entire sexual harassment proceedings need to be kept confidential by your organization.
2. Temporary reliefs: You can ask for the following temporary reliefs when the POSH proceedings are ongoing:
    i. Suspend your reporting relationship with the harasser.
    ii. Transfer either you or your harasser to a different manager or project.
    iii. Paid leave up to three months/work from home for yourself. As per the law, this is available in addition to your annual leave policy.
3. Protection against secondary victimization: Often, victims hesitate to complain because they fear backlash—colleagues whispering, the accused trying to use his power to make life difficult for the victim, etc. However, as per the law, you have protection against secondary victimization that may create a hostile work environment.

When you file a POSH complaint with your organization, mention the above-listed rights and reliefs that you seek in a polite but assertive manner. This will serve as a gentle reminder to the team dealing with your complaint that you are aware of your legal rights and that they need to adhere to the legal procedure.

How Do I Prove Sexual Harassment at Work?

'Proof kahan hai, my Lord (Where is the proof)?' is a common dialogue in Hindi legal dramas. That is because proof is the foundation in most cases. Who wins a case usually depends on who can prove their point better. This is not to scare you, but to alert you. There are plenty of tools available these days to document sexual harassment. Here are a few examples:

1. Screenshots or screen recordings
2. Call or voice recordings
3. Witnesses
4. CCTV footage
5. Previous history of harassment (to supplement your complaint)
6. Similar experiences of others (to supplement your complaint)

You may wonder what to do in case there is no evidence and it is the harasser's word against yours? This usually happens when harassment happens behind closed doors. Let us understand how to document this through an example:

Suppose a male superior calls you for a private meeting in a closed space after office hours. Simply keep the voice recorder switched on in your phone (or an extra phone, if possible, so that the recording is not interrupted). Good for you if all goes well! But if it doesn't, and you face any harassment, you can express objection then and there, knowing that the conversation is being recorded.

But what if you are caught unawares and do not have time to record? In that case, bring up the harassment later (in private) and record that conversation.

Pro tip: In case of such a conversation, start by saying, 'Rajiv, what you did the other day, holding my hand in your cabin when you called me for a discussion, made me extremely uncomfortable. I wasn't able to say anything then because I was in shock, but I want to tell you now that it is sexual harassment.'

Rajiv is sure to respond with either a defence, an argument, or denial. Whatever it is, the recording will serve as proof.

What if My Harasser Retaliates?

The culture of victim-blaming is so strong in our society that, as women, we are conditioned to suffer in silence. We always fear retaliation from the harasser. In a workplace, this can be even more complex, as the harasser could be a superior who can impact your career.

The intent of the POSH Act is to avoid retaliation. Although the Act doesn't spell this out, the POSH handbook (on pages 24 and 27) of the Ministry of Women and Child Development states that it is an employee's right to expect an assurance against retaliation when filing a POSH complaint, and that this right is non-negotiable.[4]

Therefore, if anyone in your organization tries to retaliate after you speak up, tell them that you know the law, that their action is against legal policy. Also, collect evidence of it in case you need to prove your point later.

Can I Be Reverse-blamed for Filing a Complaint?

Another worry that complainants have is not being able to prove the allegations and their complaint being declared false. Will you be penalized for filing the complaint? The answer is a loud NO.

The POSH Act makes a provision against false complaints. If the POSH committee finds the complaint to be false, or malicious, it can act against the complainant as per the rules of the organization. However, this provision comes with two important caveats.

1. '... a mere inability to substantiate a complaint, or provide adequate proof, need not attract action against the complainant.'
2. '... the malicious intent on part of the complainant shall be established after an inquiry, in accordance with the procedure prescribed, before any action is recommended.'

What this means is that just because you are unable to prove your complaint does not mean that the accused can charge you with filing a false complaint. Further, to avoid the common practice of blaming the complainant (such as, 'she is doing this for money', 'she is frustrated because she wasn't promoted', 'she is taking revenge', 'she is lying'), the law clearly states that the malicious intent has to be proven after an inquiry. Mere allegation of malicious intent is not enough.

So, you see, the law is balanced when it comes to false complaints and addresses the concerns of a complainant about retaliation.

Is Your Company Fulfilling Its Responsibility as Per the POSH Act?

The POSH Act applies to any organization that has more than ten employees (of any gender). It does not matter if only one of those ten employees is a woman. Further, it does not matter what type of organization it is—a corporate, an NGO or a start-up—the same rules apply to everyone.

Any organization with more than ten employees has to implement the following steps under POSH:

1. Provide a safe working environment for all employees.
2. Constitute an ICC to resolve sexual harassment complaints within the organization.
3. Have an anti-sexual harassment policy.
4. Display the punishment for violation of the anti-sexual harassment policy at notable places (like bulletin boards).
5. Organize workshops and programmes to create awareness among the employees about the POSH Act.
6. Help the victim if she chooses to file a police complaint.

Activity Time: Of the above-mentioned points, count how many your organization complies with.

The Plague of Poor Implementation

The unfortunate truth is that even though the law mandates every organization to comply with the POSH Act, very few organizations actually do. Even the compliant ones simply have a POSH committee and policy on paper.

I have personally heard stories of large organizations, including one that was led by a woman and had over 2,000 employees, that if a complaint comes up, they prefer to fire one or both people involved (i.e., the complainant and the accused) rather than investigating it.

Part of the problem is that organizations don't have the internal expertise to handle a POSH complaint, given that the process is almost like running a courtroom within the office. They neither want to set up a proper ICC nor do they want to invest time and money on training the committee and the employees.

I don't mean to dishearten you about the POSH Act. While there are organizations that would rather not care about it, there are those within India that are concerned about their employees and are particular about being POSH-compliant. I have served as an external member on the ICC of one of the biggest dating apps in the country, and I must tell you how proactive they are about ensuring that everyone in the organization is fully aware of their rights and trained to respond to sexual harassment. The same is the case with the big corporates, which have to follow ESG (environmental, social and governance) standards.

How Can You Make a Difference?

While you cannot change the attitude of the lakhs of organizations in the country, here's what you can do on a personal level:

1. Ask questions: When joining a company, always ask about POSH compliance and what steps they take to ensure a harassment-free environment.
2. Build your bargaining power: Make yourself so skilled and irreplaceable that you hold strong bargaining power vis-à-vis your employer. This will give you the leverage to ask for, or initiate, positive changes in the workplace, like efforts for gender equality. It is a proven fact that when empathetic women rise to the top, they take other women with them by introducing welfare and equality initiatives.
3. Build collective bargaining power: Ten voices are always stronger than a single voice. Build a support system and community of women (and other allies) in your organization. If you can't do it within your company, look beyond. There are several women's networking platforms emerging today. Take advantage of this and find your voice!
4. Support other women in your organization: It can be difficult for a woman to speak up against sexual harassment at work, for fear of losing her job or having her colleagues blame her. Your support can make all the difference between the victim choosing to suffer in silence and filing a complaint.

Remember, small steps have a big impact. Similarly, each time a woman asks her interviewer about POSH implementation, she sends out the message that this is important for her to join the organization. The more we start asking these questions, the louder and clearer our message becomes!

#WomenEmpoweringWomen

Also, it is important that we, as women, stand together and help each other. Silence is also a conscious choice; it means you stand with the perpetrator by choosing not to stand up for the victim. And we cannot expect others to take a stand for us if we don't do the same.

Finally, just like before taking an insurance policy you ask the agent about the cover, how to claim, who all does it cover, etc., when you join an organization, do your research and find out what the organization's policies are like.

Checklist for When You Join an Organization

- ✓ Do they have an anti-sexual harassment policy? If yes, what all does it cover?
- ✓ Have they constituted an ICC as required by the POSH Act?
- ✓ How do you access the HR? Are they friendly and approachable?
- ✓ What is the gender ratio? How many female employees work in the organization?
- ✓ How many women do you see in leadership positions?

- ✓ Finally, and this is something you cannot explain but only feel, do a vibe check!

> **POINTS TO REMEMBER**
>
> 1. Any place that you go to for work will be considered your workplace. This can be your office desk, canteen, office transport and video conference calls.
> 2. Every organization with more than ten employees (irrespective of gender) needs to have a POSH committee.
> 3. What matters is what the victim felt, not what the harasser meant. For example, if the harasser cracks an adult joke that makes you uncomfortable, what matters is that you felt uneasy, not whether he meant to harass you or was trying to be funny.
> 4. All POSH proceedings must be kept completely confidential.
> 5. A POSH complaint can be initiated parallel to a police complaint. You should file a police complaint if it is a serious case of sexual harassment.

EXERCISE TIME!

Workplace Warrior

Guess the letters to reveal the words related to sexual harassment at the workplace.

1. _ _ G _ _ _ V _ D   _ O _ _ N
2. H _ _ T _ _ E   E _ V _ _ O _ _ _ N _
3. QU _ _   _ _ O   _ _ O
4. C _ _ F _ D _ _ T _ _ L I _ _
5. W _ _ K _ L _ _ E

Answer key:
1. Aggrieved Women 2. Hostile Environment
3. Quid Pro Quo 4. Confidentiality 5. Workplace

Equal Pay for Equal Work

Have you ever wondered if you have the legal right to demand equal pay for doing an equal amount of work?

What is your guess? Before I give you the answer, let me share a real-life example. When I was in law school, I was working on contracts for an A-list actor and actress for a popular Bollywood movie. I was shocked to see that the actor's fee was *five* times more than that of the actress, despite both being in the lead. No wonder the gender-based wage gap in the movie industry is a huge topic of discussion these days.

Sadly, this wage gap is not limited to Bollywood. It applies across industries and organizations. It is not uncommon to see male colleagues drawing a higher salary than their female colleagues for the exact same role.

What Does the Law Say about Equal Pay?

The Code on Wages, 2019,[5] states that no employer should discriminate for wages on the ground of gender, when it comes to the same, or similar, work. Your rights to equal pay are also covered under Articles 14, 15 and 16 of the Indian Constitution, which require equality before the law, protection against discrimination and equal opportunities in public employment.

How do you ask for equal pay?
Now that you know that your demand for equal pay is not just based on moral grounds but is also backed by the law, here are a few practical steps you can take:

1. Negotiation: Ask for what you deserve. Do your research on what other people of both genders, in a similar position, are making. Negotiate with your employer accordingly. If they refuse, bring to their attention the laws that grant you the right to seek equal pay for equal work.
2. Gather evidence: If your employer refuses to budge, then it is time for you to take action. Start by gathering evidence of the gender-based wage gap. This can include paychecks, employment contracts, descriptions of job profiles, designations, scope of work, roles and responsibilities, etc. Once you have proof of the discrimination, it is on the employer to justify the basis for the difference in wages (except gender).
3. Gather support: If you can, gather the support of other female and male colleagues who believe in equal pay for equal work and would like to demand the same. This will make your ask much easier. An employer can risk losing one employee over failed negotiations, but it cannot risk losing ten employees in one go. Strength in numbers will put you in a better bargaining position.
4. File a case: Lastly, if nothing works, you can file a case with a labour court (lower courts dedicated to employment and labour disputes) in your jurisdiction, under the Code on Wages, 2019. For this, you may need the assistance of a lawyer, especially one who specializes in labour laws. When filing a case, you will need to submit all the evidence possible to demonstrate gender discrimination in wages.

Pro tip: Given India's complex legal and government systems, filing a complaint or a case may not always get you the relief you are looking for. However, it will make your employer take your demand seriously. Most likely, your employer will come forward for a negotiation and settlement post this.

Food for thought

Sometimes, filing a complaint could have a counter-effect, where you burn bridges with your employer and face discrimination in other ways. As a result, most people remain silent in such cases, especially if they don't have financial backing. This is why I have suggested filing a case as the last step.

Maternity Benefits at Work: From Conception to Compensation

Have you ever met a new mother? Most of them spend sleepless nights, awakened every hour by a baby wanting to feed, navigating physical and emotional changes, and facing societal pressure to shed pregnancy weight rapidly. Their entire life is turned upside down by the demands of a tiny new human. Yet, some people believe that 'maternity leave' is like a paid holiday! Little do they know that taking care of a newborn is more strenuous than office work!

On that note, let us understand the rights granted under India's Maternity Benefit Act, 1961.

Which employer has to give maternity benefits?
Every organization that has ten or more employees of any gender, must grant maternity leave.

How many months leave can you get?
First- and second-time mothers can avail twenty-six weeks of paid leave. Of this, eight weeks (two months) can be before childbirth, and the rest after it.

Mothers with two children get twelve weeks of paid leave. Of this, six weeks can be taken before childbirth.

How much do you get paid?
You get paid the same amount as your average daily wage over the three months preceding your maternity leave. In simple words, you will get the amount that you were drawing immediately before your leave started. This includes not just the basic salary component, but every other component, such as allowances and bonus.

Pro tip: Maternity leave is only available after you have worked in your office for a minimum of eighty days in the twelve months preceding your delivery date. If you are planning a child and this leave is important for you, keep this in mind.

Did you know that the law also gives rights to mothers who have children through adoption or surrogacy? Adopting and surrogate mothers get twelve weeks of maternity leave, from the date of delivery of the child. In cases of adoption, the child must be less than three months old.

> **Maternity Leave for Female Students**
>
> MPhil and PhD students are permitted a maternity leave of up to 240 days, once in the entire duration of their course, as per Rule 4.4 of the UGC Regulations, 2016. This benefit is especially useful in the medical field, where women often have to balance their studies with family planning.[6]

Rights under maternity benefits that no one tells you, but you should know:

Apart from paid leave, you have other rights as an expecting and new mother. These are:

1. Right to job security: You can neither be fired nor demoted during your maternity leave. You should be able to join back at the same designation that you held when you went on your maternity break.
2. Amenities and comfort: Pregnant women need extra care. To ensure that they can work in a safe and healthy manner, the workplace has to provide certain amenities such as hygienic restrooms, comfortable seating or working arrangements and safe drinking water.
3. Leave for miscarriage: A woman is entitled to six weeks of leave from the date of miscarriage.
4. Right to crèche: If an organization has fifty or more employees, it needs to provide a crèche, or at least offer access to such a facility nearby.

5. Nursing breaks: A new mother has the right to four nursing breaks per day, in addition to her regular breaks, once she rejoins her company.
6. Additional leave for illness: In addition to the maternity leave, if a woman has postpartum illness extending beyond her maternity period, she is eligible for one more month of paid leave.

Pro tip: Beware of sneaky tactics. Some workplaces, especially those dominated by men, attempt to avoid granting maternity rights to their female employees. Knowing they can't demote you directly, they might slyly shift you to a less crucial project or keep you stagnant in your current role. Keep an eye out for these strategies to ensure that you don't unknowingly fall victim to 'pregnancy discrimination'.

> **Activity time:** Round up your female colleagues for a quiz. Ask yourselves how many of these rights did you know? Brainstorm ideas to ensure that your employer gives you your statutory maternity benefits!

What can you do if your employer is not giving you maternity benefits?

1. Know your rights: First, ensure you are well-aware of the maternity rights as per the law, so that you can demand the same from your employer.
2. Ask for it: If you work for a big company, which has an HR team, you will need to take this up with them. If there is no HR, or it is not effective, speak to the

senior management. Understand if your company has a maternity benefit policy, and if it is in line with the law. If your company does not have one, you will need to ask for your maternity benefits.

Pro tip: To begin, have an informal chat to establish an amicable discussion. You can document the chat over email as a follow-up. You could always say, 'Thank you for your time today. I wanted to summarize what we discussed about my maternity benefit …'

> Don't start the discussion with an accusation. This could put your employer on the defensive.

3. Legal notice: If internal discussions are unsuccessful, you can send your employer a legal notice, asking them to grant you maternity benefits, failing which you will take them to court. Get this notice drafted from a lawyer. The notice will also help you if you have to go to court.
4. Court case: If nothing works, file a case against your employer in the labour court under the Maternity Benefit Act, 1961. In this case, you should ask for maternity leave and other benefits, for your organization to form a maternity policy in line with the law, monetary compensation if you were not granted leave and had to continue working, and monetary compensation for the mental agony caused.

Should you file a case?

While not many cases of maternity benefit are filed, the ones that did reach the Supreme Court and high courts have generally leaned in favour of the mothers. For example, in a 2023 case (*Dr Kavita Yadav vs Ministry of Health and Family Welfare Department*),[7] the Supreme Court held that even if a woman's contract is expiring, and she applies for maternity leave towards the end of the contract, the employer must pay her salary for the full term of the maternity leave. In this case, the woman's contract was ending one week after her leave started. Her employer decided to give her only one week's worth of maternity benefit and did not renew her contract. This action was quashed by the Supreme Court, holding that maternity benefits apply regardless of the duration of the contract.

While the Kavita Yadav case is pro-women, the outcome in such cases can depend on the judges and how they interpret the law. When you file a case, you also need to keep in mind that the case can outlive your pregnancy. It is possible that you get the final judgment when you are celebrating your child's first or second birthday! Nevertheless, a court case can put pressure on your employer to give you your rightful leave/compensation. If you get a favourable judgment from the court, it is a bonus!

Pro tip: Hire a good lawyer to represent your case. Also do a cost–benefit analysis and decide whether you are willing to wait for the result, and if the result is worth the wait.

>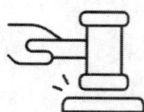
> **Supreme Court Grants Childcare Leave for Mothers**
>
> In a recent 2024 judgment (*Shalini Dharmani vs State of Himachal Pradesh*), the Supreme Court held that denying a woman 'childcare leave' is a violation of her constitutional right to equality and her right to participate in the workforce. Childcare leave is to take care of a child, in addition to maternity leave. In this case, a government college professor was granted this leave to attend to her child with special needs.
>
> While this judgment is a great start to more equitable workplace policies, it is just *one* judgment, without any concrete guidelines or laws. Therefore, it may not translate into reality for most women.[8]

'*Beta, good news kab de rahe ho?* (When are you giving us good news?)'

Sooner or later, all of us are faced with this question. When are you getting married? When are you having children?

These questions come not only from nosy relatives but also from recruiters during job interviews! As preposterous as it may sound, many women have been subjected to these invasive 'interview questions'.

Understand that it is not okay for a recruiter to ask you about your personal life. Next time you or someone you know faces this, politely tell the person asking you that you are not comfortable discussing something so personal, but you can assure them that your personal life will not affect the professional front.

Are you winning in office but losing at home?

There is no doubt that motherhood is rewarding, but this reward comes with the loss of career and earnings. Harvard University professor Claudia Goldin was awarded the Nobel Prize in Economics in 2023 for her research on the 'motherhood penalty'. Goldin demonstrated that women earn less than men after the birth of their first child, often having to leave the workforce or significantly reduce their work hours. Consequently, they miss out on the career advancement that their male counterparts continue to experience.

The motherhood penalty is also one of the reasons why we mostly see men holding top management positions and women retaining entry- and mid-level positions.

You know why this happens, right? It is because even if both parents are working, the primary responsibility still falls on the mother. Therefore, the mother either must cut down on her workplace responsibilities or stretch herself to balance both the personal and professional fronts perfectly.

The 'bare minimum father'

Raise your hand if you have heard of men being praised for doing the bare minimum for their child. 'Oh my God, he changed a diaper?', 'Your husband fed your baby a meal?', 'He took the kids out for dinner (instead of cooking)? What an involved father!'

Society has double standards when it comes to expectations from a mother and father. The mother's labour goes unnoticed, while even the 'bare minimum' from the father is applauded and praised. Relatives and neighbours are always quick to exclaim, '*Kitna help karta hai woh* (He helps so much)!'

The thing is, this is not 'help.' It is 'contribution'. When we say the husband is helping his wife out, it implies that childcare is the mother's job and the father is being generous enough to assist her. The truth, however, is that both parents chose to bring a child into the world. And contribution to childcare should be the duty of both parents, irrespective of gender.

Case in Point

A woman in the US asked her husband to compensate her with $50,000 a month for having their baby!

The wife and husband, who were both earning the same amount per year, kept their individual expenses separate and combined all joint expenses before they had a child.

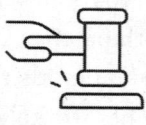

During her six-month maternity leave, the wife stood to lose 50 per cent of her earnings, apart from being set back in her career. Hence, she wanted her husband to compensate for the 'motherhood penalty' that she would have to bear. This news was hotly debated on the internet, with users writing in support of and against the woman.

What are your thoughts on this?[9]

The bottom line is that we need, and have on paper, maternity rights at our workplace. But more importantly, we need equality in our homes. Women should not have to choose between a fulfilled family life and a flourishing career, the same way that men never have to make this choice. And this change will not come until we, as a society, learn to accept that childcare is not a mother's job alone. Just like charity begins at home, change also begins from home.

> **POINTS TO REMEMBER**
>
> 1. You get twenty-six weeks of paid maternity leave (eight weeks before childbirth and the rest after it).
> 2. Your employer can't fire you while you are on maternity leave. Once you return to work, you must be reinstated in the same role (you cannot be demoted).
> 3. You must be paid the same salary that you were drawing before your maternity leave.
> 4. You are entitled to nursing breaks when you return to work after your maternity leave.
> 5. Maternity leave is also granted to a woman who suffers from a miscarriage.

4

Behind Closed Doors: Domestic Violence

In this chapter, we will understand what counts as domestic abuse, what action can you take against it, and what happens when you file a police complaint or court case.

Introduction

In March 2020, when I launched Pink Legal, I assumed we would receive the maximum queries for sexual harassment. I mean, we see it almost every day, right? It starts as soon as we step out into a public space. But what happened within the first month of Pink Legal's launch shocked me and opened my eyes to a startling reality. Within a week, our website (www.pinklegal.in) received 60,000 (yes, SIXTY THOUSAND) organic hits from all over the country. Our inbox was flooded with emails from women seeking legal help. And guess what 90 per cent of the emails were about? Domestic violence!

Till date, the maximum grievances that we receive at Pink Legal are for domestic violence (usually involving the husband or in-laws). Almost every other day I have some well-meaning neighbour, aunt or friend reaching out to help a victim. It is like what Bulbul Jauhari, a character in the web series *Made in Heaven*, said, '*Hamaari society beemar hai* (As a society, we are unwell).'

I truly believe that domestic violence is an epidemic in our country, with countless women falling prey to it every single day. The only way to beat an epidemic is to vaccinate the population. In our case, awareness and action are the best forms of vaccination. Let us understand domestic violence and our legal rights with regard to it.

What Is Domestic Violence?

Close your eyes and picture a scene of domestic violence, based on how you understand it. You may picture a hapless woman being beaten by her husband. But, domestic violence is much more than that.

The Domestic Violence (DV) Act, 2005, protects a woman from all kinds of abuse, broadly categorized as:

1. Physical abuse: Physical abuse means any kind of physical or bodily harm, such as beating, slapping, kicking, punching, etc. Any type of, and any degree of, physical harm counts. It need not be violent or extreme, nor does it need to cause severe injuries.
2. Mental abuse: This includes insults, ridicule, humiliation, name-calling, taunts with regard to not having a child, or a male child, or verbal threats about physical harassment.
3. Sexual abuse: This means any sexual conduct that is abusive or violates the woman. This can include forcing her to have intercourse or engage in any sexual activity without her consent, showing her pornography against her will, forcefully filming any sexual act, etc.
4. Financial abuse: This one is VERY important and often ignored. The provision against financial abuse is meant to protect every woman who is financially dependent on her family members, or whose money and assets are controlled by them, to ensure that they do not use financial threats to mistreat her. It includes:
    i. Depriving the woman of financial resources (any form of money), which she is entitled to. This includes earnings/savings/stridhan.

ii. Not giving the woman financial support, which she needs for maintenance. For example, money needed for monthly expenses, running the household, taking care of children, etc.
iii. Disposing of any property, jewellery, money, shares, bonds, or other financial assets that belong to the woman, or in which she has a share as a wife/daughter/daughter-in-law. For example, selling a house she might own without her permission, or not giving her a rightful share in the family property.

#ReelToReal

If you have seen the Bollywood movie *Thappad* (which literally means 'slap'), the message is loud and clear: even one slap counts as physical abuse. In the movie, the husband slaps his wife in the middle of a party, in a fit of rage. The wife, played by Taapsee Pannu, files a case against him for domestic violence. Her plea is clear: '*Usne mujhe mara, pehli baar. Nahi maar sakta. Bas itni si baat hai, aur meri petition bhi itni si hai.* (He hit me, for the first time. He cannot hit me. It is as simple as that, and my petition is also as simple as that).'

If only every woman could be as empowered as Taapsee's character, the epidemic of domestic violence would have been eradicated ages ago!

Who All Am I Protected against When It Comes to Domestic Abuse?

How about I don't answer this question for you, but help you do it yourself? Just like every recipe requires certain ingredients, and without the right sugar/salt/spice combination it will not be complete, the Domestic Violence Act requires two 'ingredients' for physical, mental, sexual and financial abuse to qualify as domestic violence.

1. The abuser should be related to you and be a family member. You could be related by blood (your own family members), by marriage (anyone from your in-laws' side), by adoption, or in a live-in relationship (your live-in partner).

    To leave no room for doubt, it will include your own family members (parents, siblings, grandparents, aunts, uncles, etc.), your husband or live-in partner (the law does not explicitly include live-in relationships, but since they are treated like marriage your live-in partner will also count) and your in-laws (mother-in-law, father-in-law, sister-in-law, brother-in-law, etc.).

2. You need to live in the same house or have lived together when the abuse took place. Basically, you need to share a roof with the abusive family member for it to qualify as 'domestic' abuse. How long should you have lived together? The law does not specify a time limit. It is decided on a case-to-case basis. However, it is safe that a 'visit' will not count as living together.

To summarize, the abuser should be related to the victim and they should share a roof. If these two criteria are satisfied, then any abuse falling under the above-listed four categories (physical, mental, sexual and financial) will qualify as domestic violence.

Applying the above two points, will abuse by your live-in house help (in a hypothetical situation) qualify as domestic violence? No, it will not! Why? Because the law does not consider her a family member.

So, now can you answer the question about who all does the Domestic Violence Act protect you against? Look around, see who you live with and you will have your answer.

You may well ask, are you protected from domestic abuse by female family members also? Yes, of course. The gender of the abuser does not matter. What matters is that they should be a family member and you both should live in the same house.

Which Laws Protect Me against Domestic Violence?

1. Domestic Violence Act, 2005: This is the main law of the country, which protects all women from any form of domestic violence.

Note: As of 2024, the Domestic Violence Act is not even twenty years old. Until then, there was no dedicated law in our country to protect women against domestic violence. Even the law we have today is thanks to women's rights activists who had to fight with their blood, sweat and tears. We owe them a big thank you for this crucial step.

2. Sections 85 and 86 of the Bharatiya Nyaya Sanhita: This law protects all married women against serious forms of physical and emotional abuse from their husband or in-laws.

Note: Before the DV Act of 2005, the only law that protected women against domestic violence was Section 498A of the Indian Penal Code (now sections 85 and 86 of the BNS).

Although both laws protect women against domestic violence, they are different. Let us understand the difference between the DV Act and Section 498A.

DV Act	Section 498A
Protects *all* women against *any* family member (not just husband and in-laws).	Protects only *married* women against their husband and in-laws.
Covers *all types of abuse*: physical, mental, sexual and financial.	Covers only *physical* and *emotional* (mental) abuse.

If you are an unmarried woman, you should turn to the DV Act. If you are a married woman, you can use both the DV Act and sections 85, 86 of the BNS.

What Can I Do against Abuse by My Husband and/or In-laws?

If there is one epidemic plaguing most women in our country, it is domestic abuse after marriage. The saas–bahu TV serials that we would watch in the '90s and early 2000s were not all fiction. What they showed in those serials is very much a reality in many Indian households. I know many women who are educated and well-to-do, and some who had a love marriage, and are still victims of domestic abuse.

> #### #TrueStory
>
> Let us take the real-life case of my friend Kareena (name changed). Kareena got married to Saif (name changed), who she was in love with. She dreamt of building a life with him, where the two of them would spend weekends with breakfast in bed, come home to each other every night and share a loving relationship. However, Kareena's mother-in-law—let us call her Cruella—had other plans. Cruella was basically looking for a housemaid in the form of a daughter-in-law. The minute Kareena moved into their house after marriage, Cruella fired all the maids and expected Kareena to cook and clean. Kareena would be expected to serve the other family members first and eat leftovers herself. Added to this were daily taunts and insults, openly calling her names and threatening to throw her out of the house on a daily basis. It became so bad that, one night, Cruella locked Kareena out of the house and refused to let her in. The domestic abuse not only affected Kareena's marriage, but also took a severe toll on her mental health.

What should Kareena do?
First, let us identify the type of abuse at play here. This is clearly a case of emotional abuse, which is a type of domestic violence.

Second, does it satisfy the all-important two criteria of domestic violence? Yes, it does. Kareena's mother-in-law is considered a family member and they live in the same house.

What legal action should Kareena take?
1. Start collecting as much evidence as possible: Whether it is audio recordings, video recordings, photos, messages, anything and everything helps. This is possibly the most important step that can help prove all allegations in court.
2. File a police complaint: Once Kareena decides that she has had enough of Cruella's ways, she can file a police complaint under sections 85, 86 of the BNS.
3. Speak to a lawyer to file a case: A good lawyer will help you build your case, be able to advise you the right course of action and tell you when to file a case under the Domestic Violence Act. If you don't have access to a lawyer, there are some helplines like Project Nyay'ri (run by Pink Legal in collaboration with Project Naveli) that provide women free legal consultation.

What happens after you file a police complaint under sections 85, 86 of the BNS and a case under the Domestic Violence Act is explained a little later.

If it is possible for you to move out of the house and the toxic environment, do that. Sometimes that is the best solution. It's like the Hindi saying *'Na rahega baans na bajegi bansuri,'* which roughly translates to 'if there is no bamboo, you cannot make a flute out of it'. Basically, if you are not in front of your abuser, they can't abuse you. You know what Kareena did? She bought a house for herself and shifted there with her husband! What a slap-in-your-face move! Now, Kareena could do this because she was earning well, and that is why I stress on the importance of financial independence for women in multiple places in this book.

Can my in-laws or husband throw me out of the house?
Consider Kareena's case, where her mother-in-law would keep threatening to throw her out of the house. Luckily for Kareena, her parents lived close by and were supportive of her. However, in many cases, victims of domestic abuse have nowhere to go. Their parents either don't stay in the same city, or they don't support their daughters coming back home thinking '*Log kya kahenge* (What will people say)?'

What rights does Kareena have in such a situation?
1. Once you are married, you have the right to live in your matrimonial house, i.e., your husband's house. No one can take this right away from you. Therefore, if the in-laws threaten you, tell them strongly that you have the right to stay there and they can't ask you to leave.
2. If your in-laws pull stunts like Cruella, like locking Kareena out of the house, you can file a police complaint under sections 85, 86 of the BNS. In most cases, victims take legal action as the last resort as it can spoil relationships. Therefore, this is your choice. If you don't want to file a police complaint, at least collect evidence of what is happening. Bring in your husband or other relatives to mediate.

> **#TrueStory**
>
> Another friend of mine, Ashima (name changed), became a victim of domestic abuse at the hands of her husband and in-laws. She had moved to her husband's house in Punjab, from Hyderabad, after marriage. One day, Ashima just couldn't take the torture any more. She booked her tickets to Hyderabad and returned to her parents' house, with just a small carry-on bag and her purse.
>
> All of Ashima's belongings, including her jewellery, clothes, documents and other valuables were still at her matrimonial house. Her in-laws did not allow her to come back to the matrimonial house. It took her over six to eight months to get her belongings back.

Again, Ashima's case is not uncommon. In many cases, victims of domestic abuse pack and leave when they can't take the abuse any more. However, most women leave in such distress that they forget to take the essentials. All they want is to escape the torture. While this is understandable, leaving without your belongings can create problems for you in the future, when you want your valuables and documents back.

What should Ashima keep in mind when moving out of her matrimonial house?

1. Ashima should not leave her matrimonial house without taking all her stridhan, jewellery, cash, etc. Once the woman leaves, it becomes extremely difficult to retrieve her belongings.
2. Ashima should take all important documents with her, like her passport, Aadhaar card, driving licence, PAN

card, educational and professional certificates, and documents related to assets and properties (like share certificate, sale deed, etc.).
3. If possible, Ashima should take her clothes and other valuable, or sentimental items, with her.
4. If there are any joint properties between Ashima and her husband, she should take copies of those documents as well. If possible, she should also take copies of documents regarding her husband's assets. That might help if she files for maintenance later.

Basically, if you plan to move out, 'plan' to move out. Don't leave without items 1 and 2 from the list above. How do I carry all my things without raising suspicion, you may ask? Pull an overnight coup if you must! Like how Simran and her family shifted countries overnight in *Dilwale Dulhaniya Le Jayenge*. Trust me, you would rather be out of the abusive environment, safe with your belongings, than be stuck worried about what your in-laws will think.

#TrueStory

My friend, Mohini (name changed), called me one day. She sounded extremely distressed. Her parents were forcing her to get married. Her father locked her up in her room and took away her phone. They were not allowing her to speak to anyone or step out of her room, fearing she would run away. Her uncle even raised his hand on her when she questioned their behaviour.

I have heard of several such cases through friends and acquaintances. Forced marriage is only an example.

What can I do against domestic violence by my parents?
Domestic abuse by parents can take on many forms. I have explained these in detail in a section called 'Forced Marriage' later in this book (under the chapter titled 'All About Marriage'). The same steps will be applicable, more or less, for any kind of domestic abuse by one's parents or family members.

What can I do against domestic violence by my live-in partner?
While I have covered everything you need to know about live-in relationships, and how to protect yourself legally if you are in one, in a later chapter, here's an outline of how to safeguard your rights in such a situation.

If your live-in partner is being abusive, think about whether you want to continue the relationship. Very often, we mistake abuse or aggression for love. Don't get swayed by movies like *Kabir Singh* and *Animal*, which may influence women into believing that it is okay for your partner to slap you, that it is his way of showing love. No, it is not!

From a legal perspective, your first steps will be the same as a case of domestic violence: collect evidence, file a police complaint, file a court case. The laws that protect you against domestic abuse apply here too—the Domestic Violence Act and sections 85, 86 of the BNS.

However, in a live-in relationship you may face an added legal step, proving your relationship itself. If you go to court, your partner is sure to try and deny the fact, so that he can show that no live-in relationship implies no domestic abuse.

You can prove your live-in relationship by presenting any address proof that shows you both live together, like your

Aadhaar or driving licence. You can also show electricity or phone bills that have your address on it. The idea is to show that you both have the same address and live together. Also, you can ask others to testify that you were in a live-in relationship and not simply friends or flatmates. This can include neighbours, friends or family members.

> ### Common Myths about Domestic Violence
>
> **Myth 1:** Domestic violence only means physical abuse.
> **Truth**: According to the law, domestic violence can be physical, mental, sexual and financial.
>
> **Myth 2:** The Domestic Violence Act only protects married women.
> **Truth**: The Domestic Violence Act protects all women and girls, irrespective of their marital status or age.
>
> **Myth 3:** Domestic violence is perpetrated only by the husband or in-laws.
> **Truth**: Domestic violence can be perpetrated by *any family member* who lives in the same house. This means not only in-laws but also one's own family members (parents, uncles, aunts, siblings, etc.).
>
> **Myth 4:** Only male members are responsible for domestic violence.
> **Truth**: Any family member can be a perpetrator of domestic violence, *regardless of their gender*. This means that even female family members can be responsible for domestic violence (aunt, mother-in-law, sister-in-law, etc.).

Action to Take against Domestic Violence

A domestic violence case can take anywhere between one and three years, or more, depending on the court. Again, this is not to scare you but to prepare you. *'Tareekh pe tareekh'* (date upon date in court cases) is an unfortunate truth in domestic violence cases, where the lawyer of the accused party keeps seeking future dates to delay the case. What can you do to prevent this, or make the journey easier for yourself?

1. First, I would highly recommend getting a strong lawyer. Why? To file your case in the best way possible, oppose delaying tactics from the other side and to ensure that you get some relief during the pendency of the case.

    Can't I fight the case on my own, you may wonder? Yes, you can represent yourself in court. However, court procedures are complex. In the absence of a lawyer, the other side can easily take advantage of you.

2. Second, understand the legal procedure. Whether or not you have a lawyer, it is important for you to understand the procedure so that you can take informed decisions.

What Happens after Filing a Police Complaint?

You can file a police complaint under sections 85, 86 of the BNS against your husband and in-laws. I have explained the steps on how to file a police complaint, and what to expect, in the last chapter.

Before 2014, the police had the authority to immediately arrest the accused based on a complaint registered under

Section 498A of the IPC. However, in 2014, the Supreme Court (while hearing *Arnesh Kumar vs State of Bihar*) held that no arrest can be made unless it is extremely necessary. This was re-iterated by the Supreme Court in a 2023 case and by other high courts in several other judgments. Since 2014, upon filing a police complaint, the accused and the victim are sent for counselling. The police also issue a warning to the accused, but no arrests are made unless it is an extreme case.

Considering this, should you even file a police complaint? Yes! All is not lost just because there will be no immediate arrest. A police complaint is the first step for filing a criminal case against your abuser(s). For more on what happens after filing a police complaint, see the last chapter.

In any case, a police complaint serves as a strong deterrent to the accused. It sends out the message that you will not suffer in silence, that there will be consequences to their abusive actions.

Food for thought

While it is important that no innocent person is arrested, isn't it ironic that in a country where women constantly struggle for justice every day, courts have been extremely proactive in enforcing the Arnesh Kumar (i.e., no arrests) judgment? If only the courts showed the same enthusiasm towards ensuring that the accused persons don't keep delaying the case, our world would be a better place!

What If I Wasn't Able to Collect Evidence?

Don't worry, just write everything down. Each time an incident of domestic violence occurs, write down all the details in a safe place (and keep a backup). Make sure to write every small detail like the time, place, date, who all were there, what happened, were there any witnesses, etc. These details will help you substantiate your testimony if you approach a court.

Pro tip: Write down the details ASAP. After all, memory fades with time. Remember, the devil lies in the details. Details are very important in law. The date, time, place and other such small things, can be used to establish consistency on your part. If there is any inconsistency, the opposing party can use it against you. Therefore, keep the details true and consistent. If you can't remember something, it is better not to include it rather than writing something wrong.

What Happens after a Case Is Filed under the Domestic Violence Act?

The step-by-step process of how to file a case is mentioned in a later chapter.

For now, let us start with where you should file a case against domestic violence. The answer is family court. It is usually a magistrate's court (we have a three-tier court system: the Supreme Court, high courts and lower courts like the magistrate's court). You can either file the case on your own, or through a lawyer. I would highly recommend going through a lawyer because the Indian court system is very complex.

Alternately, you can seek a protection officer. A protection officer is a designated officer, usually appointed by the police, to assist women facing domestic violence and other related issues. You can find a protection officer through a google search for your city, or by going to a police station or the national/state commission for women, asking them to get you in touch with one. You can file a Domestic Incident Report (DIR) with the protection officer. A DIR is like a police complaint and contains all details of the domestic abuse. The protection officer is supposed to file the DIR with the family court to initiate a court case under the DV Act.

Technically, each district is supposed to have a protection officer. However, in many jurisdictions, this role either exists on paper alone or is not adequately serviced, causing victims further anguish. If you can't find an efficient protection officer, I would suggest approaching a lawyer.

What Happens in a Court?

While this is explained in a later section of the book, let us take a quick look at the procedure here.

1. The court will send a notice to the accused person(s), asking them to appear before the court on a particular date. This is called summons.
2. Once the accused person(s) appears in court, they are given time to file their reply to your complaint.
3. After you receive their reply, you can submit a counter-reply.
4. After the complaint and reply stages, the case moves towards oral hearings (arguments).

What is important during this entire procedure is to ask the court for relief, right from the beginning. These are called interim reliefs, which mean reliefs granted to you when the case is still going on. Once you get interim relief, you will have some respite while the case continues.

What Kind of Relief Can the Court Grant?

Based on your situation, you can ask for any or all of the reliefs listed below:

1. Right to stay in the matrimonial home, i.e., the house you have been staying in after getting married.
2. You can ask for monetary compensation for physical or mental injuries, loss of earnings, destruction of property, medical expenses, etc.
3. Apart from monetary compensation, you can also ask for maintenance for day-to-day living expenses for your children and yourself.
4. You can ask for custody of your children during the pendency of the case. The perpetrator may be granted visitation rights, depending on safety implications.
5. You can seek a protection order against the accused. For example, you can ask for the accused to be stopped from contacting you, visiting your workplace, etc. If you are staying in a separate house, you can also ask for an order to stop the harasser(s) from visiting.
6. You can ask the court to direct the accused persons to undergo counselling.
7. You can request the court to conduct the case proceedings 'in camera' (i.e., in the privacy of the judges' chamber and not in an open court).

Note: Each of these can be granted as interim relief (i.e., during the pendency of the case) as cases often go on for long.

> 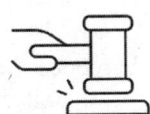 **Bombay High Court Awards Three Crore as Compensation to Victim of Domestic Abuse**
>
> In a recent case in 2024, the Bombay High Court ordered a man, who had inflicted mental, physical and financial abuse on his wife, to pay her three crore as compensation for the trauma. This case made headlines because it is possibly the first domestic violence case where a victim has been granted such a large sum. In this case, both husband and wife were well-to-do, educated and living and working in the USA. The court considered the severity of the abuse, the financial position of both parties and their high social standing while deciding the compensation amount.
>
> However, as usual, things look better on paper than in real life! After this order, the husband challenged the order in the Supreme Court and the case is now on hold. We will have to wait and watch if the woman gets her compensation.[1]

When Do People Typically File a Domestic Violence Case?

Although a domestic violence case can be filed by itself, to raise one's voice against the trauma, women typically file it along with a divorce case. This is because it is considered taboo to file a case against one's family members, including one's husband or in-laws. Also, once a case is filed, the marriage is as good as over. Therefore, most domestic violence cases in India are filed as an addition to a divorce case, usually to get a better settlement.

Let us understand some technical points.

1. Any case you file under the Domestic Violence Act, and any reliefs you ask for in this case, are available in addition to the relief you get under other laws. For example, if you have also filed a case for dowry harassment, you will be entitled to relief under those provisions separately.
2. You can file a police complaint under sections 85, 86 of the BNS and a case under the Domestic Violence Act simultaneously.
3. You can also file a petition against domestic violence as part of any other related case that is ongoing. For example, if you have already filed a divorce or dowry case, you can file the domestic violence petition along with it. All the cases will be clubbed at the time of hearing.

Section 498A of the IPC (Now Sections 85, 86 of the BNS): A Boon or a Bane?

These days, it has become fashionable to talk about Section 498A of the IPC in a negative light. A Google search about this section throws up more results about how it is misused, rather than explaining the provision. There is no doubt that some people use it for the wrong reasons, but if we were to compare, the number of cases of misuse may constitute a miniscule percentage of the domestic violence cases filed.

I must add a line of caution here. Do not abuse the protections granted to women against cruelty. Domestic violence is a horrible epidemic that plagues several women who really need these laws and the protection they offer. The last thing we need is for someone to abuse these provisions for a selfish motive, create mistrust in the law and, as a result, deny an actual victim protection.

What Should I Do if My Case Is Taking Forever?

You are not alone. Our courts are chock-a-block with cases, reliefs are not granted quickly and the opposition always uses delaying tactics or tries to character assassinate the complainant. Many victims and their families either get stuck with never-ending cases, leading to frustration and emotional and financial drain, or end up letting go of the cases, thereby giving up on their rights. Domestic violence cases, like most other cases in India, can take years. To fight it, you will need *emotional and financial support*. This is not to scare you but to prepare you, so that you can gather all the armour possible.

You should prepare yourself:

1. Emotionally: Find someone you can rely on, discuss things with and vent to. It could be family members, friends, neighbours or any well-wisher. You can even approach mental health counsellors.
2. Financially: You will need money to file a court case, pay a lawyer, obtain documents, etc. If you are going to move out of your matrimonial home and do not have a family home to live in, you will need to plan how you are going to support yourself (and children, if any).

Lastly, if you don't want to take on the emotional and financial pressure, opt for an out-of-court settlement. Make sure you seek enough monetary compensation to help you maintain your standard of living. For more details, read the 'Maintenance and Alimony' section in the chapter on divorce. I know that money cannot heal scars, but it can save you from enduring further emotional and financial strain.

Does domestic violence exist only among the uneducated?

If this is what you think, you are sadly mistaken. Domestic violence does not discriminate. It exists in every class, community and social strata. A classic example of this is the second episode of the web series *Made in Heaven* (Season 2). In this episode, a supermodel (Adhira) is in an abusive relationship with her boyfriend, Anik, a motivational speaker. Both Adhira and Anik come from educated and well-to-do backgrounds. To the world, their relationship looks perfect; they project the image of a power couple. One day before the wedding, when Anik beats up Adhira, her family insists that she leave him. However, Adhira goes ahead and marries him, thinking she can fix him.

Adhira is a classic example of why even educated and financially independent women continue to endure domestic violence, because they believe they can change the man, and that it won't happen again. Little do they realize that it never stops. If women understand that a wife is not a rehabilitation centre for a badly behaved husband, many more will walk out of abusive relationships.

> **Women**, you are not rehabilitation centers for badly raised men. It is not your job to fix him, parent him or raise him.
>
> **You want a partner, not a project.**

POINTS TO REMEMBER

1. Domestic violence is not only physical. It can also be mental, sexual or financial abuse.
2. The two main ingredients for an abuse to qualify as 'domestic violence' are: (i) the victim and abuser should live in the same house, (ii) they should be related by blood or through marriage.
3. The Domestic Violence Act, 2005, protects girls from abuse by their own family members.
4. Serious physical and mental harassment by the husband or in-laws also comes under criminal law.
5. You have the right to stay in your matrimonial home; no one can ask you to leave.

> **EXERCISE TIME!**
>
> Unscramble the following words related to domestic violence based on the clues provided.
>
> 1. **MLATMIORANI HSOUE**
>   *Clue:* The house where a married couple lives together.
> 2. **LMNTEA BUESA**
>   *Clue:* Insults, ridicule, humiliation, etc.
> 3. **CODMEITS IOELVCEN CTA**
>   *Clue:* The main law in India to protect women against domestic abuse.
> 4. **ILACNNFIA BUESA**
>   *Clue:* Denying a dependent woman the means to financially maintain herself.
> 5. **IFYMLA CURTO**
>   *Clue:* Court where you can file a domestic violence case.
> 6. **NOCASOTEMIPN**
>   *Clue:* Amount awarded to a victim of domestic violence.

Answer key:
1. Matrimonial House 2. Mental Abuse 3. Domestic Violence Act 4. Financial Abuse 5. Family Court 6. Compensation

5

All about Marriage: How to Safeguard Yourself

This chapter is all about your rights in a marriage, busting patriarchal myths and understanding how to exercise your right of choice for a ceremonial or court marriage, or interfaith marriages.

Introduction

Marriage is one of the most important decisions of your life. Marrying someone means choosing a partner, housemate and co-parent to share a major chunk of your life with. It goes without saying that you should get married only if you are absolutely sure of the person and the idea of marriage and not because 'time is running out' or your family is pressurizing you. If we think ten times before choosing a roommate or giving our house to a paying guest, just imagine how many times we need to think before choosing someone as a spouse.

Come to think of it, legally speaking, why should you get married? Well, the law considers marriage an important union. Getting married gives you certain rights that bind you, your spouse and children as a family unit. These are:

1. The official right and responsibility to live together as husband and wife.
2. The right to inherit each other's property. (See the chapter titled 'Money Matters' for details.)
3. Your children born out of this marriage are automatically recognized as your legally born children.
4. Your children also get the right to inherit property from the parents.

Did You Know: Marriage Law depends on your religion

Believe it or not, but marriage, divorce and property rights in India are governed by your religion. For example, if you are a Hindu woman, you will get married under the Hindu

Marriage Act. Similarly, a Christian woman will get married under the Indian Christian Marriage Act.

So who falls under which law?

Hindus (including Sikhs, Buddhists, Jains)	The Hindu Marriage Act, 1955
Muslims	Muslim marriage is mainly governed by traditional customs. These customs have been given the status of law by the Muslim Personal Law (Shariat) Application Act, 1937.
Christians	The Indian Christian Marriage Act, 1872
Inter-faith marriages	Special Marriage Act, 1954

What are the legal requirements for any marriage?

The basic principles for a valid marriage are the same across all religions, whether you opt for a court marriage or a ceremony.

1. Both bride and groom must be of legal marriageable age. As of June 2024, it is eighteen years for girls and twenty-one years for boys. For Muslims, the age limit is fifteen years, or puberty, for any gender, as per their uncodified customary law.
2. The marriage should happen out of the free will of the bride and groom, without any force. Also, both spouses must be mentally sound and capable of giving consent.

3. Neither spouse should be in a pre-existing marriage, i.e., if you are already married, you cannot marry again unless the previous marriage is dissolved. (Under the Muslim Personal Law, however, a man is allowed to have up to four wives.)
4. The spouses should not be immediate relatives. E.g., parent and child, uncle and niece, aunt and nephew, step-parent and child, siblings, etc.). However, in some communities, marriages between close relatives—like first cousins and uncle and niece—are common. If it is the custom of that community, the law will not prohibit such a marriage.

Note: As of June 2024, the marriageable age for girls and boys is different (eighteen and twenty-one respectively). However, the Indian Parliament is contemplating raising the marriageable age for girls also to twenty-one. If this comes into effect, young girls will get more breathing time to complete their education, explore career opportunities and gain financial independence. It will also reduce the occurrence of child marriages.

Have you ever thought about how deeply the law penetrates your personal life without you realizing it? For instance, your marriage, and even your wedding ceremony, is governed by law! The interesting part is that the law recognizes and incorporates the difference in ceremonies across religions. If you choose a ceremonial wedding, you need to meet certain legal requirements. For a registered marriage, this will not be necessary. In both cases, you should register your wedding and get a marriage certificate that serves as proof, the process for which is outlined a little later.

Hindu Marriages

If you opt for a ceremonial marriage (i.e., a wedding ceremony as opposed to a registered marriage), your marriage can be solemnized after performing the customary ceremonies followed by your community. If *saptapadi* (where the bride and groom take seven steps before a sacred fire) is a customary part of the ceremonies, then it is a must for solemnizing the marriage.

Pro tip: Almost all Hindu communities have saptapadi as part of their custom, deeming it a necessary step.

Muslim Marriages

A Muslim marriage, called 'nikah', is like a contract. For a legal contract, there must be a proposal, acceptance and witnesses. One party must propose the marriage (*ijab*) and the other party must accept (*qubul*). There should be a minimum of two witnesses, both of whom must be adult Muslims of sound mind.

Muslim marriages also have the concept of *mahr*, a gift given by the husband to the wife at the time of the wedding. This can either be money or property. There is no fixed mahr amount as per the law; it is up to both the parties to mutually decide. The main purpose behind fixing mahr is to ensure that the wife can financially support herself if her husband dies, or if the marriage is dissolved.

Note: Mahr need not be paid during the wedding. It can be done later. During the wedding, the husband needs to commit the amount he will pay.

Since Muslim marriages are considered a contract, the parties also sign a marriage deed, or the *nikah nama*. This deed lays down all the conditions of the marriage (just like you would prescribe terms and conditions in any other contract), such as the mahr, child custody, or other conditions like the wife's maintenance, or granting her the right to divorce if the husband takes a second wife, etc.

Since a Muslim marriage is governed by a mix of customs and laws, there are two exceptions compared to other religions:

1. Age of marriage: According to Muslim traditions, a person who has obtained puberty, or is fifteen years of age, is eligible to marry. They do not need to be eighteen (in case of a girl) and twenty-one (in case of a boy), as required by other religions. There is an ongoing case in the Supreme Court[1] to make the marriageable age same for all religions, to prevent young Muslim girls of fifteen being married off by their parents.[2]

2. Polygamy: This is the practice of having more than one spouse. Though it is not codified under any law, it is permitted as a religious practice. As per Muslim customs, men are allowed to marry up to four wives at a time. I know this sounds bizarre in today's day and age, but the original intention of this provision was to provide security to young widows back in the day. This custom has also been challenged in the courts by Muslim women and is currently under review.[3]

Note: Muslim customs vary based on the sect (Shia and Sunni). Most customs are not codified as law but are practised as a part of tradition (and not as a legal requirement). While this section is a broad overview about Muslim marriages, it is best to check with an expert if you plan to get married under Muslim laws.

Christian Marriages

Christian law requires one of the parties to give a written notice to the religious minister of his/her church, about the intention to marry. This notice must include the names, professions, addresses of the bride and groom, along with the name of the church in which the marriage is to be solemnized. The notice is then put up in the church for a few days to invite objections. If there are none, the parties make a declaration to go ahead with the marriage. The minister issues a certificate, after which the ceremony can be performed. It is followed by registering the marriage in a registrar book maintained by the church.

Incidentally, the law does not require a Hollywood-style you-may-now-kiss-the-bride moment!

See how the law incorporates the requirements of each religion? While these are the basic legal procedures, the actual process may vary from state to state and community to community.

What If I Want to Marry Someone from a Different Religion?

Since the laws of marriage are governed by religion, both spouses need to belong to the same religion. But what if you want to marry someone outside your religion? There is good news! In matters of love and marriage, you hold the ultimate freedom to choose your partner, free of the constraints of religious boundaries. There are two options available to you:

1. Change your religion: Either one of you may decide to embrace your partner's faith, convert to their religion and get married under the religious law concerned. In this case, you will be governed by the laws of the religion that you convert to. E.g., if you are a Hindu woman and convert to Islam, you can get married as per the Muslim law.

Remember, when you convert to another religion, you will no longer inherit from your birth family as per your original inheritance law. You will inherit from your partner as per your new religion, but to inherit from your parents, they will need to write you a Will. See the section on inheritance under the chapter 'Money Matters' later in the book. Conversion could also affect other aspects of your life like burial rights, ceremonial rights and acceptance within your religious community. Always weigh the pros and cons, and make an informed decision.

2. The Special Marriage Act (SMA): There is a special religion-neutral law called the Special Marriage Act, 1954, which allows two people of different religions to marry each other without having to change their religions.

Again, similar to the above situation, once you get married under the SMA, you will not be able to inherit from your birth family under your original inheritance law. You will now inherit as per the Indian Succession Act (explained in the inheritance section in the 'Money Matters' chapter). However, unlike above, since you are not converting your religion, other aspects of your life will not get affected.

We know that celebrities like Kareena Kapoor Khan and Saif Ali Khan, Shah Rukh Khan and Gauri Khan (née Chhibber), Aamir Khan and Kiran Rao, etc., had interfaith marriages. In such cases, each partner holds on to their faith, embracing a multi-faith family. It is possible that they chose the Special Marriage Act to solemnize their marriages.

What is the step-by-step process under the Special Marriage Act?

Getting married under the Special Marriage Act, 1954, involves a specific procedure that ensures the legality and recognition of the union. Here's what it entails:

1. **Application and documents:** You need to fill an application form for registering your marriage and submit it to the marriage registrar as notice of your intention to marry. You can get your marriage registered in any place where you, or your partner, have been residing for at least thirty days (with proof of residence). You can do this online (visit the government website of the state where you want to register) or visit the marriage registrar's office.

    You will also need to submit other documents with the form:
    i. Affidavit: You can get an affidavit prepared from any local lawyer or court. Do this locally because the format varies from jurisdiction to jurisdiction. Your affidavit also needs to be notarized.

ii. Identity documents: You will need proof of identity, age, residence (Aadhaar, passport, voter ID/driver's licence) along with passport-sized photos.
  iii. Witnesses: Details and identity documents of three witnesses (this can be anyone, not necessarily family) who will need to sign.
2. **Publication and objections:** After receiving your form and documents, the marriage officer will publish a public notice about your intended marriage in his office for a period of thirty days. During this time, any person may raise objections to the marriage, if they have valid reasons to do so. This thirty-day wait is a formality the marriage registrar carries out.

Note: Objections to an intended marriage can only be on legal grounds. For example, if either partner already has a spouse, is a minor, or the parties are immediate relatives. It CANNOT be on the ground that the parents don't agree with their child's choice of partner.

3. **Sign and marry:** After the thirty day-wait, you need to visit the same registrar's office again for final signatures, along with your witnesses. Both partners, along with the witnesses, will sign a declaration in the presence of the marriage officer, stating that they are marrying of their own free will and without any coercion. The registrar will go through your file again, confirm that everything is in order and then sign the documents.
4. **Marriage ceremony:** You can choose to get married however you like. It can be a religious ceremony, a

celebration, or a simple registration at the office of the marriage officer.

5. **Marriage certificate:** After the ceremony, the marriage officer will register the proceedings and issue a marriage certificate, which serves as legal proof and is essential for various purposes such as obtaining passports, visas or changing the marital status in official records.

It is important to note that the specific procedures and requirements may vary slightly, depending on the state or district you are in. It is advisable to consult the local marriage officer or seek legal advice for accurate and up-to-date information regarding the process in your specific jurisdiction.

Food for thought

Don't you think it is strange that if someone wishes to marry under the Special Marriage Act, they need to issue a public notice? Not only is this requirement against a couple's right to privacy, but it is also wrongly used by families to deny their children the choice of marrying outside their religion. Also, this requirement is not part of any other religious law. It was probably added as a caution against forced marriages, or religious conversions, but it is time to amend the law!

Note: As of now, there is a petition in the Supreme Court to remove the requirement for a public notice under the Special Marriage Act. Let us wait and see what the court finally decides.

How Do I Register My Marriage?

Till 2006, most couples in India did not register their marriages. Back then, inviting their near and dear ones and getting married in front of them was proof enough.

Each state government had the choice to decide whether to make marriage registration compulsory or not. Only five out of twenty-eight states (Maharashtra, Gujarat, Karnataka, Himachal Pradesh and Andhra Pradesh) had done so. However, in 2006, the Supreme Court made it compulsory for every marriage to be registered, irrespective of religion (*Seema vs Ashwani Kumar*).

Why is it important to register your marriage?
When you register your wedding, you get a marriage certificate. This document serves as proof of your marriage. It also helps you add your spouse's name to legal and other documents like your passport, bank account, insurance policy, etc. Earlier, when people would not register their marriages, it became an excuse for husbands to desert their wives and re-marry without divorce (and without consequences), leaving their wives helpless in the absence of proof.

> **Activity Time:** Ask your parents, or grandparents, if they registered their marriage. It will be interesting to know how things have changed over generations.

What is the process to register your marriage?
1. Identify the marriage registrar: Generally, you approach a marriage registrar of any of these two jurisdictions:

where you get married (i.e., the jurisdiction under which the venue of your wedding falls) or where you will live after marriage. You can do an online search to identify where the marriage registrar is located.
2. Collect documents: You need documents to show proof of identity, proof of address, proof of age (like Aadhaar), either a wedding invitation card or photographs of the wedding, two witnesses (this can be anyone, not necessarily your family) and passport photographs. If you have a temple wedding, you can show receipts.
3. Marriage certificate: Once you pay the fees and fill a form, the registrar will give you both your certificate to sign. When filling the form for the certificate, you should specify if you want to change your surname. If you don't clarify, your name will automatically be changed from your maiden name to your husband's surname.

Registration is usually a straightforward and hassle-free process. However, you may have to wait in queue at the registrar's office, maybe even tip someone. While the steps given above outline the general process, each state government may prescribe rules with slight variations. You can check this for your state online (many states have their own website) and proceed accordingly. You can google marriage registration <state> to find the website of your state.

Can I register my marriage online?
Nowadays, many states have started online registration for marriages. You will need to visit the website of the state government or registrar (where you wish to register your marriage) and locate the form. You can then fill and submit

the form online, along with all the supporting documents. In some cases, the process may be completely online, while in other states you may have to visit once.

When should you get your marriage registered?
You can get your marriage registered any time after your wedding. Of course, the sooner you do so the better, not only for your documentation but also to avoid being questioned about the delay. Any time between one week to two or three months is typically when couples get their marriage registered.

Can you register your marriage before the ceremony? Yes, you can! I have seen many couples who complete the registration process and then go ahead with the ceremony according to 'favourable dates'. The process for this is the same. You can show your wedding invitation as proof.

What if I Want a Court Marriage?

A court marriage happens when a couple skips the wedding ceremony and directly registers their marriage. It comes under the Special Marriage Act (already explained earlier).

Why don't the religious marriage laws apply for court marriage?
If you recall, the marriage law of each religion requires you to perform essential ceremonies for the union to be solemnized. For example, in a Hindu marriage, saptapadi is essential. Now, in a court marriage you are skipping the religious ceremony, which is why you will not be eligible to register your marriage under any religious law.

Note: Your divorce and inheritance rights will also be decided as per the Special Marriage Act.

Step-by-step process for court marriage
The process for a court marriage is the same as a marriage solemnized under the Special Marriage Act. You will begin by submitting your application and documents, waiting for thirty days for objections (if any) and then signing in front of a marriage registrar with your witnesses.

The Hadiya Case and the Constitutional Right to Choose Your Partner

In the sensational Hadiya case (*Shafin Jahan vs Asokan K.M.*), which was widely covered by the media, a Hindu girl Akhila Ashokan converted to Islam and married a Muslim man, Shafin Jahan, at the age of twenty-five. She changed her name to Hadiya Jahan after converting. Hadiya's father objected to the marriage, stating that his daughter had been brainwashed. The case went all the way to the Supreme Court.

Hadiya consistently maintained in court that she had married Shafin Jahan out of her own choice and wanted to live with him. Based on her testimony, the Supreme Court not only decided to not interfere in the marriage, but also held that each individual has the right to choose their own partner, within or outside marriage, as per Articles 19 and 21 of the Constitution.

What do you think? While I feel for the parents, this judgment is a landmark case for interfaith couples who wish to get married.

Can we exchange garlands?
Yes, of course! The marriage registrar's office is usually full of couples in a celebratory mood. Feel free to exchange garlands or distribute sweets.

You can also call the registrar to a designated venue, instead of going to the office to sign, for an additional fee. For instance, you may want to celebrate with your near and dear ones and sign in front of them. You can understand the procedure from the local marriage registrar's office.

The whole process, aside from the thirty-day waiting period, will take two to three days (when you have to visit the registrar's office). It is quite a straightforward process, but be prepared for *sarkari* behaviour!

What if I Want to Elope?

Some couples choose to elope, or run away, and get married secretly, mostly because their families do not agree with their choice of partner. Movies serve as a good example of this. In many such cases, the couples get married secretly, often in temples, exchange garlands and perform a basic ceremony.

In such a case, what are their options?

1. Have a small religious ceremony as per the religious law (if both are from the same religion) and then register the marriage. If they have a temple wedding, that will count as a religious ceremony. They can click photos with timestamps as proof (since there will be no invitation card stating a date).
2. Opt for a court marriage, the procedure for which has already been explained.

If both partners are from different religions, they will need to get married under the Special Marriage Act. This will require the couple to give the registrar notice of their intention to marry, which the registrar will publish in his office. If a couple has eloped, their families could track the registrar's office and raise an objection.

#MovieTime

Have you watched the Bollywood movie *Dhadak*, in which two lovers run away from their families because they belong to different castes? They run from a village in north India and end up in West Bengal.

In such a situation, they can either perform a quick ceremony under the Hindu Marriage Act and register their marriage in Kolkata (after collecting proof of residence there, like a lease agreement or electricity bill) or they can directly head for a court marriage. Worst case, if they are struggling to find a house or are in hiding, they need not register their marriage immediately. They can always do it later, once they feel it is safe to do so.

Life after Getting Married

Do I need to change my surname after marriage?
No, not unless you want to! There is NO law in India that requires you to change your surname after marriage. You can very well retain your maiden name, choose to hyphenate it with your husband's, or use your husband's surname only. Remember, the choice is yours alone. No one should force or

try to influence you otherwise. You have lived with a certain identity all this while; don't let anyone take that from you!

If you do change your surname, to maintain uniformity, update your name on all your personal identity documents (passport, PAN card, Aadhaar card, driving licence, bank accounts, etc.).

How to change my name legally?
To legally change your name in India, you need to follow a specific procedure. Here is a general outline of the steps involved:
1. Affidavit: Prepare an affidavit stating the reason for changing your name. In this case, it will be marriage. This affidavit should be typed on non-judicial stamp paper and notarized.
2. Newspaper publication: Publish a notice in at least two newspapers (one local and one national), stating your intention to change your name. The notice should include your current name, the proposed new name and the reason for the change. Preserve the original newspaper clippings as they may be required for further documentation.
3. Gazette notification: Apply for a name change in the central government's official gazette. You will also be required to pay the prescribed fee.
4. Supporting documents: Gather the supporting documents, which will include a copy of the affidavit, newspaper clippings of the name change notice, identity proof (such as Aadhaar card, PAN card or passport), address proof, passport-sized photographs and any other documents required as per the specific guidelines of your state.

5. Submission and verification: Submit the application, along with the supporting documents, to the authority responsible for name changes. The application will undergo verification. If everything is in order, a gazette notification will be issued with your new name.
6. Update official records: After receiving the gazette notification with your new name, update your name in all official documents, such as your Aadhaar card, PAN card, passport, driver's licence, bank accounts, etc.

There are websites like VakilSearch[4] these days which help you do this easily online.

Food for thought

Many women are influenced into changing their surnames by their husband or families, saying it will 'make her feel more like a part of the family'. Ask yourself this: does a name change on paper determine how close-knit your relationships are? And if that is the case, why don't husbands also adopt their wives' surnames, to equally feel like a part of their wives' families?

If I retain my maiden name, what about my child's surname?
Did you know that you can give your child ANY name and surname, irrespective of your and your spouse's name? For instance, Hollywood actress Gwyneth Paltrow and her ex-husband, Coldplay singer Chris Martin, named their daughter Apple! If they did that, what stops you from naming your child Jamun!

A child's surname is decided by the parents and it need not include either's surname. The reason that children are automatically given a parent's surname (mostly father's) is because of tradition, because families want to keep their surname alive. It is not a legal requirement.

In case both parents have different surnames, you can decide whether your child takes your husband's surname, your surname, or both! *You can even choose a completely random third name!* The trend of hyphenated surnames is also becoming increasingly popular among couples, to ensure that the child derives his/her name from both parents instead of using only the father's.

For example, tennis star Sania Mirza's son is called Izhaan Mirza Mallik, taking both his parents' names. But, you may ask, now that Sania Mirza and Shoaib Mallik are officially divorced, what happens to their son's surnames? Well, he can continue using his name as is, or he can change it later in life.

When it comes to your child's documents, the birth certificate will have the names of both parents and will serve as proof of the parent–child relationship. In addition, you should add your name to a couple of your child's documents (in the section that says 'daughter/of', 'son/of'), wherever there is an option to write the parent's name, instead of the father's name. This way, you will have at least one or two documents as proof, which will make it easier for you with regard to other documents.

Do I need to live with my in-laws after marriage?
No and maybe. Why do I say so? Because there is no law that requires a wife to live with her in-laws. But there is a catch.

Typically, after marriage in India, the woman is expected to shift to her husband's house. Very often, it is a home shared with the in-laws and other family members. If the relationship between all the family members is pleasant, and the daughter-in-law feels at home in her matrimonial home, then it is great! But the sad reality is that the daughter-in-law is often not treated as an equal. She is burdened with responsibilities, treated like a second-class citizen and not made to feel 'at home'. In many cases, she is also subjected to harassment and cruelty by her in-laws.

You may also want to live independent of your in-laws to have your own space as a couple or to live life on your own terms. Whatever your reasons, no one can force you to live with your in-laws.

What is the catch?
While the law does not require you to live with your in-laws, our patriarchal society and culture expects women to comply. A daughter-in-law who wishes to live separately is seen as 'breaking the house', 'breaking the family' and 'separating the *ladla* son from his parents'. It is an entirely different matter that no one notices that the wife, too, left her parents and family to move in with her husband. In matters of divorce, the husband's lawyers often get him to say 'she made me separate from my parents, which proves she is evil' as grounds for cruelty by the wife. It is used to paint the wife's character in a bad light.

Incidentally, in 2016, the Supreme Court indirectly mandated that a woman should live with in-laws by making it a ground for divorce (while hearing *Narendra vs K. Meena*). The court held that the husband was being forced to separate from his family. As per traditional Indian values, the court said, it is the son's duty to take care of his parents, making the wife's demand to live separately from her in-laws, cruelty under Section 13 of the Hindu Marriage Act, 1955.

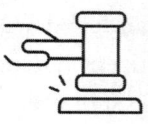

> **'Wife's effort to separate her husband from his parents amount to cruelty'**
>
> While hearing the case, the Supreme Court held that:
>
> '11. ... in a Hindu society, it is a pious obligation of the son to maintain the parents. If a wife makes an attempt to deviate from the normal practice and normal custom of the society, she must have some justifiable reason for that and, in this case, we do not find any justifiable reason, except monetary consideration ... In our opinion, normally, no husband would tolerate this and no son would like to be separated from his old parents and other family members, who are also dependent upon his income. The persistent effort of the wife to constrain the husband to be separated from the family would be torturous for the husband and in our opinion ... this constitutes an act of "cruelty".'

Food for thought

What do you think of this Supreme Court judgment? Do you agree or disagree with the judge? Do you think it is okay for a husband to demand to live with his parents after marriage, while the wife is expected to leave her parents behind and move to his house?

All about Marriage

#MovieTime

Recall Amitabh Bachchan's dialogue from the Bollywood movie *Piku*, where he says, '*Arey, dekhbal karna hai toh mera karo. Shaadi ke baad father ka ghar chodke doosre ghar mein jaana, udhar dekhbal karna*, how foolish!' What he meant was that it is equally important for a daughter to take care of her parents, whether or not she is married. Yet, society expects her to move out of her parents' home, denying her the opportunity to take care of them, while the husband continues to live with his parents.

Pro tip: Always have a conversation about where you want to live as a couple before getting married. Since it is two people getting married to each other, it is important that both spouses have an equal say in the decision. It is unfair to expect the wife (by default) to leave behind everything and move to the husband's house, just because she is a woman.

What if my husband won't let me move for a job?
This is a tricky situation. Of course, there is no law that stops you from moving for a job, whether or not you are married. However, the law expects a husband and wife to live together in their matrimonial home. If the couple lives separately for any reason (such as a job in another city), it needs to be a mutual decision. If one of the spouses does not agree, they can go to court and seek 'restitution of conjugal rights', a legal

remedy by which one spouse can demand the other spouse's physical company and cohabitation. Of course, if a spouse goes to court asking for the restitution of conjugal rights, they may be assured of their partner's physical presence but not emotional or mental attachment.

Try to handle such a situation with care and find the sweet spot between maintaining your independence and keeping your marriage intact.

What if my husband wants to move for his job, and I don't want him to? Or, what if I don't want to move with him?
From a legal perspective, this situation is similar to the one above. The law expects you to live together, but you can choose to live apart if it is a mutual decision. If you don't agree with his decision to move, your legal remedy will be to file for restitution of conjugal rights.

Practically speaking, it is very rare for someone to file a case of restitution of conjugal rights against their spouse, because it is considered taboo. And be prepared, if you do go to court, it could cause your marriage to collapse. Therefore, most people try to resolve such situations without involving the law.

Conversations to have before you say 'yes' to marriage

If I could, I would make compulsory some important conversations to have with your partner before getting married. Many couples jump into marriage thinking it is all about romance, or worse, about a grand wedding. No!

Marriage is about building a life together, sharing your life with someone and being able to navigate the ups and downs together.

Here are some questions you should discuss before you get married.

1. Are you expected to change your surname? What about the surname of the kids?
2. Are you expected to leave your family and move in with your husband's family?
3. Will you be free to make your own decisions about work and career?
4. Are you both on the same page about kids?
5. How do both of you plan to manage your finances? Will your husband let you handle your own finances/will you both handle your finances as a couple jointly?
6. What are his parents' thoughts on the above (this matters if you will live in a joint family)?
7. What are the differences in both your lifestyles? How do you plan to achieve common ground?
8. How are important decisions going to be made? Will they be joint decisions, or will he expect you to agree with him? This will give you an idea whether your partner wants an equal partnership or a puppet he can control.
9. What are each of your non-negotiables, i.e., something that is a dealbreaker for you and your partner? For example, smoking or drinking. For some, it could be about where to live or the spouse's profession.

> **Activity Time:** Get together with your girlfriends and make your own list of questions to discuss with your fiancés before you get married. It will be interesting to share what is important for each one of you! More importantly, make sure you have these conversations before you choose your life partner!

Prenuptial Agreements

A prenuptial agreement is a contract signed by both spouses, which lays down the terms and conditions of the marriage and what happens to finances, assets, etc., in case of separation. Prenups are a common phenomenon in the West, and you may have seen them in movies or heard about them during celebrity divorces.

Are they legal in India? This is a grey area; our law is silent on prenuptial agreements. The Indian Contracts Act, 1872, which governs all contracts, states that you cannot enter into a contract that is against public policy. Since marriages are considered a holy union under Indian law, any agreement that is seen as encouraging separation can be invalid.

However, things are changing. There have been instances of family courts acknowledging prenuptial agreements to determine the intention of the spouses. In a 2013 case in Mumbai,[5] a family court held that although the prenuptial agreement between the spouses cannot be held as a binding contract, it can help the court understand the intentions of the parties involved.

So, can I sign a prenup?
You can if you want to. You can sign a 'Memorandum of Understanding (MOU)' agreement with your fiancé that sets certain ground rules for your marriage, finances, assets and what happens in case of a divorce. This will require both partners to be transparent with each other, have difficult conversations and come to a consensus on important matters. As part of a prenup, you cannot sign anything that goes against the law. For example, if the law says adultery is a ground for divorce, you cannot sign a prenup saying that the partner cannot seek divorce in case of adultery. Similarly, if you sign a prenup saying your spouse will not be an heir to your property, while the law makes the spouse an heir, the law will prevail. A prenup is mainly for you to sort out assets and finances in case the marriage ends.

Note: Since the law is not clear on prenups, such an agreement can always be challenged in court by any spouse. In case of any conflict, the law will always trump the prenup.

Remember, DO NOT sign a prenup if you have the slightest doubt that it can put you at a disadvantage or take away your rights. Never sign anything you are not comfortable with.

Pro tip: A prenup agreement is almost always drafted by a lawyer. Make sure you have a lawyer go through the agreement and advise you on it.

>  **Food for thought**
>
> A Muslim marriage is considered a contract. The spouses sign a deed called the nikah nama, which lays the terms of their marriage, such as the mahr (maintenance) that the wife will get, grounds on which the wife can ask for divorce, restrictions on polygamy, etc. This is actually a prenuptial contract, worded differently, very much legal in India!

Wedding Gifts

'All the gifts and jewellery I got for my wedding are under my husband/in-laws' control.'

This is a very common problem faced by women in India. Due to the customary practice of moving to the husband's house, and consequently the relative lack of financial independence, it is common practice for a woman to deposit all her jewellery and gifts with her husband or in-laws. Sometimes, this is done out of goodwill, but in many cases the daughter-in-law is forced to do so.

While this practice is fine if the relationships are positive, more often than not, we see cases of the husband or in-laws using this to deprive the woman of her rightful assets. It is a tool for financial control. The thought process is that if the woman doesn't have access to her jewellery or assets, and if she is not financially independent, what can she do? These cases are more common that you would imagine. Jewellery, in fact, becomes a key area of control if a marriage goes bad.

Here are a few pro-tips to safeguard yourself against a situation like this:

1. During the wedding, ask your parents/family members/friends to give the gifts in your name, so that they serve as financial security for you.
2. Instead of cash (which can be used by anyone), encourage your family members to give a cheque in your name.
3. If they gift you expensive items or jewellery, make sure to immediately deposit these in a bank locker that is in your name/your family's name. If you don't have your own locker, make sure to deposit it in a joint locker that you have the right to operate.
4. After the wedding, as soon as possible, make a list of all the gifts that you have received (including cash, jewellery and other valuables). Make sure you and your parents sign this document, with the date and place mentioned. Get two neutral witnesses to sign as well. If possible, try to get the husband's side also to sign this document, so that they cannot dispute it later. Keep one copy with you and one copy with your parents.
5. Take pictures of everything. If it is jewellery, take pictures of you wearing it, so that no one can swap it or pretend that it never existed.

Remember, all the gifts that you receive in your name during the wedding become your stridhan. Only you, and no one else, have rights over it.

The issue of stridhan usually comes up in cases of divorce, where the wife demands that it be returned. Courts, too, usually ask for the stridhan to be returned to the wife, unless it can't be done for some reason. For example, if the gold was melted to convert it into something else, or if something is lost (and there is proof of a police complaint). In such cases, the court can ask the family to pay the wife compensation equal to the value of the stridhan. However, what is most important is that you will need to be able to prove your stridhan, so make sure that you follow the steps mentioned above.

Forced Marriage

What if my parents are forcing me to get married?[26]
'Help! My parents are forcing me to get married to a man of their choice. They are not letting me leave the house. They have taken away my phone.' If reading this surprises you, let me tell you such a situation is not uncommon in India. Parents often force their daughters to get married against her wishes. Remember the last episode of the web series *Made in Heaven*, where the girl's politician parents drug her and force her to marry as part of a political alliance? In true filmy style, she hatches a plot with the wedding planners and runs away from the *mandap* one night before the wedding! While a reel character could do that, running away may not be possible in real life. This is when the Indian law comes to your rescue.

Which laws protect you against forced marriage?
While there is no direct, single law that explicitly bans forced marriages in India, you can locate your rights against it under several different laws.

Constitutionally, you have the fundamental right to live with dignity under Article 21 of the Indian Constitution. This includes the right to choose one's partner, which implies that no one can be forced to marry against their will. Under Section 24 of the Guardians and Wards Act, 1890, parents, as your guardians, have a legal duty to look after your health and education, and to support you. Further, the basis for a valid marriage under any religious law in India is that the two parties do so with 'free consent', without any force. Principally, these legal provisions make it abundantly clear that no one, not even your parents, can force you to marry.

There are more provisions that protect you:

1. Domestic Violence Act: This Act protects any girl/woman against any kind of violence (physical, mental, sexual, financial) from any family member she shares a house with. If you live with your parents (and/or other relatives), then you can use this Act to protect yourself.

Note: Forced marriage often involves harassment of various kinds—restricting the girl's movements, not allowing her to leave the house, taking away her phone, cutting her off from friends and controlling her access to money. Sometimes it even involves physical violence. All of these actions qualify as abuse under the DV Act.

2. Bharatiya Nyaya Sanhita: Section 127 (1) of the BNS makes wrongful confinement of a person, i.e., restricting their freedom of movement, a criminal offence. Section 87 makes it criminal for anyone to kidnap or abduct a woman to force her into marriage,

or knowing that she will be forced into marriage. The above two provisions can come into play if your parents, or anyone else, locks you up in the house or your room.

Note: If you are a minor, i.e., below the age of eighteen, forced marriage will also attract the Prohibition of Child Marriage Act, 2006 and the Indian Majority Act of 1875.

What should you do if you are being forced into marriage?

1. Try to find a mediator: A forced marriage is a tricky and sensitive situation. If possible, identify a reasonable adult, whom your parents also respect and trust, to mediate. Sometimes difficult situations can be resolved through a neutral third party stepping in.
2. Escape safely: If nothing works out and you intend to leave your parents' home, make sure you have another safe place to go to. This can either be a friend's place, a trusted relative or elder, or a neutral place like a hostel or hotel, wherever you are comfortable.
3. Have financial backup: You will need money to support yourself and for legal proceedings till such time that you find an alternative. This can be in the form of money in your account, cash, jewellery, etc. Be careful about taking any jewellery that does not belong to you as this could amount to stealing and give your parents a counter-allegation against you.
4. File a police complaint: You can file a police complaint under the BNS. A complaint should be filed either where you were living with your parents, or in your new

place of residence. When you file a complaint, the police will most likely call your parents to the police station to question them and attempt a settlement. It is up to you, whether you want to have a talk with your parents at the police station.
5. File a domestic violence case: You can also file a case against your parents for domestic violence. For this, it will be better to consult a lawyer as they will be able to tell you the exact procedure, create a strong complaint and appear in court on your behalf. Remember, when it comes to court cases, the procedures and rules vary from state to state. You can consider this option as a last resort, if nothing else works.

While on paper you have several legal and practical remedies, filing a complaint against one's parents can have far-reaching implications. It may permanently affect your relationship with them or make them vengeful. It is obviously a difficult decision to make and must be made after careful consideration.

What should you do if you are in a forced marriage?
In some cases, you may not be able to escape the situation and may have to go through with the marriage. Sometimes, for your safety, it is better to go ahead with the marriage and then take steps immediately after to annul it.

Annulment is a legal procedure of cancelling a marriage, as if it never existed. It is different from a divorce where it is considered that the marriage did happen but is being dissolved. Apply for an annulment as soon as possible.

Practical points to consider if you want to annul your marriage:

1. Apply as soon as possible. The sooner you seek an annulment, the stronger your case will be. The longer you wait, the more you give the other party a chance to prove that you gave consent for the marriage. After one year of marriage, you cannot apply for an annulment.
2. Do not let any sexual relations be established between you and your forced husband. If the marriage is consummated, it becomes difficult (nearly impossible) to seek an annulment.
3. Make sure you have custody of your money, jewellery, wedding gifts and other assets. This will help you remain financially independent. If you hand everything over to your forced husband/in-laws, it is possible that they use your financial helplessness to make you stay.
4. If you had already filed a police complaint or domestic violence case against the forced marriage, these documents will come in handy as evidence to prove that the marriage was without consent. Also, try to live separately from your spouse if possible. This will help your case.

While the concept of annulment remains the same across different religions, the procedure is different. It is recommended that you consult a lawyer for specific knowledge of your religious law.

Non-Resident Indian (NRI) Marriages and Marrying Foreigners

What if you are an NRI who got married in India? Which law applies to you?

Hey, global citizen! Don't worry, we have your back. Did you get married in India and then move abroad? Or took a quick vacation from your life abroad, came to India, got married and went back? Whatever your situation, there is always a solution.

If you get married in India, and register here, your marriage will be governed by Indian laws. For all matters related to the validity of your marriage, separation, divorce, child custody, property rights and inheritance, Indian laws will apply. By Indian laws, we mean the laws of your religion (as explained earlier). However, for matters such as domestic violence you will get protection under the local laws of the country you reside in.

Pro tip: Don't just have your big fat Indian wedding and catch the next flight out! Ensure that you get your marriage registered in India (compulsory for all marriages since 2006).

What if you got married outside India? A destination wedding?

Destination weddings abroad have become quite popular. What is the legal status of your destination wedding, you may wonder? It is the same as any other wedding, if you both are Indian citizens living in India. You will simply have to register your marriage the way anyone else who got married in their hometown would. You can register in the jurisdiction where you will be living after your marriage.

What if you are an NRI who got married in the country where you live?

The Indian diaspora has spread across the globe, and we have second- and third-generation NRIs who are settled and married abroad.

If you got married under the laws of another country and got your marriage registered there, your marriage will be considered valid in India. You can use your foreign certificate of marriage as proof in India.

> **#TrueStory**
>
> One of my Indian friends, Saloni (name changed), got married to her German boyfriend. They both live in Singapore and got married, and registered their marriage, there. When they came to India, she used her Singaporean marriage certificate to get her husband's name added as a spouse on her passport. The passport office did not raise any objection to the Singaporean marriage certificate. My guess is that this is because Singapore is a well-recognized country. One can never be sure if Saloni would have had the same hassle-free experience if her marriage certificate was from Uzbekistan, for example.

I would suggest getting your marriage registered in India as well and obtaining an Indian certificate. A marriage certificate is not only an important document to prove your marriage but also comes in handy at banks and for matters related to insurance, property inheritance, etc. In some cases, it might become difficult to prove the authenticity and validity of a foreign marriage certificate in India, especially if it is from a less-recognized country. For example, one registrar may recognize a marriage certificate from Uganda or Vietnam as valid proof, but another may not. In fact, the Indian Parliament is contemplating making it compulsory for NRIs to register their marriages in India.

How do you register your foreign marriage in India?
You can do so under the Foreign Marriage Act, 1969. You will need to produce your foreign marriage certificate before the marriage registrar, along with an application seeking an Indian certificate. If your marriage certificate is not in English, get it translated, and signed and stamped, in the country of its origin as a valid proof of your marriage.

What if you want to marry a foreigner?
If you want to marry a foreigner (i.e., a non-Indian citizen) and you are a resident of India, you will need to get married under the Special Marriage Act, 1954. The conditions for getting married under the SMA are:
1. Both partners must be of marriageable age in India, even if the foreigner's country prescribes a higher or lower age.
2. Neither partner should have a living spouse, i.e., both should be unmarried.
3. They must both give valid consent and not be of unsound mind.

The procedure to get married under this Act is the same as explained earlier in this chapter. Apart from that,

since one partner is a foreigner, you will need the following documents:
1. Birth certificates of both parties (as proof of age).
2. The foreigner must have a valid Indian visa of more than thirty days.
3. An affidavit stating that both parties are single (not married), which is signed by both parties.
4. Both parties must stay in India for thirty days prior to the application and submit proof of this stay. This can be in the form of tickets, hotel bookings or local bills.
5. A no-objection letter from the embassy/consulate of the foreigner's country, stating that they have no objection to the marriage in India. (This step is to ensure that a foreigner is not committing marriage fraud in India.)

How to Avoid the NRI Marriage Scam?

There are cases where NRI men abandon their wives after marriage. What can the woman do in such a situation?[7]

You will be surprised to know how common the NRI scam is. NRI bachelors come to India, get married, tell the wives that they will go back to their countries of residence to get things in order and then call them. Except, they never call. They abandon the wives in India and remain untraceable. It later turns out that these scamsters are either already married abroad or never intended to marry in the first place. Sometimes, an NRI takes the wife abroad and abandons or isolates her there, leaving her helpless. Most of these scams are done for dowry or to wash family pressure off their backs.

> **#TrueStory**
>
> In one case, the NRI husband (let us call him Rajiv) took his wife (let us call her Priya) with him to a small town in the US. Within a few days, Rajiv's behaviour towards Priya became weird. She found out that he already had a wife and children in the US. Rajiv took away Priya's phone, locked her up in the house when he left for work and subjected her to physical and mental abuse. According to Rajiv, Priya was only supposed to cook and clean for him. Isolated, away from family and friends, without any phone or money, Priya suffered silently for a few months, until one day, Rajiv left a phone behind by mistake. Priya immediately called up Rajiv's friend and informed him about the situation. Rajiv's friend then informed Priya's parents, who flew Priya out on the first flight back to India. Luckily, Priya had her passport with her and could escape.

Priya's case is not an exception. Every year, several innocent girls and families fall prey to the NRI marriage scam.

First steps to take if a bride is abroad and a victim of the NRI wedding scam:

1. Hold on to your passport. It is the most valuable asset in such a situation.
2. Come back to India at the earliest. It is easier to take action from the comfort and support of one's home rather than being alone in a foreign land.
3. When coming back, bring back as many of your important belongings, especially your jewellery and

personal documents. It may not be possible for you to retrieve them later.
4. If you can, before coming back, file a police complaint with the local police abroad. Keep a copy of this complaint and bring it with you to India. This will serve as evidence when you initiate legal proceedings in India.
5. Approach the Indian embassy/consulate of the country you are in. Register a complaint with them. Keep a copy of any acknowledgement you receive from them.

What Are the Legal Options?

There is no specific law protecting women against the NRI marriage scam and we need to locate our legal remedies across legal provisions. Here are a few options below:
1. File a police complaint against the husband on grounds of cruelty (sections 85 and 86 of the BNS). Since he will not be in India, you will need to include his immediate family members (parents, mostly) in the complaint.
2. File for divorce on the grounds of desertion. This will be done as per your religion. The court will issue summons (an order to appear before the court in person or through a lawyer) against the husband. This can be sent to his address in India (where his parents live) and to his last-known address abroad. You will have access to a copy of the summons issued and can send it to him via email or WhatsApp. If he

does not come for the case or send a lawyer, you can ask for an ex-parte order. This means the judgment can be given even in the absence of the other party's representation.

3. Seek reliefs during the pendency of the divorce, like maintenance. Ask for the amount you need to financially support yourself and cover legal costs. You can also seek compensation for the mental harassment you undergo. It is always better to take all the maintenance upfront, rather than in instalments, because it is difficult to chase the other party for the payments, which they mostly don't pay. If the husband says he does not have money to pay maintenance, or does not turn up in court, you can ask for his properties to be attached.

4. Ask for impounding (i.e., cancelling) his passport. You can apply to the local passport authority (which issued your husband's passport) for impounding his passport. The Passports Act, 1967, allows for impounding a person's passport if:

   i. There are criminal proceedings pending against the person in any court in India. For this, you have to file a police complaint under sections 85, 86 of the BNS.

   ii. A warrant or summons for appearance has been issued against this person by any court in India. For this, you need to file a case for desertion in court, so that the court may issue summons against your husband.

What Happens if the NRI Husband's Passport Is Impounded?

He will no longer be able to travel abroad from India. If he is already abroad, his stay there will be considered illegal from the day his passport is cancelled. He can be deported back to India.

Along with pursuing legal remedies, you can parallelly exert pressure through other means:

1. Try to find common connections in society with the husband or his family, whom you can inform about the scam. They may be able to pressurize him and his family, since their reputation will be at stake.
2. Contact someone from his workplace, preferably the HR of the company. You can find contact details on the company's website or locate them on social media platforms like LinkedIn, Twitter, Instagram and Facebook. Inform them about the scam. Many companies have strict rules against their employee's involvement in a court case, especially criminal matters. They may take action against him.
3. There is usually an Indian association, or community WhatsApp groups, of Indians living abroad. If you can contact them, you may be able to get their help in finding more details about the scamster.

Precautions to Take against the NRI Marriage Scam

The biggest precaution to take against the NRI marriage scam is an extremely thorough background check, even if the alliance comes through a known source.

Pro tip: Here is a checklist of documents to verify before marrying an NRI.
- ✓ Visa.
- ✓ Passport.
- ✓ Social Security Number, or an equivalent for the country concerned.
- ✓ Tax returns for the past three years.
- ✓ Address proof in the foreign country.
- ✓ Proof of his employment, issued by the employer.
- ✓ Proof of his and his family's address in India.
- ✓ Common connections that your families share in society.
- ✓ Ask to speak with any of his friends or connections abroad.

Remember, there is no need to feel awkward while asking for all these details. Your intention is not to offend the other party but to safeguard yourself. After all, marriage is a life-long decision and you are well within your rights to make an informed choice.

Note: If an NRI alliance is asking for a dowry payment, especially upfront and into their bank account, watch out! It could be a scam! Ensure you do an extremely thorough background check.

Dowry

You may wonder what to do if your husband, or his family, demand dowry or unreasonable gifts.

Dowry has been banned in India since 1961 (Dowry Prohibition Act, 1961). It has been six decades since, but the practice is far from abolished. A World Bank study[8] done in rural India found that dowry was paid in 95 per cent of marriages. Statistics[9] by the National Crime Records Bureau (NCRB) reveal that nineteen women are killed each day due to dowry demands.

Let us understand the legal details of this rather grave situation.

What qualifies as dowry?
As per the Dowry Prohibition Act, 1961, dowry means any kind of money, goods, cash, jewellery or property, which the husband's side demands from the wife's side. The keyword here is 'demand'. This demand can be made to anyone on the wife's side (the wife herself, her parents, relatives, guardians) at any time. It need not be as dramatic like the movies (exactly before the *baarat* [celebratory procession] enters the venue, or just before the *phera*s) but can be made at any time, i.e., before, during or after the marriage.

Dowry disguised as 'gifts'
If money, assets and other gifts are *willingly* given to the bride or groom at the time of marriage, *without any demand* from the other side, then it is not considered dowry. Again, the keyword here is 'willingly'. Nowadays, dowry is innovatively disguised in ways like making the bride's side pay for the entire wedding expenses, making unreasonable demands for gifts, etc. Remember, you are not required to make any arrangements that exceed your budget. If the groom's

side makes demands on you or your family for expensive arrangements, it can be considered as dowry demand. You have every right to refuse.

What are my rights against dowry demands?
Not just accepting dowry, but even demanding, giving or helping someone give/take dowry is illegal. So, the next time you hear someone make a dowry demand, make sure to let them know that it is a crime and that you will not participate in one!

If the groom or his family demand dowry, you can file a police complaint against them. If you can, collect evidence (such as recordings, messages) that will help with your complaint. The alliance may not go ahead if you file a complaint, but think about whether you even want to marry someone who asks for dowry? Moreover, filing a complaint will give the groom's party a strict warning that their demands are illegal, hopefully acting as a deterrent in the future.

There is no shame in filing a complaint against someone for their illegal actions. In this day and age, it is the dowry demanders who should feel ashamed!

Have you watched that episode in the web series *Made in Heaven*, where a young couple has a love marriage? The groom (showed as a 'humble' IAS officer) and his parents demand 4 crore from the bride's family, just before the ceremony after all the guests have arrived. Hence, her parents are forced to give in to the demands on the spot. When the bride finds out, she walks out of the wedding with the powerful line, 'I am not going to pay anyone to marry me.' Be that bride—know your self-worth!

Which law protects women against dowry demands/harassment for dowry?
1. The Dowry Prohibition Act, 1961: This law makes it illegal for anyone to demand, take or give dowry.
2. Section 85, 86 of the BNS: These provisions protect married women against serious forms of physical and mental harassment from husband or in-laws.
3. Section 80 of the BNS: This provision deals with dowry deaths.

How do I prove dowry harassment?
If you want to take action against dowry demands made before or during the wedding (when you haven't given dowry yet), a police complaint will suffice.

However, if you have a divorce case going on and want the groom's side to return the dowry they had forcefully taken, then you should collect proof. This can be given in the form of receipts, photos of the jewellery, messages or recordings of the dowry demands, bank transfer details, etc.

Dowry deaths
A dowry death is said to have occurred when a married woman dies within seven years of her marriage under abnormal circumstances, or because of bodily injuries or

burns. The law specifies seven years as it assumes that dowry demands are likely to be made within this time frame. In such a case, it is assumed that her death was a result of dowry being demanded. Anyone responsible for such a death stands to be punished with imprisonment for a minimum of seven years, which may extend to life imprisonment (Section 80 of the BNS). Also, it is a non-bailable offence.

> **POINTS TO REMEMBER**
>
> 1. Marriage gives you the legal rights to inherit property from your husband. Children born out of a marriage also have clearly defined inheritance rights from both parents.
> 2. The law governing your marriage depends on your religion. Each religion has its own requirements. Broadly, all religious laws allow marriages only between consenting adults of sound mind.
> 3. You can either choose to have a ceremony as per your religious law, or have a court marriage under the secular Special Marriage Act.
> 4. There is no law that requires you to change your surname after marriage or stay with your in-laws.
> 5. Asking for dowry is illegal. Wedding gifts demanded out of pressure can also be considered dowry. All gifts that a woman receives as part of her marriage are considered her stridhan, over which only she has rights.

6

Divorce: The Exit Option

This chapter will answer your questions about divorce and how to navigate these rough waters smoothly, with the least possible damage. Divorce doesn't always have to be a dirty word. Read on and find out for yourself.

Introduction

No one gets married with divorce on their minds. After all, marriage is considered a union of a lifetime. While that is the case for many people, not all marriages are made in heaven. Some appear to be a slice straight out of hell!

Fortunately, divorce is no longer considered a taboo. More and more people are now opting to get out of marriages that only bring them misery. I am sure you have seen this happening around you; suddenly all of us know at least one person who has gotten a divorce. Although India still has one of the lowest divorce rates in the world, the number is definitely on the rise.

When we picture a typical divorce, what comes to mind is a bitterly fought case, toxic accusations, and extreme mental and financial drain. But a divorce doesn't always have to be a nightmare. It can also be a ticket to freedom and a happier life! Think of it like an option to exit a marriage that is no longer working.

Just like marriage is governed by personal laws according to religion, divorce is also covered by personal religious laws. Here is an outline for quick reference:

Religion	Law
Hindus (including Sikhs, Buddhists, Jains)	Hindu Marriage Act, 1955
Muslims	Muslim divorce is governed partly by traditional customs and partly by the Dissolution of Muslim Marriages Act, 1939

Religion	Law
Christians	Indian Divorce Act, 1869
Inter-faith marriages	Special Marriage Act, 1954

Under the Hindu Marriage Act and the Special Marriage Act, you cannot ask for a divorce within the first year of marriage. The law wants you to give your marriage at least one year before you decide to call it quits. This requirement can be waived off by the court in exceptional circumstances, on a case-to-case basis.

With that in mind, let us understand how you can exercise this option.

Mutual consent vs contested divorce

Can I ask for a divorce simply because I am no longer happy in my marriage? What if my partner wants to divorce me, but I don't? If both of us can no longer stand each other, what type of divorce should we opt for? The answers to all your questions are right here in this chapter!

Getting a divorce in India boils down to two main options: the mutual consent route and the contested divorce route.

A mutual consent divorce is when both spouses agree to exit the marriage. They can draw up the terms of exit, such as division of assets, alimony and custody of children, and present it before a court to get divorced. In this case, the mutual desire of the parties is enough. No other legal grounds are necessary.

A contested divorce, on the other hand, is when one of the spouses (either the wife or the husband) wants an exit, but the other one does not. The one who wants to exit can ask for a divorce only on legally permitted grounds. The other spouse can fight the divorce and ask the court to not grant it. Or the two parties can come to an agreement and ask the court to settle the divorce after accounting for division of assets, alimony and custody of children.

Practically, a mutual consent divorce is a lot quicker (one year or less), smoother and less toxic. Contested divorces can get extremely messy, with spouses airing dirty laundry in court and take much longer (think two to five years). I have seen several divorce cases where accusations expected only from a television drama are levelled. As they say, no one can be a worse enemy than an estranged spouse, because s/he knows your deepest, darkest secrets.

Pro tip: In my opinion, a mutual consent divorce is always better. Why? In both cases (mutual or otherwise), you need a lawyer to help you navigate court procedures and important issues like property, alimony and child custody. Also, in both cases, you must go to a court. However, in a contested divorce, the case drags on for years and the only person to benefit from this is your lawyer! Instead, use your lawyer's services to negotiate favourable terms in the settlement deed and move on with your life.

Contested Divorce

The grounds for a contested divorce are given in Section 13 of the Hindu Marriage Act, 1955.[1] Since a contested divorce is one-sided, it is allowed only on legally permitted grounds. These are similar under most religious laws, with just a few minor differences:

1. Adultery: If cheating in a marriage is a dealbreaker for you, you can ask for a divorce. Adultery means having sexual intercourse with another person outside the marriage.
2. Cruelty: Your safety is in your hands! If your spouse assaults or harasses you, physically or mentally, you don't need to stay in the marriage. Divorce may just be a better option.
3. Desertion: If your spouse has abandoned or wilfully neglected you for a period of two years, you have a valid ground for divorce.
4. Conversion to another religion: Since marriage is so closely tied to religion, if your spouse converts to another religion, or renounces the world and religion altogether, you can choose to divorce him/her.
5. Spouse gone missing: What if your spouse vanishes and nobody—you, the family or friends—has heard from him/her for seven years or more? You can use divorce as your way out. While this sounds similar to desertion, desertion usually applies when your spouse actively abandons you, whereas this ground applies when the person goes missing, like in true crime shows.
6. Mental instability: If your spouse is suffering from a serious mental disorder, like schizophrenia, abnormal aggression, etc. such that it becomes impossible to live with him/her, then you can seek a divorce. (This is not a ground for divorce as per the Indian Divorce Act applicable to Christians.)

7. **Physical disease:** If your spouse has a communicable STD (sexually transmitted disease), it is a valid ground for divorce.
8. **Non-consummation:** If your spouse wilfully refuses to engage with you sexually, you can seek a divorce. This ground is only available for Christians, under the Indian Divorce Act.
9. **Imprisonment:** If your spouse has been sentenced for seven years or more, you can ask for a divorce. This ground is only available for marriages registered under the Special Marriage Act.

Note: All the grounds listed above are available to both the husband and wife equally.

In addition to the above, the law provides women the option to walk away from a marriage if the husband is found guilty of rape, sodomy or bestiality.

The Curious Case of Cruelty in Indian Courts

Cruelty is one of the most used (and abused) grounds in a contested divorce. Since the law vaguely defines it as physical and mental cruelty, if a spouse can't find another valid reason, they use cruelty as a reason and say 'my partner is evil' (or something on those lines). This has led to some of the most bizarre and random judgments emerging from across the country. For example:

1. In March 2024, a family court in Indore said that since the wife did not wear sindoor, it meant that she had abandoned her husband, as wearing sindoor is the religious duty of the wife.[2]

2. The Madras High Court made headlines in 2022 for apparently stating that removing the *mangalsutra*, or *thali*, amounts to the highest form of mental cruelty by the wife.[3]
3. Cricketer Shikhar Dhawan got divorced from his wife, Ayesha, in 2023, on the grounds of mental cruelty. The cruelty here, according to him, was that Ayesha was living in Australia for several years, forcing Dhawan into a long-distance marriage and keeping him away from their son, Zoravar.[4]

The above examples are only illustrations of the myriad kinds of judgments on cruelty that come out of Indian courts on a daily basis. It is best to take them with a pinch of salt and not think about them too deeply. As I said, every situation is decided on a case-to-case basis.

What if My Husband Wants a Divorce, But I Don't?

You may ask why you should agree to a divorce when you don't want one? The simple truth is that if your spouse has decided to divorce you, you are anyway going to get dragged to court. The end of the marriage seems inevitable. The court may grant him a divorce, and if it doesn't, would you want to be in a marriage with someone who went to court against you?

Instead of being stuck in a dead relationship, focus on sorting out important issues like alimony and child custody. Use the mutual consent option to negotiate favourable terms for yourself.

> **When 'Not in Love' Is Not a Good Enough Reason for a Divorce #MovieTime**
>
> Have you watched the Bollywood movie *Dil Dhadakne Do*? In that movie, Priyanka Chopra's character, the daughter of a successful business family, wants a divorce from her husband because she doesn't love him and they lack compatibility. When she breaks this news to her parents and mother-in-law, their response is not only hilarious but also sheds light on the way most Indian families perceive marriage and divorce.
>
> Her father asks, '*Kaise compatible nahin hai? Tum dono young ho, successful ho, Punjabi ho, squash khelte ho.* (How can you both not be compatible? You both are young, successful, Punjabi and play squash.)'
>
> Her mother-in-law asks, '*Kanjoos hai yeh? Tumhe shopping karne nahi deta?* (Is he a miser? He doesn't let you shop?)'
>
> If only these factors were enough to spend a lifetime with someone!

How Does a Contested Divorce Go Through?

Let us understand a contested divorce through the example of a fictional couple, Rohit and Sheela, where the latter seeks a divorce.

1. Finding grounds: Sheela first needs to identify the legal grounds she can file a divorce under. Cruelty is the easiest option, unless there is another strong reason like adultery.

2. Filing a petition: Sheela appoints a lawyer and files a divorce petition in the family court. This can be the family court, which has jurisdiction over where Sheela and Rohit live, or where Sheela is currently staying (if she is not with Rohit), or where they got married.
3. Serving divorce papers: Once the court admits Sheela's petition, she will have to serve a copy of her divorce petition to Rohit. This is usually the part you see in movies, where an unassuming spouse opens the door and is caught off-guard by divorce papers.
4. Reply to petition: Rohit will file a reply to Sheela's petition through his lawyer. He can choose to challenge the divorce, or challenge the grounds on which Sheela has asked for it, or even the terms she has proposed. Along with filing his reply, Rohit can also file a counter-claim against Sheela, alleging his own grounds for divorce.
5. Arguments: Skipping a few procedural steps, we come to the arguments. Thus begins a long-drawn and bitter legal battle between Rohit and Sheela, as they 'expose' each other in court and fight over alimony, division of property and custody of children. The case goes back and forth between both parties as they make allegations and try their best to prove them, simply to have an upper hand on the settlement terms. Some couples even hire private detectives to dig up dirt on their spouse.
6. Divorce decree: Finally, after years of legal battle, the court grants a divorce to Rohit and Sheela, and pronounces the terms. Once the court passes the decree, the divorce is final, unless either of the parties is unhappy with the

terms of divorce and files an appeal in a higher court. If an appeal is filed, the entire process of arguments starts again.

The above is a zoomed-out version of what actually happens in a divorce case. There are several procedural steps in the middle, but you don't need to burden yourself with that information right now. The idea is to give you a basic idea of what to expect.

How Long Does It Take?

It can take anywhere between two and five years, or more. It depends on the complexity of the case, how bitterly the parties argue, delaying tactics used by the parties and the workload of the court. Further, if one of the spouses files an appeal against the original divorce decree, then you will need to account for the time the appeal will take.

How Much Will It Cost?

A contested divorce costs an arm and a leg, and your peace of mind. Monetarily, you must factor in minimal court fees and a lawyer's fees. Since contested divorces go on for long, the lawyer fees can really pile up. In addition, there are other out-of-court expenses like living costs, providing for children, paying for private detectives, etc.

Mutual Consent Divorce

Although a mutual consent divorce does not call for any legally permitted grounds, you must fulfil certain requirements.

1. The couple should have been living separately for a year before filing for a mutual consent divorce. For Christians, it is two years. Living separately does not mean that they have to physically be in two different houses, or that the wife has to move out and return to her parent's place. It means that the couple has not been able to live like a 'married couple' and has no desire to perform marital obligations. Living in two different rooms in the same house is considered as living separately.
2. Both agree to the divorce. This is the underlying principle of a mutual consent divorce.

How Does a Mutual Consent Divorce Go Through?

Let us employ Rohit and Sheela's example again to understand the step-by-step process for filing a mutual consent divorce.

1. Discussions: Rohit and Sheela (or their lawyers and family members) discuss all the terms and conditions of the divorce, like maintenance, child custody, division of assets. (This can be done on the basis of the 'Hard Talks' section a little later in this chapter.)
2. Drafting a joint petition: Once their terms are final, Rohit and Sheela get a joint petition for divorce drafted from a lawyer. Sheela, being a savvy girl, goes through the petition to ensure it contains the same terms that she agreed to.
3. Filing the joint petition: Rohit and Sheela jointly file the divorce petition (signed by both) in a family court, stating that they have not been able to reconcile and have been living separately for a year. This can be filed in the

court having jurisdiction over where they are currently residing, or where Sheela is residing, or where they got married.

4. First motion: For the first hearing, both Rohit and Sheela need to be present in court, along with their lawyers (or joint lawyer). The court will verify the documents and petition, and confirm from the parties that they both agree for the divorce. They may also have to sign a joint statement recorded on oath. Then the first order is passed, granting them six months' time, in case they change their minds.

   Pro tip: Most couples request the court to waive off the six months' waiting period. You have to clearly tell the court that there is no scope of reconciliation. Most courts do away with the waiting period.

5. Second motion: After six months, and within eighteen months of the first hearing, Rohit and Sheela need to file another petition for the second hearing, to confirm that they still want the divorce. Both need to be present before the court again to record a joint statement, on oath, that they have not changed their minds.

6. Final order: If the court is satisfied that both parties mutually and truly want this divorce, and all issues related to alimony, child custody, properties, etc., are settled, then a final decree dissolving the marriage is issued. The court can pass this decree after the second motion itself, or it can ask for additional hearings if any clarifications are needed. These hearings can be attended by the lawyers, without Rohit and Sheela being present.

The final order—the divorce decree—serves as proof of the divorce. This order is important to show your change of marital status and even for getting remarried.

Pro tip: Get your own lawyer. I have seen many women skip this step when it comes to a mutual divorce. Usually, the husband's family appoints a lawyer and gets everything drafted. The wife just signs. Sometimes, this can get you the raw end of the deal—be it alimony, maintenance, child custody, division of assets, etc. If you have your own lawyer, you will be better equipped to put forward your points and ensure that they are incorporated into the divorce petition.

How Long Does It Take?

It can take anywhere between six and eighteen months, depending on your case and the workload of the family court concerned. If the cooling-off period is waived, the divorce can come through in just a few months.

How Much Does It Cost?

Since a mutual consent divorce involves minimal hearings, you will only have to pay basic lawyers' fees and court fees. The process itself is not expensive. You can get an idea of the lawyers' fees in the last chapter.

Divorce in Cases of Muslim Marriage

Just like marriage, divorce for Muslims in India is governed by a mix of customs and statutes. Initially, as per the customs, Muslim women did not have the right to initiate divorce. The only way for them to get a divorce was if their husband agreed. This left Muslim women helpless and vulnerable.

It was after the Dissolution of Muslim Marriages Act (DMMA) was introduced in 1939 that Muslim women got the right to ask for a divorce on certain grounds. After all, nobody should have to stay in a bad marriage.

Before we move to the grounds of divorce, let us understand the difference between customary divorce (i.e., as per customs) and a divorce granted as per the DMMA. Primarily, for a divorce under customary law, you need not go to court. The marriage can be dissolved by religious leaders without any legal intervention. A divorce under the DMMA, however, must have court approval, like any other divorce.

Also, there is no codified law requiring a Muslim man to go to court for a divorce. He can simply do so through customary law. A Muslim woman, since her options under customary law are limited, must go to court if she seeks a divorce under the DMMA.

When Can a Muslim Wife Ask for Divorce?

Now, Muslim women in India have the right to seek divorce under both customary practices as well as the DMMA. As per Section 2 of the DMMA, a Muslim woman can ask for a divorce for any of the following reasons:

1. Cruelty: Under the DMMA, the following acts are classified as cruelty:
    i. If your husband habitually assaults you, or repeatedly harasses you, physically or mentally.
    ii. If the husband disposes of his wife's property and prevents her from using it. So, if your husband is messing with *your* property, it is a big no-no.

iii. If the husband is known to sleep with 'women of evil repute' or lead a life of debauchery.
iv. If the husband obstructs the practice of religion by the wife.
v. If the husband takes on more than one wife and fails to treat you equally! (Basically, the law tells husbands that they can have more than one wife, as long as all of them are treated equally.)

2. Non-payment of maintenance: If your husband has neglected or failed to provide you maintenance (financial support) for two years, you have the right to seek a divorce.
3. Failure to fulfil marital obligations: If your husband fails to fulfil his marital obligations to you for three years or more, you can ask for a divorce. The law does not define marital obligations, but they are generally understood as cohabiting, consummating the marriage or paying the promised mahr.
4. Impotency: If your husband was impotent at the time of marriage, and continues to be, that is a legitimate ground for divorce.
5. Desertion: Imagine this. Your husband has been missing for four years and no one knows where he is. This is a valid ground for divorce. After all, it takes two people to make a successful marriage!
6. Disease: Healthy partners make healthy relationships. If your husband has been mentally unstable for two years or more, and is suffering from leprosy or a venereal disease, you have the right to seek a divorce for your safety and well-being.

Note: The DMMA does not include adultery as a ground for divorce, unlike other religious laws, because Muslim men are allowed to have up to four wives. However, it makes sleeping with 'women of evil repute' a ground for divorce!

Coming to customary law, Muslim women have the following options to initiate divorce:

1. Talaq-e-tafweez (TET): A TET divorce is when the husband allows the wife to ask for a divorce. A Muslim woman can initiate a TET divorce only if her husband gives her this right.

    Think of it this way. You and your husband are joint owners of a car (your marriage). Normally, only your husband has the keys and authority to drive it (initiate divorce). You can drive it only if your husband gives you a spare key and says, 'If you ever feel the need, you have my permission to drive this car (seek a divorce).'

    Pro tip: A smart girl should always get the TET included in the nikah nama (marriage deed), along with the grounds based on which she is entitled to initiate a TET.

2. Khula: Under khula, a Muslim woman can unilaterally initiate divorce by stating her reason. She needs to pay the husband in this case, either by returning the mahr amount, or any other agreed financial settlement. It is like her saying, 'Let me go. I am paying you back the money you gave me during the marriage.'

    Interestingly, the divorce between Indian tennis star Sania Mirza and Pakistani cricketer Shoaib Malik was supposedly done by way of khula.[5]

>  **Food for thought**
>
> Since khula has its origins in customs, there are two schools of thoughts about the husband's agreement to it. Some believe that khula is the woman's absolute right to get a divorce. Others believe that the husband must accept the request for the divorce as final.
>
> As of July 2024, the question is pending before the Supreme Court. Interestingly, the Kerala High Court had recently held that the right to invoke khula shouldn't be subject to the husband's will.[6] Since the case is yet to be decided by the Supreme Court, the high court's judgment is only applicable to Muslim women in Kerala and not binding across India.

3. Lian: If your husband hurls accusations of adultery against you, why should you sit back and take it? Lian gives you the right to sue your husband for this false charge. Not only can you clear your name, you have the right to ask for a decree of divorce on these grounds. After all, no relationship is worth sacrificing your honour and dignity for! This type of divorce is very specific to allegations of adultery and nothing else.

When Can a Muslim Husband Divorce His Wife?

Under customary Muslim law, your husband can pretty much decide to divorce you whenever he wants, using multiple ways. He neither has to go to court nor prove anything.

The commonly used methods have been explained below:
1. Talaq-i-Ahsan: In this form of divorce, the husband makes a single pronouncement of divorce (talaq). He then must wait for three menstrual cycles of his wife, during which the couple should not engage in sexual intercourse. If the husband changes his mind during the waiting period, the divorce is cancelled. If not, after the waiting period, the divorce is final. It's like hitting the pause button and waiting to see if things get better.
2. Talaq-i-Hasan: This form of divorce is like the first one, except that instead of saying 'talaq' once and waiting for three months, the husband says it thrice, i.e., once every month for three months. After the third month, the divorce is final, unless he changes his mind and revokes it.
3. Ila: Your husband takes an oath to abstain from sexual relations with you. If you don't engage in sexual activity for four months, the marriage stands dissolved. However, if he resumes cohabitation within these four months, the marriage stays intact.

Note: In all of the above forms of divorce, it is important to abstain from sexual relations between the husband and wife. If sexual relations are resumed, the divorce process will stand cancelled.

Notice the stark difference between the grounds of divorce for Muslim women and men? Often, Muslim men don't even need to give reasons to initiate divorce. All they have to do is say it and wait for three months! Man proposes, law disposes!

> **Triple Talaq: Instant Divorce in a World of Instant Gratification**
>
> Triple talaq, or talaq-e-biddat, was a form of instant divorce where the husband would say 'talaq' thrice in one go and the marriage would be over. It did not involve any waiting period of three months. Imagine a tower of cards, painstakingly built with love and care, sent crumbling with just one sudden gust of wind. Talk about taking instant gratification to a whole new level!
>
> What was more was that the husband could send his rendition of 'talaq, talaq, talaq' however he wished—whether spoken, written, or via phone, SMS, email or social media. Imagine opening your Facebook or Instagram account and finding out that your husband has divorced you! Sounds bizarre, doesn't it? What is more bizarre is that triple talaq was a legally valid form of divorce in India until as recently as 2017, when the Supreme Court declared it invalid while hearing the landmark case of *Shayara Bano vs Union of India*.
>
> It was after this that the Parliament passed the Muslim Women (Protection of Rights on Marriage) Act, 2019, popularly known as the 'Triple Talaq Act', to make it abundantly clear that triple talaq is not acceptable!

Mutual Consent Divorce for Muslims

There is no codified law about mutual consent divorce for Muslims. Instead, under customary law, they have *mubarat*, a form of mutual divorce where both the husband and wife agree to a divorce and decide the terms. Some say that mubarat is a form of khula, where the other party accepts the request for a divorce. However, as part of khula, the wife must return the mahr. Under mubarat, there are no payment conditions. Once the mutual offer is accepted and after observing the mandatory *iddat* period (usually three months), the divorce is considered final.

What if I Want to Walk Out of My Marriage?

It is not uncommon for distressed women, mostly victims of domestic violence, to walk out of a marriage when they can't take it any more.

One of my friends, Nirmala (name changed), whose husband used to ill-treat her, was going through a divorce. One day, when she had had enough, she booked a flight from Delhi and came back to Hyderabad with a small bag. She left all her clothes, jewellery, etc., in Delhi, at her husband's house, because obviously when you are in distress, you do not think about these things. During the course of the divorce, she wanted to get her things back. But it was difficult for her to go back to Delhi just to collect her belongings. Also, she didn't want to interact with her husband's family and have them hovering around while she collected everything. To top it all, her husband's family sent her pictures of her wardrobe with half the things missing. She had no way of finding out what happened to the other half.

This is a very common scenario. As time passes, it becomes increasingly difficult to get your things back.

Pro tip: Just like an expecting mother prepares a hospital bag closer to the delivery date, keep aside a bag with all the essentials if you know that you may eventually walk out. Here is what it should have:
1. Take all your documents with you (passport, Aadhaar, educational and professional certificates, driving licence, marriage certificate, etc.).
2. Take all your jewellery, cash and other valuables.
3. Take as many of your belongings as possible with you.
4. Whatever you cannot take, pack it in a suitcase or cupboard and lock it. You don't want anyone messing around when you are absent.

Hard Talks: Important Conversations to Have in Case of a Divorce

Apart from the emotional baggage, there are certain important terms of settlement in a divorce. These include division of assets, maintenance and alimony, full and final settlement, child custody and providing for children, if any.

Division of Assets

Navigating the division of assets can be a challenging and emotionally charged process.

You have two types of assets: immovable property (real estate and property) and movable property (jewellery, cash and all other valuables).

Both types of assets are divided during a divorce. How does that happen? Who gets how much? What factors are considered? You will be able to answer all these questions yourself. Just read on!

1. **Immovable property**

   Think of immovable property as a baked pie. What you need to decide is the share of pie each partner gets. Like you have different types of pies—apple pie, banana pie, cherry pie—there are different types of properties. Your right to a share depends on the flavour.

   i. **Ancestral pie** (aka ancestral property): This is the pie baked by the husband's previous generations (parents, grandparents). For example, a joint family home.

      You will not be entitled to a share in this pie, unless your husband's share has been carved out and handed over to him.

   ii. **Self-made pie** (aka self-acquired property): This is the pie your husband baked himself, i.e., the property acquired by him and in his name. It is a different story that, behind the scenes, you purchased the ingredients, helped him mix the dough, etc. If he registered the property only in his name, it is considered *his* self-acquired property.

       You can claim a share in this pie, but your share will depend on factors like your earnings, other properties, etc. However, your children will directly have a claim over this pie, as the heirs of the father.

   iii. **Couple pie** (aka joint property of the couple): This is the pie both of you baked together, i.e., property registered in the name of both spouses. It can include the home you live in together.

You can easily claim a 50 per cent share in this pie, especially if you contributed towards it in any manner. Your children will also have a claim over this pie, as heirs of both parents.

>  **#MovieTime**
>
> Let's go back to *Dil Dhadakne Do*. In this movie, Anil Kapoor's character is a businessman and his wife (Shefali Shah's character) is a homemaker. During an argument about money, he says, '*Tumhare paas paise isliye hain kyunki maine kamaye hain* (You have money because I have worked to earn it).'
>
> To this, the wife says, '*Aur tumhe support maine kiya hai* (And I supported you through it).'
>
> This is a common scenario. A homemaker makes the house a home, she runs it, maintains it and takes care of the family. Don't let anyone tell you that just because you didn't contribute financially, you don't deserve a share in the pie.

Pro tip: What happens often with a married couple is, when they buy a house together, they use the husband's earnings to pay for the mortgage and the wife's earnings to pay for day-to-day expenses. As a result, on paper it looks like the husband has bought the house, whereas the fact is that both partners have contributed in their own way.

This can come in the way of you getting your rightful share. Therefore, always ensure that your earnings are also used towards the mortgage and the property is registered in both your names.

2. **Movable property**

   With movable property, follow one simple rule: if it is yours, it is yours! If it is not, it is not. This means that any jewellery, cash, etc., that you have earned, bought yourself or received as a gift (even if it is from the husband's family) is yours. The same thing applies for your husband. Whatever is his, is his.

Alimony and Maintenance

While alimony and maintenance are often used interchangeably, they have slightly different meanings as per the law. Generally, maintenance is the support money paid by one spouse to the other while the couple is married and when the divorce proceedings are ongoing. Alimony is the support money paid after a divorce.

The idea behind maintenance and alimony is that if either spouse is not able to support herself or himself during or after the divorce, the other spouse should provide this support. The concept comes from the age-old tradition where women were expected to take care of the house and the husband was the breadwinner. The woman had no means to support herself financially. Hence, maintenance and alimony came into the picture.

So, who gets it? If you opt for a mutual consent divorce, you can sit across the table and discuss who gets maintenance and alimony, and how much. If the court is deciding for you, in case of a contested divorce, it will be decided based on who earns more, who needs maintenance more and who is self-sufficient.

Here, I have used maintenance and alimony interchangeably.

>  **Food for thought**
>
> It is a myth that the wife is always granted maintenance. Courts nowadays grant maintenance to whichever spouse appears to need it more.
>
> For example, if the wife is a homemaker and financially dependent on the husband, the court will grant her maintenance. If both the husband and wife are earning almost the same amount, the court may not grant maintenance to any of them.
>
> Always remember, maintenance is an extremely subjective matter and is decided on a case-to-case basis and also depends on the court hearing it.

> **Wife Ordered to Pay Maintenance to Husband**
>
> In a recent 2024 divorce case before the Bombay High Court, the court directed the woman to pay a monthly maintenance of Rs 10,000 to her former husband, who was unemployed and unable to earn due to his ailments.
>
> It is interesting to note that the judge who passed this order, Justice Sharmila Deshmukh, is the same judge who, in another case, asked the husband to pay the wife a compensation of Rs 3 crore for domestic violence. Anyone who would have accused her of bias in the domestic violence case will probably have no answer here![7]

Maintenance can be paid monthly, periodically (for example, quarterly) or in a lump sum. It is often up to the parties to decide. You can ask the court for what you need. In the case of a mutual consent divorce, put it down in the settlement agreement.

Maintenance looks good on paper, but looks even better in the bank. However, practically speaking, maintenance is often delayed or left unpaid. If your ex-husband is not paying the promised maintenance or delaying it, you will have to go to court again for an order asking him to pay on time. This means wasting time and money again, and who wants to do that!

Pro tip: Instead of a monthly maintenance, ask for a lump sum alimony. Lump sum means you get the entire chunk in one or few instalments in a short period of time, instead of small monthly payments. This way, you will get the money upfront, it is a sizeable enough amount for you to invest/use and you don't need to keep running after your ex-husband asking for maintenance. Less hassle, isn't it?

Full and Final Settlement

All this talk about property and maintenance brings us to what we shall call the 'full and final settlement' or FnF.

Are you familiar with the full and final settlement paid to an employee who leaves a job? The company rounds up the employee's salary, any pending arrears, provident fund payments, etc., and hands over everything to the employee. This marks the end of the company's relationship with the employee.

An FnF in a divorce is similar. Both spouses round up what is owed to the other, put it down on paper, make the transfers and close the chapter of marriage.

Think of your FnF like an empty pot that is to be filled with your share from the divorce. In goes a bag containing your share of the immovable property. Next goes in the bag with your jewellery, cash and other valuables. Finally, you put in your alimony.

Each of these three bags go into filling the same pot. Therefore, the size of one bag will increase or decrease depending on the size of the other bags. Every couple will have their own permutations and combination for this pot, depending on their circumstances. For example, if you get to keep the house you are living in, you will get a smaller alimony. If your husband is keeping the house, you should ideally get alimony worth your 50 per cent share in the house, plus some more.

Remember, the purpose of dividing assets is to give each spouse what is rightfully theirs. The purpose of maintenance is to ensure that if one of the spouses is financially dependent, they are taken care of. The size of each bag should depend on their purpose and what you need.

Pro tip: I have seen a few mutual consent cases getting stuck in court and turning into a contested divorce because the spouses don't agree on the settlement terms. For example, Sheela expects Rs 25 lakh in settlement, but Rohit agrees to Rs 15 lakh only.

Should Sheela go to court for this? No! If Sheela goes to court, she will get stuck in a huge backlog of divorce cases.

Even if the court grants her Rs 25 lakh after three years, Sheela needs to ask herself what will be the value of those additional Rs 10 lakh after three years? More importantly, is it worth the added stress?

If Sheela is a savvy girl, she will get her lawyer to negotiate. Even if her lawyer is able to settle for Rs 20 lakh, it is a win for Sheela! She will end up saving precious time. And if the case were to get dragged in court, she would have to pay most of the balance Rs 5 lakh to lawyers.

Watch Out!

There are some dirty tactics commonly deployed to avoid paying the other partner their rightful FnF. These include:
1. Transferring assets to other family members.
2. Claiming lower income than actual figure.
3. Diverting funds to other accounts.
4. Claiming that assets are owned by family business.

Custody and Visitation

'Just have a baby, everything will be fine.' This is the WORST advice anyone can give a warring couple and the worst reason to have a child! If a couple is headed towards divorce, having a baby not only ties you down to your spouse, whom you want to divorce, but also brings a child into an unhappy family.

What happens to children of divorce, you may ask? Till the child turns eighteen, the court grants custody to one of the parents. Usually, it is the mother, at least until the child turns five. Once the child turns eighteen, they are free to vote, drive a car and choose which parent they want to live with.

Is it always the mother? No. When granting custody, courts only care about one thing and that is the child. The egos of the parents don't matter. The courts mainly look at two factors:

1. Welfare of the child: This ensures that the child stays with the parent who will be able to take care of him/her better. It doesn't have to do with which parent earns more. It means which parent can grant a safe and comfortable environment for the child to grow up in.
2. The child's wish: If the court feels the child is old enough to decide which parent they want to live with, the court can consider that. This obviously applies for older kids, like teenagers.

If the court believes that neither of the parents are fit enough to raise the child, it can grant custody to someone else, like grandparents, uncle and aunt. This, however, is very rare.

If you are in a contested divorce, it is likely that both parents will fight for custody. The court will then decide for you. In a mutual divorce, the spouses will decide between themselves and the court will rarely interfere.

If parents could, they would divide the child! After all, nobody wants to lose their child. Thankfully, the child is not a pie that can be cut into two halves!

While one parent gets full custody of the child, what about the other? That's when visitation rights come in! The other parent always has the right to have the child visit and stay, or to meet the child at his/her place of residence.

For example, if the mother has custody during school term, the child can live with the father during holidays. If things are not cordial, the father may be allowed to visit the child only at the mother's house.

How visitation plays out completely depends upon the relationship between the ex-spouses, their trust in each other and, most importantly, the child's welfare. Again, it is very subjective and depends on the unique circumstances of each case.

Don't Use Your Child for Revenge

I have seen several divorce cases where the parents get unreasonable about child custody, to the extent of completely denying the other spouse access.

Remember, the custody of a child is not a tool for you for to seek revenge. You may have your own (justified) grudges against your ex-husband. However, even if he is the first person on your 'hate list', he is the father of your child. A bad husband doesn't have to be a bad father. Don't be unreasonable about visitation rights. Instead, address your concerns about the child's welfare through the settlement terms.

Of course, there are cases where the husband simply washes his hands off the children. In such a case, make sure that your ex-spouse shoulders some part of childcare responsibility. You can set up a co-parenting system where both parents contribute towards raising the child, even if the custody lies with only one parent. Or ensure that he pays towards supporting the child, along with creating a support system for childcare (like hiring help).

> ### Bitter Custody Battle over Henry the Dog
>
> Member of Parliament Mahua Moitra and her estranged ex-lover, lawyer Jai Anant Dehadrai, fought bitterly over the custody of their dog, Henry, in what became quite a public battle.
>
> This case brought to light the issue of custody of pets. What happens when pet owners split up? Anyone who has a pet knows that they are a part of the family and no one would like to lose their custody. India has no custody laws on pets, the way we have for children. It is left to the couple to draw up settlement terms for custody. If they can't, the court decides for them on a case-to-case basis. It is safe to say that unlike custody of children, where the welfare of the child is the primary goal, the custody of pets is more about negotiation and bargaining power. For example, 'I will give you the pet if you let go of these demands.'[8]

Providing for Children

Getting custody is only the first step. Providing for them till they become independent is a whole other ball game. Apart from school fees, children have a multitude of needs. It is important to set up a system, at the time of the divorce itself, to ensure that your child's financial needs are taken care of.

In a mutual consent divorce, the parents can decide on a system through negotiation and submit it to court. In a contested divorce, the court will decide, based on the submissions of the parties.

So, what expenses should you consider? Here are a few examples of the broad categories that a child's expenses will fall under. Based on your standard of living, you can draw up a rough estimate of the total expenses that will be incurred for the child.

1. Living expenses for basics like food, clothing, shelter.
2. Education costs all the way up to college or higher education.
3. Healthcare and medical expenses.
4. Recreational and extra-curricular activities, such as hobbies, clubs, travel, etc.
5. Special needs. For example, if the child needs therapy or counselling.
6. Most Indian parents pay for their children's marriage, so you need to account for that, too.
7. Costs related to birthday parties, gifts and holidays are essential for maintaining a sense of normalcy and joy in the child's life.
8. There may be unforeseen expenses, such as medical emergencies, that require both parents to contribute.

It is important for divorcing parents to work together or through legal channels to establish a fair and comprehensive plan for sharing these expenses. The goal is to ensure that the child's needs are met and that s/he receives the care and support required.

To provide for your child's financial needs, you need to set up a system that works almost on autopilot. Your child's needs should be taken care of without you having to beg your ex-spouse for funds. To ensure this, opt for a lump sum amount over periodic payments.

Here is how you can set up a system for your child's maintenance:

1. Create a trust fund: Imagine a trust to be a treasure chest. You and your ex-spouse (the 'settlors') fill it with treasure (like money or property) for your child (the 'beneficiary'). You ask a neutral trustworthy friend (the 'trustee') to keep an eye on it. Your friend's job is to ensure that the treasure is used for the child's benefit. The rules for how it is to be used are written down in a special document.

   A trust fund is ideal to provide for the long-term expenses of your child, such as higher education and marriage.

2. Investments: Another hassle-free route is to have investments in your child's name. For a minor child, either parent can be the nominee and operator. The interest and maturity amount from these investments can pay for your child's periodic expenses.

3. Money in the bank: For day-to-day and regular expenses, the best option is to have the funds accessible. You can either hold this amount in a designated account of the parent who has custody of the child, or a joint account operated by both parents. If you are financially dependent and your ex-spouse is unable to set aside a chunk of money, set up a system where, each month, a fixed amount is auto-deducted from his account and deposited into the child's expenses account.

From the examples above, figure out which system works best for you. But remember, don't fall into the trap of 'I'll pay you Rs 25,000 out of the promised Rs 1 lakh now and the remaining Rs 75,000 over a period of six months.' The balance almost never comes on time. You will end up losing not just time but also mental peace.

Pro tip: Don't combine your FnF settlement and childcare expenses. Often, women are shortchanged by combining these two, to make it look like she is getting the world. Whereas, in reality, most of the settlement goes towards providing for the children and she is hardly left with anything. This is especially important if the wife was financially dependent on the husband.

This is also why the book lists the FnF section before custody of children.

How Do You Secure Yourself in a Divorce?

We get into a marriage with the idea that it will last forever. Sometimes, it does not. It's like getting into an accident without wearing your seatbelt. To keep yourself secure in the car that is your marriage, here is what you can do:

1. Mortgage: If you take out a mortgage for your home, both of you should contribute to it (if the wife is also earning). Very often, what happens is that the wife pays for day-to-day running expenses of the house while the husband pays for the house. When things go sour between them, the wife gets the raw deal. She does not have any rights on the house, leaving her helpless.

Therefore, both partners should contribute towards the mortgage and the living expenses.

If you are not earning, you should still ensure that your name is added to the property documents as a co-owner. Or you should have security in some other form, like mutual fund investments or a fixed deposit in your name. As a homemaker, you contribute time and effort towards building a home, so get the thought out of your head that you don't deserve financial security.

I have seen several husbands who add their wife's name to each property they buy, even if she did not contribute towards it monetarily. This shows that they value her efforts in building a life together. Such husbands truly are treasures to be cherished.

2. Children: Secure your children's present and future through investments, or a trust fund in their name. Tomorrow, if things go south and you assume responsibility for your child, these investments will ensure that you are not struggling without the father's support.

3. Transparency: Ask for complete transparency on business and money matters. Very often, we see that the wife has absolutely no idea about her husband's bank accounts, insurance, medical policies, business accounts, etc. You need not be involved in the day-to-day business, but you should know how much your husband/family members are drawing from it for personal use. One of the easiest ways to understand this is through income tax returns.

As partners, you should maintain transparency in this regard.

What if You Are Going through a Divorce, but Did Not Know about Any of This?

1. Keep ALL your documents, jewellery, belongings and valuables with you. This way you will not have to start your battle by trying to get custody of your things.

> **#TrueStory**
>
> My friend, Akriti, got divorced from her husband whom she had dated for six years before marriage. As is customary, she had kept her jewellery with her mother-in-law for safekeeping. When they were getting divorced, Akriti asked her mother-in-law for her jewellery. However, she got only one of the two expensive necklaces that Akriti had handed over to her and was told that the other was 'misplaced'. Akriti was so fed up because of the process that she let it go. She didn't have the energy to fight any more. The thing is, if such an expensive necklace was actually missing, her mother-in-law would have filed a police complaint or called attention to it much earlier.

2. Try to access your husband's income tax returns and bank statements. If you don't understand them, seek help. This will help you counter any claims of 'I am so poor that I can't pay maintenance' in court. It is funny how husbands become bankrupt overnight when it comes to divorce cases.

3. Look out for any property transactions, or large bank transfers, taking place around you. Many husbands resort to transferring all their properties and assets to their parents and siblings, so that they can show the court that they don't have any money to pay maintenance.
4. When you file a domestic violence or divorce case, ask for an immediate freeze on the transfer of any personal assets that are in your husband's name. You can also ask for a freeze on banking transactions beyond a certain limit, to ensure that he doesn't empty his bank account overnight.

Be careful before signing any document. Get it reviewed by a lawyer, or a financial advisor, whichever is applicable. It is better to pay professionals to safeguard your interest than to lose much more by trying to do it all yourself.

Difference Between Divorce, Separation and Annulment

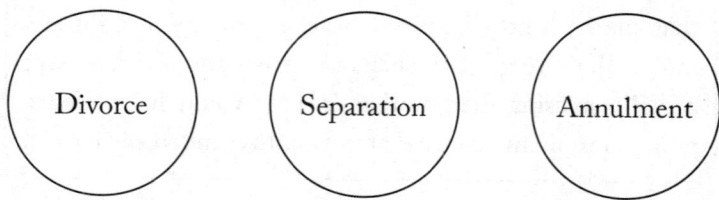

Wait a minute, aren't they the same thing? Generally speaking, they could be. Legally speaking, they are not.
1. **Divorce:** This is a legal process that formally ends a valid marriage. It acknowledges that a valid marriage existed, but it stands terminated through a court order.
2. **Separation:** This is a formal arrangement in which a married couple decides to live separately but remains

legally married. Unlike a divorce, legal separation does not terminate the marriage. The grounds for separation, and the process, is like a divorce. It involves getting a separation order from the court to settle matters such as division of property, custody, maintenance, etc.
3. **Annulment:** This is a legal declaration that a marriage is void or invalid, as if it never existed. It essentially erases the marriage from a legal standpoint. Annulments are relatively rare compared to divorces and separations. They are often sought when there is a fundamental defect in the marriage.

So, which one is for you? That depends on your specific situation.

If you choose a divorce, you formally end your marriage and cut all legal ties with your spouse. Go for a divorce when you want to close that chapter, put it behind you and move on in life.

Opt for separation when you and your spouse are considering reconciliation but want some time apart to work on your relationship, or when divorce is not an option due to personal or religious reasons. Separation is usually opted for by couples in long-term marriages, where they want to live separate lives but don't necessarily need to move on to a new relationship. Being legally married does not affect them. Couples with children sometimes opt for a separation instead of divorce for legal convenience.

You can get an annulment only if the law permits it for your specific situation and if you have been married for a year or less.

1. For an annulment, the most important factor is whether your marriage can be considered 'void', or 'voidable', under the law. Here is how that happens:
   a. Void: If one spouse is already married (this does not apply to men governed by the Muslim law), or if the spouses come within the ambit of prohibited degrees of relationship (i.e., they are very close relatives).
   b. Voidable: This includes non-consummation of the marriage due to the impotence of one of the spouses. If already consummated, there should be no sexual relations after you find out about the voidability.
   c. The wife was already pregnant with someone else's child at the time of marriage.
   d. Consent for marriage was obtained by force or fraud.
2. The second important factor is time. You can get an annulment only within the first year of marriage, or if you started living separately after you found out that the marriage is void/voidable.

Remember, like marriage, divorce and its cousins (separation and annulment) are also governed by specific religious laws.

The Divorce Landscape in India

According to newspaper reports,[9] India is the only country where men initiate most of the divorces. In other countries, it is women. Isn't this ironic for a country that records high rates of domestic violence and marital rape? This tells us that we live in a society where women would rather suffer in a bad marriage than walk away from it.

The two main factors contributing to this are societal pressure and lack of family support. But, in my opinion, the biggest factor at play is the lack of financial independence. When a woman is independent and self-reliant, she can fight the world, including her own family. However, if she is financially and emotionally dependent, she will be forced to put up with anything and everything. This is why, later in the book, I emphasize the importance of financial independence for women and the need to know your rights related to matters of property.

#MovieTime

Let us return to *Dil Dhadakne Do*, to the scene where Priyanka Chopra's character tells her parents that she wants a divorce. Their response is a stark reminder of how families fail to support their own daughters.

Her parents say: '*Hamare mehman kya kahenge? Iss family mein na kabhi divorce hua hai, na hoga* (What will our guests say? There has been no divorce in this family, and there never will be).'

To make things worse, they add, '*Yeh mat samajhna ki tum hamare paas wapas aa jaogi. Ab woh tumhara ghar nahi hai* (Don't think you can come back to us. You don't belong in our house any more).'

Since Chopra's character is a successful businesswoman with her own income, she can choose to go ahead with the divorce even without her own family's support.

To end this chapter on a positive note, let me tell you about a father in Jharkhand who organized a baarat (celebratory procession) to welcome back his daughter who was allegedly being tortured by her in-laws and had filed for a divorce.[10]

On his Facebook post, the father wrote: 'When your daughter's marriage is done with great pomp and show, and if the spouse and family turn out to be wrong or does wrong things, then you should bring your daughter back to your home with respect and honour because daughters are very precious.'

I couldn't agree more! The video of the baarat, which went viral on social media, is a heartwarming reminder to families that it is more important to have a happy daughter than a happy neighbour!

POINTS TO REMEMBER

1. Like marriage, divorce is also governed by religious laws and depends on which law you got married under. Each religion has different rules, based on which you can ask for divorce.
2. A divorce can either be contested or mutual.
3. Mutual divorces are becoming more preferred these days, as they are quicker, hassle-free and less toxic.
4. Custody of children is usually given to the mother, as she is considered the natural guardian. However, courts always consider the welfare of the child first.
5. Maintenance and alimony are granted based on which spouse needs it more. If both are earning and financially independent, the court may not grant maintenance. If the woman is financially dependent on her husband, the court can ask the husband to pay her maintenance.

Remarriage

Remarriage is when someone, who was previously married but is now single (due to death of the spouse or divorce), gets married again. Divorce and remarriage are slowly gaining acceptance in our society, especially in urban India. Studies show that the percentage of men who remarry is double that of women.[11] Clearly, in our patriarchal society, the acceptance seems to be more for men than women! Another reason for this difference could be that most women take the responsibility of raising the children born out of a marriage, therefore finding it difficult to find a partner who accepts their children and vice-versa.

But first things first, is remarriage permitted in India? Yes, it is! There is no law under any religion that bars remarriage.

What is the waiting period for remarriage?

1. Divorce: In case of a divorce, either party can remarry after the waiting period, which is:
    i. For a contested divorce: When the time to file an appeal (i.e., challenge) against the divorce order is over. This is usually three months. If there is no appeal filed, then you are free to remarry. If an appeal is filed, then both spouses will have to wait till the court dismisses (i.e., does not consider it valid) or concludes (i.e., gives a judgment on) the appeal.
    ii. Mutual consent divorce: There is no waiting period. Both parties can get remarried whenever they want.
2. Death: In the case of death of a spouse, the law does not specify any waiting period. The widowed spouse can legally remarry anytime. It is society that acts as a strong

influence at this time by creating an invisible barrier for widows to rediscover their life!

The waiting period stated above is more or less universally applicable, except for Muslims.

Waiting period for Muslims
Since most of Muslim religious law is derived from customs, it is slightly different. Moreover, under Muslim customs, the waiting period is different for men and women (unlike other religions where it is the same for both spouses).

For women, the waiting period is called iddat. It depends on the circumstance of divorce:
1. In case of the husband's death, the woman must wait for four months and ten days from the date of the death.
2. In case of a divorce, the woman must wait for three months from the date of divorce.

For men (no prizes for guessing!), there is no waiting period.

Food for thought

Don't you think it is highly unfair that the men do not have any waiting period? This is because Muslim men do not have to go to court for a divorce. They can divorce as per religious practice, therefore, there is no question of 'time to appeal' like in other religions. Maybe it is time to change the law?

How can I get remarried?

The process for remarriage is the same as getting married for the first time. If you are doing a ceremonial wedding, you will do it under the religious law governing both the spouses. If you are doing an interfaith or court marriage, it will be under the Special Marriage Act.

You will need to register your remarriage. The process for registration is also the same. The only difference is that you will also need to submit your divorce order, or your spouse's death certificate in the list of documents.

Does marrying again affect your property or custody rights?

The good news is that remarriage does not affect your rights. Once you get divorced, you cut all legal ties with your husband and his family. After the divorce, you will no longer have any property rights flowing from your husband. This change happens after your divorce, which is why getting married again has nothing to do with it.

Remarriage also does not affect your rights to child custody. The only situation in which it can be impacted is if your spouse brings up a fresh challenge in court, saying your new marriage affects the welfare of the child. In such a case, the court will examine the circumstances. As long as it is satisfied that the child is not negatively affected, the court will not disrupt the child's life by shifting custody.

EXERCISE TIME!

Divorce Dilemmas: The Jumble Challenge

1. ETCONEDTS
2. TUULMA
3. EUTRLCY
4. LYAINOM
5. STYDUOC

Hints:
1. *Type of divorce where the parties cannot agree on key issues.*
2. *Type of divorce where both parties agree on all terms.*
3. *Grounds for divorce involving harsh treatment.*
4. *Financial support paid to an ex-spouse after divorce.*
5. *Legal right to care for and make decisions about a child.*

Answer key:
1. Contested 2. Mutual 3. Cruelty 4. Alimony 5. Custody

7

Live-in Relationships: To Tie the Knot or Not?

In this chapter, we will understand what makes your live-in relationships work legally, how to be smart and protect yourself, and what rights the law gives you.

Introduction

I am sure you have heard the saying 'wait until you live with someone to truly know them'. It is easy to be on your best behaviour during a date, but how long can you keep up the pretence when living together? There are only so many days until one resists the urge to throw a wet towel on the bed! So, how about testing the waters before entering them?

Today's youth have grasped this concept, with many opting to cohabit before marriage or solidify live-in relationships as a permanent set-up. In simple terms, a live-in relationship is an arrangement between consenting adults, similar to marriage but devoid of any formal ceremony or ritual. In fact, as per a survey[1] of 140,000 millennials, 80 per cent supported live-in relationships.

Now, are live-in relationships an acceptable replacement for marriage? Are they legal? Can you walk-in and walk-out as you please? What if you are living with a friend of the opposite gender (as flatmates, without being romantically involved)? Will it be considered a live-in relationship?

#ReelToReal

In the 2019 Bollywood movie *Luka Chuppi*, which addressed live-in relationships, the girl and boy fall in love. When the boy proposes, the girl decides that she wants to try living together first. They rent a flat and live together for twenty days like a married couple. They even lie to their landlord and put up fake wedding photos.

While this sounds like fun in a movie, let us see what the legal status of their relationship would be.

Before we get into the legality of it, here is a fun quiz for you. Answer the following statements as true or false:
1. Live-in relationships are illegal.
2. Simply living together means being in a live-in relationship.
3. A live-in relationship is okay as a temporary trial before marriage but cannot be a permanent relationship.
4. Children born out of a live-in relationship are illegitimate.
5. A live-in couple does not have any responsibilities towards each other.

How many of them did you answer as true? The truth is, all of the above are false! They are myths, which we are going to bust.

This chapter will answer your questions about the legality and status of live-in relationships in India, and how you can secure your rights if you are in one.

First Things First. Are They Legal?

The answer is yes and no. Well, they are legal, but as it is with everything in law, the answer is never a simple yes or no. Conditions always apply!

There is no law about live-in relationships in India yet. Surprised? You should be, considering we are in the 2020s! However, the Supreme Court has come to our rescue and created a 'law' around live-in relationships in the form of judgments. In 2010, the court had declared live-in relationships as legal (in *S. Khushboo vs Kanniammal*). Since then, the law recognizes that there can be no restriction on adults choosing to live together, with or without marriage. Sorry, nosy neighbours, you can try and impose your 'morals', but the legal verdict is clear! Just because you think it is morally wrong, does not make it legally wrong!

>
> ### Can House Owners Refuse Live-in Couples as Tenants?
>
> Several house owners refuse to rent their house to couples who are in live-in relationships. Housing societies also have rules that don't allow the owners to have unmarried couples or bachelors as tenants.
>
> Is this legal? Technically speaking, it is not. Live-in relationships have been recognized as valid and a right of choice by the Supreme Court. Therefore, no one should refuse to provide a rented space to live-in couples on the grounds of their relationship status.

What Is Your Legal Right in the Situation Outlined Above?

If you are a tenant who has been refused accommodation based on your relationship status, you can file a case against the landlord on the grounds of discrimination.

If you are a house owner whose housing complex rules prohibit you from renting your house to a live-in couple, you can challenge it in court.

However, I would not recommend the legal route unless you strongly believe in the cause and are willing to invest time and money in it. If you are already a working couple struggling to find a living space, pick your battles wisely, for our court system is tedious, slow and complex. You may or may not get justice, and it definitely will be delayed.

The sad ground reality is that legal change does not always translate into societal change. We have a long way to go before our society understands that a live-in relationship is a personal choice, that there is nothing illegal or immoral about it. Until then, maybe take a leaf out of the Bollywood movie *Luka Chuppi*?

Criteria for a Legal Live-in Relationship

The only two requirements are that both partners should be of marriageable age (i.e., adults) and they should be unmarried.

I know, this sounds too good to be true! So, what is the catch?

The catch is that while you can live together, if you want legal rights as partners, your relationship needs to be 'official enough'. It must be considered 'as good as marriage' in the eyes of the law.

But not every live-in relationship is treated like marriage. The Supreme Court has laid down certain criteria for a live-in relationship to be treated like a marriage.[2]

How Can You Make Your Live-in Relationship 'Official Enough'

1. *Officially live like live-in partners*: If you secretly live together and pretend to be single, your relationship will not be illegal, but it will not be considered like marriage.
2. *Live together long enough:* The duration is not defined and can vary from case to case. However, it is safe to assume that a few weeks may not be enough.
3. *Live together in the same house:* This is the essence of a live-in relationship!
4. *Share:* The couple should pool resources and financial arrangements to support each other, like a married couple.
5. *Get physical, but with feelings:* The couple should have a sexual relationship, not just for physical pleasure but also for intimacy and an emotional relationship, like a married couple.
6. *Get into domestic bliss:* The couple should run a house together and manage domestic arrangements, maybe like 'you do the dishes, I will watch TV'.)
7. *Have children and share responsibility:* This is a strong indication of the couple's seriousness, but not a mandatory requirement. Also, it is not just about having children but also about bringing them up. As Vidya Balan's character stated in the Bollywood movie *Paa*, 'Just because you lend me your sperm, doesn't make you a father.'

> 8. *Intention of the couple:* The relationship can only be considered to be like marriage if the partners *intend* to be in it for the long-term.

In short, the partners must live like a married couple. The only difference is the absence of religious ceremonies or registering a marriage.

Why is this important? Unless your live-in relationship is considered like marriage, you are not entitled to any 'rights' that a married person has.

Remember, the above points are guidelines issued by the court, which will play a role in future judgments. However, they are not hard-and-fast law.

What Rights Do I Have in a Live-in Relationship?

Since there is no law for live-in relationships in India, the rights of women in such relationships are derived from a mix of statutes and Supreme Court judgments. Let us understand this in detail:

1. Right against domestic abuse: The female partner is protected from physical, emotional, sexual and economic abuse under the Domestic Violence Act (explained in Chapter 3). The laws that apply in this situation are the Domestic Violence Act and sections 85, 86 of the BNS.

   However, as per a Supreme Court judgment (*Indra Sarma vs V.K.V. Sarma*), if you are in a live-in relationship with a married man, and you know

that he is married, then your rights against domestic violence are not guaranteed.
2. Right to maintenance: You can claim maintenance, i.e., financial support from your partner, if you are dependent on him and not earning (or earning enough). This is possible through the Domestic Violence Act and sections 85, 86 of the BNS.
3. Right to a shared household: You have equal rights to live in your joint home. Your partner cannot ask you to just leave based on his whims and fancies. The law applicable in this case is the Domestic Violence Act.

What Are My Property Rights in a Live-in Relationship?

Property rights in a live-in relationship are a grey area, since there is no codified law. We only have a few court judgments, which are also case-specific. However, what we can infer from the judgments is:
1. Live-in partners can inherit from each other if they have been in a long-term relationship, which can be considered like marriage.
2. Children born out of a live-in relationship can inherit property from their parents. However, whether they can inherit from other family members (like grandparents, aunts and uncles) is not clear.

The inferences above are simply interpretations and not codified law. You can derive some comfort from them, but it is not a guarantee. I would suggest that you execute a Will or gift deed in favour of your partner, or children, to ensure they don't miss out on their inheritance.

What Are My Exit Options in a Live-in Relationship?

Bollywood couples Ranbir Kapoor–Katrina Kaif and Bipasha Basu–John Abraham were believed to be in a live-in relationship for several years. What do you think happened when their relationships ended?

Unlike marriage, where there is a clear exit procedure in the form of divorce, there is no such law for a live-in relationship. This means that the couple can do as they please, even if one partner decides to abruptly walk out. This is both the pro and con of being in a live-in relationship. While this flexibility is what attracts some couples to this arrangement, it can also be unfair to an individual who needs more security.

How Can You Protect Yourself in Case of a Break-up?

Unfortunately, the law does not grant either partner any security or protection if a live-in relationship ends. This lack of security affects women the most, because the female partner is typically more dependent on the male partner. If the man decides to walk out, she is left stuck in a far from ideal situation.

This is why you need to be smart about it and protect yourself. Here's a guide to get you started.

A Smart Girl's Guide to Protecting Herself in a Live-in Relationship

1. Know what you are getting into: You know that live-in relationships are fluid and do not come with legal security. Get into one only if this arrangement works for you. If you need more security, then marriage may be more suitable for you. Choose what *you* are comfortable with.
2. Secure yourself financially: If you are earning, make sure to organize your finances to ensure you are independent and secure. If you are financially dependent on your live-in partner, make sure that he gives you some kind of security. It can be money deposited in the bank, fixed deposits/mutual funds in your name, jewellery, cash or property. God forbid, should you find yourself in a position where your relationship doesn't work out, you will be able to support yourself.
3. Property and other benefits: If you are in a long-term relationship (similar to marriage), you should ensure that both of you are each other's heirs to property. You can do this by writing a Will in favour of each other. You can also make each other the beneficiary for all banking and investment-related documents. Try to include each other's name in your life insurance policy, if the policy permits.
4. Power of Attorney: A General Power of Attorney (GPA) gives the other person (attorney) the authority to act on your behalf if you are unavailable or

incapacitated. You and your partner can execute GPAs in favour of each other. This will give you the right to take care of, and act on, the financial assets of your partner in their absence.

5. Ensure that your partner is not already married! Do a background check, hire a private detective if you must! You have seen how courts react to a woman getting into a relationship with a married man. They give her no rights!

Remember, all the tips listed above will give both partners rights over each other. And we all know that with great power comes great responsibility. Therefore, enter into a live-in relationship only with someone you fully trust.

Pro tip: If something changes in your relationship, or you become unsure, you can always amend or cancel the legal documents. You will incur expenses for the transaction, but it is better to bear that cost than to have a non-trustworthy partner benefit from you.

What About the Children Born Out of a Live-in Relationship?

Children don't choose to be born; their parents choose to bring them into this world. Therefore, the law always ensures that, no matter what, children never suffer because of their circumstances. The Supreme Court has made it abundantly clear that children born out of a live-in relationship will be treated as legitimate and will enjoy the same rights as a child born out of a marriage.

> **Rights of a Child Born Out of a Live-in Relationship**
>
> 1. Right to be treated as a legitimate, biological child of both parents.
> 2. Right to inherit property from both parents as the legal heir.
> 3. Right to inherit a share in the joint family property as a coparcener (for Hindus, see the chapter titled 'Money Matters' for more details).
> 4. Right to care and guardianship from the parents. Every child has this right, which flows from the Guardians and Wards Act.
> 5. They are entitled to the same treatment as a child born to parents in a marriage.

What if My Live-in Partner Is Already Married?

The Supreme Court, in a very questionable judgment (*Indra Sarma vs V.K.V. Sarma*), has held that if a woman is aware about her live-in partner being married, then she gets virtually no rights from the live-in, not even protection under the Domestic Violence Act. Maintenance and property rights are a distant dream.

> **#TrueStory**
>
> Vijay (name changed) has two daughters with his wife, Vineeta (name changed). Vijay starts an affair with another woman, Renee (name changed). Eventually, Vijay and Renee get into a live-in relationship and have a son.
>
> Renee knew about Vijay's marriage, but she was madly in love with him and it did not matter to her. They lived

> like a married couple and all was fine. One day, when their son was five years old, Vijay realized that he had a duty towards his wife and daughters. Vijay abruptly ended his relationship with Renee and walked out. To top it all, he threatened to throw her out of the house they lived in.
>
> Overnight, Renee became nearly homeless and a single mother. What can Renee do?

If Vijay and Renee were in a legal live-in relationship, i.e., where Vijay was not already married, Renee would have a right to live in the house that she and Vijay shared, along with a right to maintenance. However, given Vijay's marital status, their relationship will not be considered legal in the eyes of the law. In such a case, Renee should follow the steps in the Smart Girl's Guide given earlier in this chapter.

The bottom line is that don't get into a live-in relationship with a married man. Not for moral reasons, but for legal reasons. If you do, then ensure that you abundantly protect yourself, even if you are madly in love. If you didn't know he was married and were duped, then this judgment will not apply to you. You can seek all your rights in that case.

> **Food for thought**
>
> Should it matter whether the woman knew about her live-in partner's marriage, especially when it becomes a question of whether or not she is entitled to her rights?

Does Your Religion Matter in a Live-in Relationship?

It so happens that all the major Supreme Court judgments, which lay down guidelines and laws about live-in relationships, were addressing live-in relationships between two Hindus. But personal laws are based on your religion, remember? Therefore, it is unclear if these laws will apply to Muslims, Christians or any other faith.

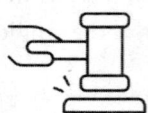 **Allahabad High Court Rejects Interfaith Couple's Plea to Protect Their Live-in Relationship**[3]

A young, interfaith couple in a live-in relationship asked the court for police protection from their families, who objected to the relationship. The Allahabad High Court refused to take their relationship seriously and did not grant them protection. The court said that in a span of two months, at the tender age of twenty-two years, we cannot expect the couple to have given serious thought to such a temporary relationship. The court asked the couple to prove their seriousness by getting married. Until then, it would not take any action.

Although this case was about an interfaith live-in couple, from the judgment it appears that the inter-religious aspect was not the focus here. Rather, it was the couple's age.

What do you think of this judgment? Do you think the couple was too young for their relationship to be taken seriously? Or do you think that age and time do not matter? If they know, they know.

As much as the law portrays that it is accepting when it comes to live-in relationships, there is a lot left to be done. There are several gaps and grey areas. Therefore, even though live-in relationships are accepted like marriage, they are not yet considered to be at the same level, especially when it comes to legal rights.

If live-in is your thing, go ahead. Don't let anyone judge you for your choice, but at the same time, don't let anyone take advantage of you for making that choice. Be smart about it and protect yourself.

POINTS TO REMEMBER

1. Live-in relationships are legal if both adults are of marriageable age and neither of them is married.
2. For you to be entitled to rights in your live-in relationship, it should fulfil certain criteria to be considered like a marriage. All live-in relationships cannot be considered equal to a relationship like marriage.
3. Children born out of a live-in relationship are legitimate and have legal rights.
4. Women in legal live-in relationships have rights against domestic violence, and can demand maintenance and a shared household.
5. If the law does not protect you, PROTECT YOURSELF.

8

Money Matters: Better Plan Than Be Sorry

This chapter will help you understand your right to inherit property, the ways you can go about it and how you can plan succession for your property.

Introduction

Do you know why most women stay on in unhappy marriages? It is mostly due to societal pressure and the lack of financial independence. While men are expected to learn how to manage their money, women are expected to find a man who can manage the money! As a result, they end up depending on their fathers, husbands or brothers (basically, male family members) in money matters.

#MovieTime

Sridevi's character Shashi, from *English Vinglish*, was an entrepreneur who used to sell homemade laddoos and other sweets. She had savings of her own, which she used to fund English language classes in the US. Through these classes, she was able to discover an identity for herself, and most importantly, gain respect from her husband and daughter. If Shashi didn't have savings and needed to ask her husband, he would have probably said no to the classes and deprived her of a life-changing opportunity!

What we can learn from Shashi is that whether you are a homemaker, entrepreneur, salaried employee, working in the family business or building spacecrafts to land on the moon, you must strive for some form of financial independence.

Why is financial independence important for women?
The short answer is, to ensure you remain the decision-maker of your life. With financial independence comes emotional

independence. When you start managing your own money, you get the confidence to take your own decisions, think freely and, most importantly, live fully.

Why, you may wonder, am I going on about the importance of managing your own money? Because I have seen a clear trend in all the cases that come to Pink Legal. When the woman is financially independent, she is able to walk out of an unhappy or abusive marriage. When she is not, she continues to suffer in silence even if she knows her legal rights. In most cases, if she leaves her husband, she has nowhere else to go. She cannot always move back to her parents' house. How is she to take care of her day-to-day financial needs? How is she to provide for her kids? Between being homeless and penniless versus having a roof over her head, she has no option but to choose the latter.

No one wakes up expecting problems or thinking they will die. Yet we take measures like insurance. Think of financial independence as your insurance. It will not only make you a strong and independent person but also keep you afloat if the going ever gets tough.

How can a homemaker become financially independent?
If your family members provide for you, instead of asking them for money when you need it (say Rs 200 for a coffee or Rs 1000 for shopping), set a monthly allowance that you will get at the beginning of the month, like a salary. This money is yours for the month. You decide how to use it and ensure it lasts the whole month! In Shashi's world, she could choose to spend it on English language classes, buy herself coffee in the US or re-invest it into her business.

To this, you can always say that you can ask your husband or parents for money when needed. Yes, of course you can, but at some point you need to learn how to manage money for yourself. You need to learn to take your own decisions about what to spend on, how much to save, what to invest on, etc.

We often see women taking the backseat when it comes to financial decisions. They end up leaving these to the men of the house. Remember, just like women are not born with cooking skills, men are not born with financial skills. These skills are acquired. If we don't take the first step, we will never learn.

> **Activity Time:** Sit down with your family and ask them these important questions:
> 1. How do we run the finances of the house?
> 2. What assets do we own and what is their value?
> 3. How much debt do we have?
> 4. What are our investments in property, stocks, gold?
> 5. What are our financial plans for the next five years?
>
> From asking these questions, you should slowly move towards participating in decision-making. Read, learn, speak to experts! There is ample information available on the internet for free. Make full use of it!

Inheritance: Inherit property, not silence

Inheritance is what you receive from someone after their death. For example, the property that grandparents or parents leave behind. Basically, it is something you get for doing nothing other than being born and loved. :) If someone wants to give you property when they are alive, they can do so as a 'gift'. This will not be called inheritance.

Women are often clueless about inheritance. Well, who can blame them? The law itself is confusing and, to top it all, women are rarely included in property and money-related discussions in the family.

But not any more! If you are reading this chapter, it means you have taken the first step towards educating yourself about your inheritance rights. Congratulations!

Before we delve into understanding your inheritance rights, here is a quick reminder. Property rights, like marriage and divorce rights, are governed by personal laws. This means the specifics vary based on your religion. Let us begin by understanding some basics that are universally applicable.

What are the types of property that I can inherit?

Property can be classified into different types based on factors like is it movable or immovable, is it ancestral or self-acquired. Let us understand this is in a little more detail:

1. Nature of the property
    i. Movable: This, as the name suggests, is anything that can be moved (jewellery, vehicles, cash, valuables, furniture, electronic devices).
    ii. Immovable: This means real estate in any form (land, an independent house, apartment, office space).

    You can inherit both movable and immovable property.
2. How you acquire the property
    i. Ancestral: This is property that is handed down to you from your ancestors. For example, the family

house you live in or land in the village that belonged to your grandparents. Basically, this includes any property for which you did not have to put in any efforts to acquire.

ii. Self-acquired: This is property that you have purchased yourself, through your own efforts. Since you are acquiring this property yourself, it is not something that you inherit.

While you can inherit ancestral property, who you can inherit from and how much you can inherit depends on your religion, gender and your relationship with that person. This will be explained in detail later in this chapter.

Stridhan: A Special Kind of Property

Simply put, *stree* (woman) *dhan* (property) is property that belongs to a woman. Stridhan is a concept under Hindu law, which emphasizes that any property of a woman is hers and hers alone. This can be movable and immovable property in any form, such as:

1. Gifts of any kind received by you in your lifetime.
2. Inheritance of any property received from anyone.
3. Self-acquired property, which you have bought through your own efforts.

Basically, each and every thing that belongs to the woman comes under stridhan. Only she has rights over it; she is the whole and sole owner who decides what to do with it. For example, women receive expensive gifts during their wedding. In many cases, the in-laws pressurize the new brides to deposit these gifts with them or the husband. Legally, they cannot do this. Even if they do, they have to hold these in good faith for the bride. It is her property.

>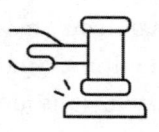
> **Husband Has No Control over Wife's Stridhan, Says Supreme Court**
>
> In a recent 2024 case,[1] the Supreme Court asked a man to pay his wife Rs 25 lakh for using her gold jewellery without her permission. This was jewellery that the wife had received as gifts during their wedding. On the first night of their marriage, the husband had taken it and given it to his mother for safekeeping. Thereafter, he had used it to clear financial obligations.
>
> The Supreme Court held that the husband has no control over his wife's stridhan. Even if he uses it during times of financial distress, it is his moral obligation to return it to her.

The concept of stridhan has its roots in old customs, when women did not have the right to property and would get gifts (like gold, cash, land in their name) for financial security. The law on stridhan ensured that no one snatched this property away from her.

How Can You Inherit Property?

There are two ways in which you can inherit property:
1. Will: A Will is a legal document by which one can decide how to pass on their property (movable and immovable) after their death. They can decide how much and who they want to give their property to.

If someone leaves you property in their Will, you can inherit this property. This is called inheritance through Will. ANYONE, be it family members or others, can leave you property this way. You will inherit whatever they leave behind as per their Will. We will delve into this more later.

2. Succession: When a person dies without a Will, their property passes on according to what is laid down in the personal, religious laws. The property usually goes to the legal heirs (people who are eligible to inherit property through succession).

Succession laws are different for each religion, which is why we will break them down on the basis of religions.

Before we begin, this is a gentle reminder that succession to (or inheriting) someone's property comes into play only after their death. Therefore, we are essentially understanding your inheritance rights after someone passes away without leaving behind a Will. Also note that succession is a highly nuanced process. Each person's rights to inherit depend on their gender, religion and their relationship with the person they are inheriting from. You should always consult an expert to find out your specific rights. This section is a good starting point for you to understand the basics.

What Are My Inheritance Rights as a Hindu Woman?

As a Hindu woman, you have two types of inheritance through succession:

1. **From immediate family members:** As a Hindu woman, you can inherit from these family members:
   1. Father
   2. Mother
   3. Husband
   4. Son
   5. Unmarried daughter

   How? You are considered a Class I heir of these relations. Hindu heirs are divided into Class I, Class II, Class III, etc., to determine the order of priority for inheritance. Class I heirs are like business-class passengers on an aircraft; only after they deplane can the rest of the passengers get off. Only if there are no Class I heirs on the list will the property go to Class II heirs. If there are no Class II heirs, then Class III heirs are considered. Usually, a person always has at least one Class I heir, which is why Class II and Class III heirs rarely come into the picture.

   However, you cannot inherit as a Class I heir from the following:
   1. Married daughter
   2. Siblings

   Simply put, you can inherit as a daughter from both parents, as a widow from your husband, and as a mother from your son and daughter (till the daughter gets married). You cannot inherit from your daughter after she gets married because you cease to be her Class I heir. Once a woman is married, her legal heirs change (more on that later). You also cannot inherit as a sister from your siblings unless they name you in their Will (explained later).

>  **Food for thought**
>
> Don't you think it is highly patriarchal that once a girl gets married, her own parents are no longer considered her legal heirs? When will we break free of the *'beti toh aakhir parayi dhan hoti hai* (a daughter, once married, belongs to someone else)' mentality?

How much share will you inherit?
You will inherit an equal share as all other Class I heirs. Think of it this way. Instead of dividing the property, you are cutting a cake. The law will round up all the Class I heirs and divide the cake into an equal number of slices for all. If there are three Class I heirs, each gets 1/3rd share; if there are four, each gets 1/4th share.

2. **Inheriting from joint family (ancestral) property:** Traditionally, Indian families lived in joint families where all the members shared a common family home. Let us get familiar with some commonly used terms in this regard:
   i. HUF: The joint family is called a Hindu Undivided Family, or HUF.
   ii. Karta: The head of the family (usually the father or grandfather) is called the karta.
   iii. Coparcener: A coparcener is everyone born into that family, up to three generations down from the head of the family. This includes the sons, daughters, grandchildren and great-grandchildren of the karta.

For example, Gopi has a son and a daughter. His son is married with two children. Gopi's son, daughter and the grandchildren are all coparceners.

You will inherit from the joint family property (ancestral property) as a coparcener. Before 2005, only sons were considered coparceners and had a right to the joint family property. However, the law was amended in 2005. Now, daughters are also considered coparceners and have equal rights in ancestral properties.

Note: A daughter's children will not be coparceners because they are considered part of her husband's family (the law is silent on this, but this is the interpretation everyone leans towards).

The rule for inheriting joint family property is simple. All coparceners have an equal right in the family's joint property at the time of partition. Think of the property as a cake that belongs to all the coparceners. When they decide to cut the cake (i.e., partition the property), it will be cut into an equal number of slices for each of the coparceners.

Let me explain through an example. Gopi lives in an HUF with his wife, daughter, son, daughter-in-law and their two children. Gopi is the head of this family, the karta.

Who are the coparceners in Gopi's HUF? His son and daughter, being related to him by birth, become the coparceners. The son's children, being related to Gopi by birth (as grandchildren), become coparceners. His wife and daughter-in-law will not be considered coparceners as they are related through marriage and were not born in this family. His wife will inherit as an 'immediate family member' as explained in the section above. His daughter-in-law will not directly inherit a share from him.

How much will each of them get when they decide to cut the cake (i.e., partition the property)? The cake will be cut into five equal slices—one for Gopi, one for his son, one for his daughter and one each for the two grandchildren. Each of them will get 1/5th share of the property.

Note: Do not confuse this section with the previous one (inheritance as an 'immediate family member'). This section is only applicable when there is a Hindu undivided family with joint property. If Gopi has a separate piece of land, in addition to the joint property, that piece of land will pass on to his Class I heirs (wife, son, daughter in this case).

How do I ask for my share in the joint family property?

As a coparcener, you have the right to ask for your share in the family property at any time. You need not wait till everyone wants to split or till the karta passes away. You can simply ask for a 'partition'. Think of it like asking for your slice of the cake early, instead of waiting for the birthday boy or girl to cut it and distribute it.

When someone asks for a partition, the family can either decide to prepone the cake-cutting and distribute the slices or they can decide to keep the cake and give you money for your slice. Either way, the transaction will be recorded through a legal agreement called a partition deed and you will get your share.

What happens to my property rights if I get married?
1. No change in your inheritance rights as a daughter (as Class I heir of parents).
2. No change in your inheritance rights as a member of the joint family (coparcener).
3. You will get additional inheritance rights from your husband and children (again, as their Class I heir).

But remember, *how* your property goes through succession will change. Your parents will no longer be your heirs. Your property will go to your husband and children.

What happens to my property rights if I get divorced?
1. Your inheritance rights as a daughter to your parents remain unaffected.
2. Your inheritance rights from your joint family as a coparcener remain unaffected.
3. You will have rights to your husband's property until the time of divorce, but not after it.
4. Your inheritance rights from your children as their mother remain unaffected.

In case of a divorce, your husband will no longer be your Class I heir. It will only be your children.

What happens to my property rights if I am widowed?
None of your property rights get affected.

> **POINTS TO REMEMBER**
>
> 1. A Hindu woman can inherit both as a Class I heir (for self-acquired property) and as a coparcener (for joint family property). The same applies to men.
> 2. A daughter has the same inheritance rights as the son.
> 3. Marriage does NOT affect your inheritance rights from your birth family!
>
> Once a daughter, always a daughter!

What Are My Inheritance Rights as a Muslim Woman?

As a Muslim woman, your inheritance rights through succession are governed by the Muslim Personal Law (Shariat) Application Act, 1937, which basically says that succession will happen according to customs.

Broadly, heirs in Muslim law are divided into three groups:

1. Sharers
2. Residuaries
3. Distant Kindred

Sharers are like Class I heirs. They are the first set of people among whom the property is distributed. After the sharers, the surplus goes to the residuaries. Distant kindred inherit property only if sharers or residuaries are absent.

I will not go into the details of who is a sharer and residuary, as that can get complicated. What is important for you to understand is who can you inherit property from as a Muslim woman.

There are two key rules to remember:
1. Females are always given half of what the males get. For example, if a brother gets 1/3rd share in a property, the sister will get 1/6th.
2. Customs and inheritance can vary based on whether you are Shia or Sunni. Although both are broadly similar, there are a few subtle differences (which we will not go into).

Who can you inherit from?
As a Muslim woman, you can inherit from the following family members:
- Husband
- Son
- Daughter
- Mother
- Father
- Siblings

You are a legal heir to all of them. To put it simply, you can inherit as a widow, as a mother from both your children, as a daughter from both your parents and as a sister from your siblings (which is not the case with Hindu women).

How much can you inherit?
This depends on the relationship through which you are inheriting, who the other heirs are and whether you fall under the sharer or residuary category (depending on who else survives, you could be promoted to sharer or demoted to residuary).

Money Matters

If the property is a cake, your slice is guaranteed as a widow, mother, daughter and sister. However, the *size* of your slice depends on how many other hands stake claim to the cake. Unlike Hindu law, the property is not divided equally among all heirs. Each heir has a predetermined share based on their gender, relationship with the person and who else survives.

I will not go into the overwhelming permutations and combinations, but here is a basic idea of what you should know:

1. From husband: If your husband dies, you will inherit 1/4th of his property in the absence of children. However, when there are children, you will get only 1/8th.
2. From parents: If you are an only child, you get half of your parent's property. If you have one or more sisters, all the sisters together get 2/3rd share in the property. If you have a brother, all the sisters will get half of what the brother gets. For example, if you are one brother and two sisters, the brother will get 1/2 and the sisters will get 1/4th share each.
3. From children: As a mother, you will get a fixed 1/6th share from your son or daughter if they have children or siblings. If your son or daughter has no children or siblings, you will get 1/3rd share in their property.

Note: These rules can differ between Sunni and Shia Muslims, so make sure to consult an expert to properly understand your inheritance rights.

What is important to take away is that in no event do you get the entire property. And rarely do you get even half of it. As a Muslim woman, your share to the property is quite limited, and therefore, you must ensure that you secure yourself in other ways, like through a Will, trust or a gift.

What Are My Inheritance Rights as a Christian Woman?

If you are an Indian Christian woman, your inheritance rights are governed by the Indian Succession Act (ISA), 1925.

Who can you inherit from through succession?
You have the right to inherit property from:
  i. Husband
  ii. Parents (mother, father)
  iii. Children (son, daughter)—if your husband is not alive
  iv. Kindred (i.e., siblings, grandparents, parents' siblings)

How much share do you get?
In case of the ISA, the share that you inherit depends on the presence of other heirs. Unlike Hindu law, where the cake is divided into an equal number of slices for all heirs, under the ISA the size of your slice will depend on who else is going to eat.

1. **From your husband:** As a widow, you get 1/3rd share of your husband's property if you have children. The remaining 2/3rd goes to the children (even if it is a single child). If there are no children, you get half of the property and the rest goes to other relatives. Only if there are no children and no relatives do you get the entire property.
2. **From your parents:** If your other parent is alive, you and your siblings combined will get 2/3rd share

of the property (with 1/3rd going to the surviving parent). The 2/3rd share will be divided equally between you and your siblings.

3. **From your children:** As a mother, you can inherit property from your children *only if* your husband (i.e., their father) is not alive. If he is alive, he will get the parents' share of the property from the children. However, the size of this share depends on the presence of other relatives. To put it simply, if your husband is alive, you won't get a slice of the cake. If your husband is not alive, you will get a slice of cake, but its size will vary based on the number of slices that need to be cut.

You can also inherit a share of property from other relatives like your siblings, grandparents, etc. However, since the share you get will depend on intricate permutations and combinations (based on who all are surviving heirs), we will not go into the details.

Remember, under Christian law also a daughter has the same inheritance rights as a son.

Food for thought

Under Hindu law, a mother can inherit from her children. Only in her absence does the father stand to inherit. Whereas, under Christian law, a father has the first right to inherit. Only in his absence does the mother get a share. Isn't it strange how the importance of your own parents changes based on your religion, although we are all citizens of the same country!

What Are My Inheritance Rights under the Special Marriage Act?

Earlier, in Chapter 5, we understood how marriages take place under the Special Marriage Act.
1. You have an interfaith marriage, i.e., both spouses belong to different religions, due to which they cannot get married under their own religious laws.
2. You have a court marriage, i.e., you choose to skip the ceremonies and opt for a simple registered marriage.

In these cases, what happens to your inheritance and succession rights?
1. Interfaith Marriages: Under the Special Marriage Act, when two people from different religions tie the knot, the Indian Succession Act (and not their personal religious laws) decides how they inherit and pass on property.

    To know more about who you can inherit from and how much, refer to the section on inheritance for Christians, which is also governed by the Indian Succession Act.
2. Hindu court marriages: When both parties are Hindus (including Sikhs, Jains and Buddhists) and they marry under the Special Marriage Act, their inheritance is governed by the Hindu Succession Act. Therefore, even if you choose to have a court marriage, your property rights will not be affected.

    To understand your rights in detail, refer to the earlier section on property rights for Hindus.

3. **Muslim, Christian and Parsi marriages:** When Muslims, Christians and Parsis marry under the Special Marriage Act, whether within or outside their community, the Indian Succession Act governs their inheritance and succession.

   For more details, refer to the section on Christian inheritance and succession.

What about Emotional Manipulation?

It is one thing to know your property rights, so that you are aware of how much you stand to inherit from your family, but it is another to stand up to your own siblings and demand an equal share. In most families, we see that the brothers are reluctant to share the property with their sisters. And sisters, to maintain a relationship with the brothers, sign away (relinquish) their share of the property.

Think about it this way. The onus to maintain a relationship is on both parties involved. A brother who loves his sister will want her to have financial security and her legal share in the property. So, the next time you hear of a woman getting emotionally manipulated into giving up her property rights, tell her to ask herself this question.

> **POINTS TO REMEMBER**
>
> 1. You can inherit property from someone who passes away either through a Will or, in the absence of a Will, through succession. As per succession laws, the property passes on to pre-decided heirs.
> 2. Your right to inherit property through succession depends on your religion and gender, and is governed by religious personal laws.
> 3. As a Hindu woman, you can inherit from parents, son, unmarried daughter and husband, as their Class I heir. You cannot inherit from your married daughter and siblings.
> 4. As a Muslim woman, you can inherit from parents, children, husband and siblings.
> 5. As a Christian woman, you can inherit from parents, husband and children. However, you will inherit from your children only if your husband is not alive.

Succession Planning

A smart woman should not only be aware of her rights to inherit but also should know about succession planning, i.e., how she wants to pass on her property and to whom.

There are three ways in which you can pass on your property, once you are no longer around.

1. Will: You can create a Will that states exactly what property and how much goes to whom. The process of creating a Will is explained a little later.

2. Trust: A trust is a legal entity you can set up for passing on property to anyone of your choice. Unlike a Will, which is a document, a trust is a legal entity managed by its in-charges called trustees. This, too, is explained later.
3. Succession: If you have not created a Will or trust, your property will pass on to your legal heirs through succession, as per your religious personal laws.

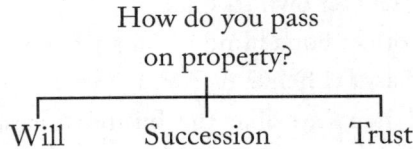

In the earlier section, we understood whose heir you are, i.e., who you can inherit from. Now we will understand who your heirs are, i.e., who will inherit from you. Your heirs and how much share they get depends on your religion, their gender and their relationship with you.

Who Will My Property Pass on to as a Hindu Woman?

Actress Sridevi passed away suddenly in 2018. She is survived by her husband, Boney Kapoor, and her two daughters, Jahnvi and Khushi Kapoor. Obviously, Sridevi would have amassed a large amount of wealth during her lifetime. She is sure to have created a succession plan, but considering she passed away suddenly, at a young age, what if she didn't? Who is entitled to her wealth? You will be answering this question yourself in no time!

A Hindu woman's heirs for succession depend on whether she is married or unmarried. This is because, in our patriarchal society, once a woman is married, she is considered a member of the husband's family and not her birth family.

A Hindu woman's heirs are:
- Class I: Husband, son(s), daughter(s)
- Class II: Heirs of husband, which will be her in-laws (mother-in law, and in her absence, father-in-law)
- Class III: Her own parents

Did you notice? For a Hindu woman, her own parents are considered Class III heirs? A friendly reminder is necessary here. Class I heirs are like the business-class passengers, they get everything first. Only if there are no Class I heirs do the Class II and then the Class III heirs come into the picture.

This means that if a woman is married, her mother-in-law (being a Class II heir) has a higher right to her property than her own mother. Isn't this bizarre? For a Hindu man, his own mother, wife and children are Class I heirs, while his father falls under Class II.

Note: The law on inheritance is more complex and full of permutations and combinations. What I have explained above will give you a solid understanding of the basic principles. However, I would recommend you consult a lawyer to understand your specific situation.

Now that we know broadly who a Hindu woman's heirs are, let us come back to Sridevi's example.

Hypothetically, who will Sridevi's property go to? She left behind three Class I heirs—a husband and two daughters.

Since she was married, her birth family will not come into the picture. In the absence of a succession plan, Sridevi's property will get divided equally between her Class I heirs, i.e., Boney Kapoor, Jahnvi Kapoor and Khushi Kapoor.

However, take the case of actress Sushmita Sen, who chose to adopt two daughters without getting married. In her case, though there is no husband, there are children. Here, her daughters will be Class I heirs. In this case, because of the daughters (Class I heirs), Sen's parents (Class II heirs) will not come into the picture.

How do I leave property for my parents?
If you are a smart girl, you must have understood that your parents will not be your legal heirs once you get married. But I am sure you would want to leave them a share, in case something happens to you. What should you do? Will it! Make a Will and demarcate clearly what you want to give and to whom. Your husband cannot contest this Will as every person is free to make their own Will.

Who Will My Property Pass on to as a Muslim Woman?

As a Muslim woman (or man), you can pass on only 1/3rd of your property through a Will. The rest will go to your legal heirs through succession, according to their predetermined shares.

Let us look at who your property will pass on to:
- Husband
- Son

- Daughter
- Mother
- Father
- Siblings—only if you don't have surviving children or father.

All those listed above will be your legal heirs. Their slice in your cake is guaranteed. However, as explained above, the size of each one's slice will depend on who else is eating and their biological relationship with you.

Let us understand briefly who will get how much:

1. Your husband: If you have no children, your husband will get half of your property. His share will reduce to 1/4th in the presence of children.

    Did you notice? If you are reading this after going through the 'who can you inherit from' section, you would have noticed that while a wife inherits only 1/4th or 1/8th share of her husband's property (depending on presence or absence of children), the husband inherits half or 1/4th from the wife. He gets double of what she would get, following the Muslim succession rule that females get half of what the males get.

2. Your children: You can pass on your property to both your son and daughter. The shares of the son and daughter depend on the total number of siblings and how many brothers and sisters there are. Keep in mind that your son will receive twice of what your daughters get.

3. **Your parents:** Your parents get a fixed 1/6th share each in your property, if you have children of your own or siblings. In case there are no siblings or children, the parents can get up to 1/3rd each.
4. **Your siblings:** Your siblings will inherit from you only when you have no children or surviving father.

Note: Unlike Hindu and Christian laws, where a married woman's primary heirs are her husband and children, and only in their absence do her parents get a share, under Muslim law, your marriage does not affect your parents' inheritance rights. Your blood relatives get a share in your property, irrespective of your marital status.

Understanding the distribution of your property is a good way for you to evaluate whether the heirs and their shares align with your personal wishes. Unlike other religions, you cannot write a Will and give away all your property to whomsoever you wish.

What can you do if you wish to control the devolution of your property? Say, for example, you want to give your daughter and son an equal share. You can do this for 1/3rd of your property through a Will. Alternately, you can also leave a gift (called *hiba*) for your daughter. There is no limitation on how much of your property you can gift, since a gift is given during the lifetime of a person (unlike a Will which is executed after their death).

Note: If you pass on property by way of a gift, you cannot get it back. So make sure to give it away with careful consideration, after retaining a portion for yourself. After all, you don't want to die without having anything to your name!

> **#TrueStory**
>
> Dr Sheena Shukkur, the head of the department of law at Kannur University, got 'remarried' to her husband on 8 March 2023, which was International Women's Day. They re-registered their marriage under the Special Marriage Act, 1954. Why did they do this?[2]
>
> They did this because Dr Sheena and her husband, both Muslim, were governed by the Muslim inheritance law that does not allow you to write a Will for your entire property and choose who you want to pass it on to. Dr Sheena and her husband wanted to leave behind their property to heirs of their choice, through a Will. Registering their marriage under the Special Marriage Act brought them under the purview of the Indian Succession Act, instead of the Muslim inheritance law, giving them the freedom to draft a Will.

Who Will My Property Pass on to as a Christian Woman?

As explained above, you can take charge of who your property goes to by creating a Will or Trust. However, if a Christian woman passes away without either, who does her property go to? It will pass on to her legal heirs under the Indian Succession Act.

A Christian woman's legal heirs include:
1. Husband and children: They are your first heirs. The share that each of them get depends on who is surviving.
2. Your parents: Your parents will get a share in your property only if neither your spouse nor children survive you.

3. Your siblings: They can inherit your property only when you have no surviving spouse, children or parents.

I am not going into the shares each of these relationships can get, as that will depend on the number of people who are surviving.

Note: Like Hindu law, your first heirs are your husband and children. Therefore, once you get married, your parents and siblings will not be on the priority list of heirs and cannot inherit property from you.

To ensure that your property is distributed according to your wishes, I highly recommend that you make a Will. Without a Will, the default rules of the Indian Succession Act apply, which might not align with your personal wishes.

POINTS TO REMEMBER

1. If you pass away without a Will, your entire property will go to your legal heirs through succession, as pre-decided by law.
2. If you would like to distribute your property differently from what is provided in succession laws, you should make a Will.
3. Your legal heirs, and the share of property they get, depends on your religious law and their gender and relationship to you.
4. As a Hindu or Christian woman, your husband and children are your main heirs. Your parents can inherit only if there is no husband or children.
5. As a Muslim woman, your husband, children and parents are your primary heirs. Your marital status does not affect your parents' right to inherit from you.

All About Wills

The best way to take charge of your estate planning is to draft your own Will. As explained above, a Will spells out what should happen to your assets and possessions when you are not here anymore. A Will gives you absolute control over who you want to pass on your property to.

What can you pass through a Will?
Any property (movable, immovable, self-acquired or ancestral) that you own. Obviously, you cannot pass on property that is not yours!

Who can you pass property on to through a Will?
You can leave your property to anyone! It need not be your close relatives. Quite like this rhyme:

> Baa baa black sheep, have you any Will?
> Yes, sir; yes sir; three bags fill!
> One for my master, one for my dame,
> And one for the little girl who lives down the lane!

How much property can you pass on?
Under all religious laws, except Muslim, you can pass on your entire property through a Will, to anyone including heirs and non-heirs. There are no legal restrictions.

Under Muslim law, you can only pass on what is left of your property after funeral expenses and clearing debts. Of this, you can only pass on 1/3rd through Will. The remaining 2/3rd will pass on to your legal heirs as per the succession rules. In the 1/3rd property, if you wish to pass it on to any legal heir, you need the consent of the other heirs. If you are passing it on to a stranger, you will not need your heirs' consent for the 1/3rd. This is probably to ensure that no one deprives any legal heir of their inheritance rights.

Note: The rules vary slightly for Shias and Sunnis—it would be best to check with an expert about your specific situation should you wish to create a Will.

Easy steps to create your Will

To put it simply, draft a list of your properties (movable and immovable), decide who your beneficiaries are and divide the property. Before you register your Will, identify a person as the executor (to ensure the Will is carried out).

Here's a flow chart to make it more comprehensive.

Consolidate assets	Take stock of all your property–movable and immovable
List beneficiaries	Make a list of all your beneficiaries
Divide	Divide your property
Identify executor	Who will carry out the contents of the Will
Will deed	Draft and register your Will

Legal Requirements for a Will

1. Written: A written Will is not compulsory. It can even be oral. For example, someone on their deathbed announces that their property will go to so and so. However, I highly recommend that you plan ahead and not leave

it for your deathbed. Also, try to write your Will down. It can be handwritten or typed. You can write it yourself or get someone else, example a family member (your grandmother may ask her children to write it on her behalf) or a lawyer to write it for you.
2. Signed: A written Will must be signed by the person making it. If someone is not able to sign, they can put a thumb impression.
3. Registered: Registration is not compulsory, but if you have a written Will and fear that some of your heirs might challenge it, or any of your heirs could be unfair to the others, you should get it registered.

    You can get your written Will registered with the registrar of properties (the same place you go to for registering property-related documents). It will cost you a fee (you have to pay stamp duty and registration charges), which varies from state to state. A Google search will tell you how much.
4. Witnesses: Have any two people sign the Will as witnesses. This grants it legitimacy.
5. Attested copies: You can create copies of your Will and get them notarized and attested, so that even if something happens to the original document, the copies are considered to be as good as the original.
6. Get your Will drafted from a lawyer, if possible: The reason I say this is because lawyers are aware of how to add the details of all your assets, how to structure things and how to ensure that the Will fulfils all legal requirements.

Tips for Writing Your Will

1. Make it as clean and simple as possible. It should be easy to understand and execute.
2. Do it in the presence of witnesses, so that there are no questions later.
3. You don't want your children or grandchildren fighting over the Will or challenging it. Therefore, if you have several heirs, get your Will written and registered.
4. Lastly, it is *your* Will, which means it should be as per your wish. You should leave your property only for those you want it to go to.

#MovieTime

Where There Is a Will, There Is a Kill!

On a lighter note, I am sure you can recall several Bollywood movies where the father threatens to remove the son's name from the Will. The son is prepared to go to any extent to safeguard his inheritance, including murdering his own father!

In *36 China Town*, a 2006 Bollywood thriller-comedy, multimillionaire businesswoman Sonia Chang is killed by her so-called loyal housekeepers. Why? All because of a Will! Sonia realized that the housekeepers were up to no good and asked her lawyer to remove their names from her Will. The housekeepers found out and were quick to kill her before she could make any changes to the Will!

When should you make your Will?
For women, the fifties are a good time to start planning their Will. By this time, they would have consolidated their assets and also have a clear idea of who they want to pass on their property to. However, given life's uncertainty, you can always write a Will (without registering it) and keep it in your locker.

I have only one child. Do I still need to leave a Will?
YES! I cannot stress the importance of having a Will. If you have a single child, obviously there will be no sibling rivalry about the division of your property. However, in the absence of a Will, your child will be buried in a mountain of paperwork after you are gone, just to prove that they are your only heir and therefore have rights over your property.

#TrueStory

One of my friends, Pallavi (name changed), is an only child. She lost both her parents suddenly during the Covid pandemic. Her parents did not have a Will and their death was sudden. Also, they were probably under the impression that they did not need a Will since they had only one child.

Pallavi's parents left behind the house in which the three of them lived, along with their dog, Tuffy. Pallavi, now alone, found it difficult to manage the house all by herself. She wanted to sell it and move into a smaller, more manageable place. In the absence of a Will, it took Pallavi almost two years to get the house transferred to her name and to be able to sell it.

Pro tip: Always create a Will and keep it ready, even if you are in the pink of health. It is not a sign that your end is near. It is just you planning ahead and keeping your children secure. Alternately, you can also execute a power of attorney in your child's name, so that if they get stuck in Pallavi's situation, they can use the power of attorney.

> **POINTS TO REMEMBER**
>
> 1. A Will lets you decide who you want your property to go to and how much share you want to give them.
> 2. Though a Will can be oral or written, it is recommended to have a written one and get it registered.
> 3. You can always update your Will if you change your mind about your heirs, or if there is a change in your assets.
> 4. You can use a Will to distribute all kinds of assets that belong to you, right from real estate and gold to your collection of artwork or saris!
> 5. Having a Will saves your heirs a lot of paperwork that would otherwise go into acquiring their share of your property. Therefore, it is always recommended to have a Will, even if you have a single child.

How Do I Create a Trust Fund?

A Trust fund is a legal entity you can set up to not only pass on your wealth but also to ensure that it is managed properly and kept safe.

Think of a Trust like a treasure chest.

Imagine that you have a valuable treasure chest filled with gold coins and precious gems. Obviously, you would want to ensure that when you are no longer here, the treasure chest goes into the right hands and benefits your family. For this, you create a Trust.

Let us understand the key players involved:
1. **Settlor:** This is the person who sets up the Trust. In this case, it will be you.
2. **Trustee:** You select a responsible person or organization, like a trusted family member or financial institution, to keep the treasure chest safe and ensure that it is handled as per your directions. These guardians are called trustees.
3. **Beneficiary:** They are the lucky ones who get to enjoy the wealth from the treasure chest. For example, if you leave a Trust for your children, they will be the beneficiaries.
4. **Trust property:** This will be the jewels and gold that you put in the treasure chest. In other words, it is the property that you transfer to the Trust, for safekeeping and passing on to the beneficiaries.
5. **Trust deed:** You establish specific rules and instructions for how the trustees should manage the Trust property. For instance, you might instruct the trustee to pay for your children's educational or medical expenses out of the Trust, till the Trust property is handed over to your children.
6. **Duration:** You decide how long the Trust will last. It could be a temporary one, until your children reach

a certain age, or even a permanent one. Until the Trust property is transferred to the beneficiaries, it is to be managed by the trustees to benefit all future generations of the family.

This way, you, as the settlor, ensure that your wealth remains a source of support and security for your family even in your absence.

In real life, Trust funds can be established for various purposes, such as preserving wealth, managing assets or providing for loved ones. They offer a structured and legally binding way to distribute and protect assets according to your desires, much like our imagined treasure chest.

What Are the Steps to Creating a Trust?

Define and Transfer the Trust Property
• Movable (like money)   • Immovable (like real estate)
Goals of the Trust + Distribution among Beneficiaries
For example: • Perpetual (enjoy the property but not own/dispose)   • Time-bound (property transferred on attaining certain age)   • Conditional (property used for certain purpose)
Trust Deed
• The rules for administering the Trust
Register the Trust Deed
• Compulsory to register unlike Will

Essentially, you should begin by defining and transferring the Trust property (including movable and immovable assets), then identify the goal of the Trust fund and its beneficiaries, and prepare a Trust Deed. Unlike a Will, this must be registered.

Consider an example. The Rajshrees are a large joint family. They own a lot of land in their ancestral village. The first generation wants to ensure that this land remains within the family as legacy and is not sold by the next generations for a quick buck. The Rajshree family can create a family Trust, add all this land to it as the Trust property, appoint trustworthy family members (or third parties) to run this Trust and then draft a deed that decides what the Trust land can be used for. The deed can restrict the beneficiaries (future generations) from selling the land, to ensure that it always remains within the family. This way, the beneficiaries can enjoy the property but do not become owners (and, thus, cannot sell it).

On a lighter note, I couldn't help but twist this iconic Amitabh Bachchan dialogue from the movie *Deewar*.

Will or Trust?

The purpose of a Will is to pass on your property to successors of your choice. Once the property is passed on to them, they can do whatever they want with it.

The primary purpose of a Trust is to *manage* the property. You want to ensure that the property is used wisely and for the benefit of your loved ones (beneficiaries). It is up to you whether you want to pass on the property to them as owners or have them enjoy it without becoming the owners.

If you just want to pass on your property, then you should make a Will. However, if you want to create a legacy, you should set up a Trust.

> **POINTS TO REMEMBER**
>
> 1. Trusts help you create a legacy and ensure the well-being of your loved ones even after you are gone.
> 2. A Trust is like a treasure chest in which you put your assets. It is managed by trustees on the basis of the Trust Deed.
> 3. A Trust helps you manage your assets and set rules on how they should be utilized. Whereas, in a Will, you pass on your assets to your beneficiaries. You have no control over what they do with these assets.

Gifts: Another Option

Until now, we discussed in detail Wills, Trusts and succession, all of which come into the picture after someone passes away. However, what if you want to transfer property to your loved ones during your lifetime? You can do so by way of a 'gift', a transfer of property to another person without expecting anything in return from them.

So, when do people gift property?
It is done for multiple reasons, including distributing assets within the family, for tax planning, or even to ensure that daughters get their due share from the parents while the parents are still alive.

The process to make a gift is:
1. Identify the property you want to gift and who you want to gift it to.
2. Draw up a gift deed, i.e., a written legal document that records the gift and all the details involved, such as the donor, donee, the gift and any other conditions attached to the gift.
3. Get your gift deed registered with the property registrar (the same place you would go to for registering any property documents in your jurisdiction).
4. Ensure that the property is transferred to the donee's name and the property records are updated.

Note: To be valid, it is compulsory for every gift of immovable property to be written and registered. For movable property, you can simply handover the gift; it need not be written.

EXERCISE TIME!

Word Search: Inheritance Insights

Find and circle the words listed below:
Will, Trust, Succession, Stridhan, Legal Heirs

```
Z  D  Z  K  H  E  R  Q  C  L
S  U  C  C  E  S  S  I  O  N
E  T  Y  C  O  D  J  D  M  S
N  B  S  L  L  I  W  M  I  X
R  X  G  U  R  N  H  B  Q  S
V  F  G  J  R  Q  S  M  M  J
N  W  R  M  V  T  Y  X  G  A
L  E  G  A  L  H  E  I  R  S
N  A  H  D  I  R  T  S  O  D
B  Q  T  M  O  E  M  G  X  A
```

9

Reproductive Rights: Your Body, Your Choice

In this chapter, we will explore different kinds of reproductive rights, such as adoption, abortion and surrogacy.

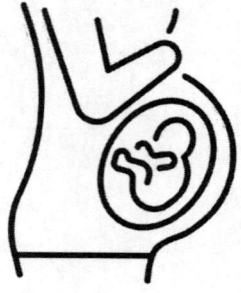

Abortion

Unsafe abortions are the third leading cause of maternal mortality in India. According to studies, nearly 67 per cent of abortions in India are unsafe, causing around eight deaths every day, says a United Nations Population Fund report.[1] These numbers are not only shocking but also deeply disturbing, considering India has decent abortion laws.

But wait, doesn't Indian law permit abortions? Yes, it does! Unlike the US, which has withdrawn the right to abortion as a constitutional right, India is moving towards making access to abortion easier and safer, as it should be.

The Medical Termination of Pregnancy Act, 1971, permitted the termination of pregnancies under certain circumstances. However, it had different rules for married and unmarried women. In 2021, the Parliament passed the Medical Termination of Pregnancy Amendment Act, 2021 (aka the new MTP Act), which made key changes to the old law. The new Act not only increased the time limit for an abortion but also treats both married and unmarried women equally (which is a big win!).

What Are My Abortion Rights?

Until the 2021 amendment, only married women were allowed a 'no questions asked' abortion, citing failure of contraception. Unmarried women could seek an abortion only on the grounds that the pregnancy/child birth would be seriously injurious to the life of the woman, the life of the child, or to the mental or physical health of the woman. Most unmarried women would have to seek an abortion on the grounds of injury to mental health. Moreover, abortion was only permitted up till twenty weeks of gestation, unless there was a threat to the mother's life.

From 2021 onwards, the gestation limit was increased to twenty-four weeks and unmarried women were also granted the right to abortion for contraceptive failure. The rights of unmarried women were reiterated by the Supreme Court in 2022 in the case *X vs Principal Secretary, Health and Family Welfare Department*.[2] To quote the court: 'The rights of reproductive autonomy, dignity and privacy under Article 21 give an unmarried woman the right of choice on whether or not to bear a child, on a similar footing of a married woman.'

I have summed up the grounds of abortion corresponding to the gestation period and the medical approvals you need in the table below (remember: the same rules apply to married and unmarried women):

Gestation period	Grounds for termination	Approval required
Up to 20 weeks	No questions asked. Failure of contraception is reason enough.	You need the approval of one doctor.
From 20–24 weeks	If you fall under the seven permitted categories (listed below).	You need the approval of two doctors.
Beyond 24 weeks	Only if there are substantial foetal abnormalities and the pregnant woman is physically fit for abortion.	You need the approval of a state-level medical board.

Terminating between twenty and twenty-four weeks—the permitted categories:

Once you hit the twenty-week mark and till you reach twenty-four weeks, you can terminate your pregnancy only under seven permitted categories:

1. Sexual assault: If the pregnancy is the result of assault or rape. This includes marital rape, which was added by the Supreme Court while hearing the above-mentioned *X vs Principal Secretary* case (2022).
2. Minors: Minors (i.e., below eighteen years of age) can terminate a pregnancy up to twenty-four weeks, no questions asked.
3. Change of relationship status: If the marital status of the pregnant woman changes during the pregnancy, i.e., she gets divorced or widowed. The Supreme Court has expanded this to apply to a break-up of a live-in relationship also (*X vs Principal Secretary*).
4. Foetal problems: If the foetus is unlikely to survive after being born, or will be born with serious physical or mental abnormalities.
5. Physical disability: If the pregnant woman has physical disabilities that make it difficult for her to carry the pregnancy or bring up the child.
6. Mental disability: If the pregnant woman is mentally ill (including mental retardation), which makes her mentally unfit to carry the pregnancy or bring up the child.

7. Extraordinary situations: If the pregnancy occurs during a disaster or emergency situation (like a war or earthquake).

Note: The Supreme Court has also included marital rape under the permitted categories. This is a huge step in the law recognizing that marital rape exists and that a married woman should not be forced to have a child born out of rape, just because she is married.

What about Terminating My Pregnancy beyond Twenty-four Weeks?

Termination of a pregnancy beyond twenty-four weeks is permitted only if there are substantial abnormalities in the foetus, such that it won't survive or will be seriously mentally or physically handicapped. For this, you will need to apply to a state-level medical board. Your doctor will help you with the paperwork. If the board refuses, you will need to file a writ petition in the high court concerned, asking the court to direct the medical board to permit the termination.

There have been quite a few cases where the court has been approached for termination. The court usually defers it to the opinion of medical practitioners and the case is decided based on the recommendation of the doctors. What is important here is swift action, for each day's delay is significant in a pregnancy. You should try and get a skilled lawyer to help you with your case.

>  **Food for thought**
>
> In April 2024, France became the first and only country in the world to make abortion a constitutional right. What is the difference? Legal rights come from regular laws, which can easily be amended by the Parliament. Constitutional rights, on the other hand, are protected by the Constitution and cannot be amended easily. Abortion used to be a constitutional right in the US, till it was repealed by the US Supreme Court in 2022. In India, abortion is a legal right.
>
> How do you feel about men in places of power (like judges and lawmakers) deciding about women's bodies?

Do I Need My Partner or Family's Consent to Terminate a Pregnancy?

The simple answer is NO. Besides the doctor, you don't need anyone else's approval. Not your spouse. Not your parents. Not your in-laws. And you definitely do not need the opinion of your neighbour's aunt's cousin's daughter! The law understands that terminating a pregnancy is a very personal decision and since the pregnant woman is the one bearing the foetus, it must be her decision only. The whole *mohalla* (neighbourhood) need not be involved.

Doctors or hospitals, too, cannot impose extra-legal conditions like spousal or family consent, additional paperwork, or requirement of police or court permissions.

Do I Have a Right to Confidentiality in Case of an Abortion?

You have the right to complete confidentiality for the entire procedure. To allow women access to safe abortions, without the fear of social stigma, the law mandates that every procedure of abortion be kept confidential. Let us read what the law says. As per Section 5A (1) of the MTP Amendment Act, 2021, 'No registered medical practitioner shall reveal the name and other particulars of a woman whose pregnancy has been terminated under this Act, except to a person authorised by any law for the time being in force.'

This means that the doctor and the hospital/clinic must keep the pregnant woman's details confidential. They should not even be a part of the hospital records.

What Happens on Ground When You Seek an Abortion?

I consulted a senior gynaecologist working with a reputed hospital and this is what she explained:

1. You register with the hospital, in the same way that every patient does. You give your name and particulars at the time (while registering, you don't have to mention the reason for your visit).
2. The doctor conducts a scan to check the gestation period of the foetus.

3. The doctor then sits down with the patient to understand why she would like to terminate the pregnancy. For example, contraceptive failure, medical reasons, victim of rape, etc. If the reason for termination is that you simply don't want to have a baby, then they will put down contraceptive failure as the reason. There is no requirement to prove that this was actually the case.
4. The doctor may counsel the woman to confirm if she wants to go ahead with the termination. If she does, the doctor fills a 'Form C', which takes the woman's consent and states all the details of the procedure (like the doctor's opinion, recommended procedure and reason for termination). The woman must sign this form, along with one witness (need not be a family member). This is the only document on which the woman's name is written. This form then must be kept in a closed envelope.
5. Post this, the doctor will carry out the termination as per medical procedure. If it is through pills, the prescription is handed over to the woman. If the woman needs to get admitted to the hospital for the procedure, her name is not mentioned anywhere in the register. They write a number against it (like the hospital registration number).
6. At the end of the month, the hospital is required to send all Form Cs to the District Medical Health Officer for records.

Note: They take your Aadhaar card for registration. However the Aadhaar must also be placed in the closed envelope which only your doctor will have access to. The Aadhaar number is not quoted anywhere and the termination procedure will not reflect on your records.

This is broadly the procedure to be followed by doctors, as required by the law. If your doctor denies you abortion, you should change your doctor and go to another one. Here is a crowd-sourced list of trustworthy gynaecologists, started by Twitter (now X) user Amba Azad.[3]

If your doctor refuses to maintain confidentiality, you could file a complaint with the hospital and possibly even the Medical Council of India.

Pro tip: Find a medical doctor, not a moral police!

The Supreme Court has clearly stated that doctors (i.e., registered medical practitioners) should respect the choice of the pregnant woman and offer abortion services without extra-legal conditions. The doctor's 'approval' should be on a medical basis only, to assess if the termination is medically safe or not. They are not supposed to impose their moral opinion on the woman.

The only exception arises if doctors need to reveal the details to a 'person authorized by law', such as the police. In cases of pregnancy arising out of sexual assault or rape, the doctors must file a police report against the assault/rape since it is a criminal offence. In such cases, they may need to reveal the particulars of the pregnancy to the police.

Are There Any Special Provisions for Minors?

In case a minor girl (under eighteen years of age) gets pregnant, the law assumes that the pregnancy is out of rape. This is because the age of consent in India is eighteen years.

Sex with a minor girl below eighteen, even with her consent, is considered statutory rape.

Therefore, when a minor approaches a doctor to terminate a pregnancy, the doctor is obligated to report it to the police. This requirement often scares minors or their parents from taking a formal, legal way of terminating a pregnancy.

However, the Supreme Court, in *X vs Principal Secretary*, has clarified that the minor and the guardian can request the doctor not to disclose identity and other personal details in their report to the police.[4] If your doctor is not aware of this, show them Paragraph 81 of the judgment.

> ### Beti Bachao, Beti Padhao
>
> Revealing the sex of the foetus is not permitted as per the Pre-Conception and Pre-Natal Diagnostic Techniques (Prohibition of Sex Selection) Act, 1994. This law ensures that the female foetuses in our country have a chance to be born, that their lives are not ended in the womb because of their sex.

Conclusion

I will leave you with the Supreme Court's quote from a landmark case (*Suchita Srivastava vs Chandigarh Administration*, 2009), where the court said that reproductive choices are a part of personal liberty: 'A woman's right to make reproductive choices is also a dimension of "personal liberty" as understood under Article 21 of the Constitution of India.'

A pregnancy is not only about the months of gestation or the process of giving birth; it is about bringing a whole new human being into this world. A human being who deserves to be cared for, loved and wanted, in the first place. Creating life and embracing motherhood can be a wonderful journey for those who seek it, however, no one should be forced into it if it was unplanned for. Therefore, the law allows every pregnant woman the choice to carry out the pregnancy or terminate it. It is a choice meant to be exercised by the pregnant woman, judiciously and without any force or coercion.

> **POINTS TO REMEMBER**
>
> 1. As per the amended MTP Act, 2021, married and unmarried women have the same abortion rights.
> 2. You can terminate a pregnancy up to twenty weeks with one doctor's approval for any reason whatsoever. Between twenty and twenty-four weeks, termination can be carried out on the basis of seven permitted grounds and with the approval of two doctors.
> 3. Only the pregnant woman's (and no one else's) consent is required for terminating a pregnancy.
> 4. You have the right to complete confidentiality for the entire abortion procedure.
> 5. In the case of minors, pregnancy can be terminated up to twenty-four weeks, no questions asked. However, the doctors must file a police report under 'statutory rape' (even if there was no rape).

Adoption

Adoption is when a person takes another person's child and brings him/her up as their own. Under Indian law, when you legally adopt a child, s/he is treated like your biological child. The law does not differentiate between adopted and biological children.

Actress Sushmita Sen made headlines in 2000, when she decided to adopt a daughter as a twenty-five-year-old single woman. In an interview, Sen said she started the adoption process at the age of twenty-one and it took almost four years for her to get custody. Not only this, but when she had a final hearing in court, Sen had even made plans to run away with the baby if the court refused to grant her adoption rights! Sounds daunting, doesn't it?

How does the adoption process work in India? Who is eligible to adopt? Can you adopt whichever child you find the cutest? You'll find the answers to all your questions in this chapter.

Under Which Laws Can You Adopt in India?

As always, we don't have a one-size-fits-all law. There are two laws under which you can adopt in India—the Hindu Adoptions and Maintenance Act, 1956 (HAMA), and the Juvenile Justice Act, 2015 (JJA). The law that will apply to you depends on, guess what, your religion!

Originally, we only had HAMA that, as is obvious by its name, is religion-specific. As per this, only Hindus could adopt. Non-Hindus were only permitted to take up guardianship of children under the Guardians and Wards

Act, 1890. Why this discrimination, you may ask? Well, most of our old laws were enacted by the British based on their understanding of our religions and what suited their needs. This left a vacuum in the law for adoption by non-Hindus. In 2015, the Parliament amended the Juvenile Justice Act to open up adoption for non-Hindus. Since then, people from every religion can adopt children as their own.

What Is the Difference between Adoption and Guardianship?

Let us understand this through an example. Say you want to add a new plant to your home-garden. You can go to a nursery and bring one home. Or you can take a sapling from your friend and plant it in your garden. In both these cases, the plant becomes yours. You can keep it for life, nurture it and help it grow. This is adoption.

In another scenario, suppose your friend is moving abroad and may or may not come back. She gives her plant to you to take care of till her return. You take care of the plant as your own, watering and nurturing it. You are the caretaker till your

friend comes back, however, you don't become the 'parent'. This is guardianship.

Under adoption, the child becomes your biological child. You will share a regular parent–child relationship for life. Under guardianship, the child is your ward, i.e., someone you are legally responsible to take care of and protect. But this does not make them your child. They cannot inherit from you or be considered your family member. Moreover, once the child turns twenty-one, the guardian–ward relationship comes to an end; you no longer share a legal relationship with the child.

You can work around guardianship and provide the child inheritance rights by gifting the child your property or leave a Will. However, in the absence of a gift or Will, the child will not stand to inherit as per law.

Luckily, we now have the Juvenile Justice Act. We don't need the century-old Guardians and Wards Act any more! The JJA is a secular law that allows people of all religions (including Hindus) to adopt children of all religions. The HAMA allows only Hindu adopting parents (including Buddhists, Sikhs, Jains) to adopt Hindu children.

> **If you are a Hindu:** You can adopt under the HAMA or the JJA
> **If you are a non-Hindu:** You can adopt only under the JJA

Who Is Permitted to Adopt under Indian Law?

Any person is eligible to adopt irrespective of their religion, gender or marital status. However, there are certain restrictions and requirements that the adopting parent(s) must fulfil. The adopting parent(s) must be above eighteen years of age and should be physically, mentally and financially fit to adopt a child and provide him/her a good upbringing.

While the above two points are the basic boxes you need to check, the procedure for adoption, including who and how many children you can adopt, depends on your gender and marital status.

1. Can a married couple adopt?
   Yes, of course! For a married couple, the requirements under HAMA and JJA are:

   HAMA:
   i. If you already have a child, you cannot adopt a child of the same sex. E.g., if you have a daughter, you cannot adopt a daughter. You will have to adopt a son. There is no such restriction under the JJA.

   JJA:
   i. Must be in a stable marriage for at least two years.
   ii. Minimum age gap of twenty-five years between the child and parents.
   iii. Should not have three or more children already (either biological or adopted). Hollywood actors Brad Pitt and Angelina Jolie have six adopted children from around the world. Needless to say, if they were in India, they would have had to stop at three.

Spousal consent: Under both HAMA and JJA, a married person cannot adopt a child without the consent of his/her spouse. This means your partner must agree to the adoption. This could be a hurdle if a couple is separated (but not divorced) and one of the spouses wants to adopt.

Note: At present, since the Indian law does not legally recognize same-sex marriages, a married couple is considered to be heterosexual (man and woman).

> **#TrueStory**
>
> Adoptions are sometimes done to 'legitimize' children from outside the marriage. Let me tell you a story about my colleague, Isha (name changed).
>
> We have Isha, her parents and her brother. Isha's father had an extra-marital affair, from which he had a daughter, Diya (name changed). Isha's father wanted Diya also to be considered his biological daughter (in the eyes of the law), so that Diya could inherit his property. He decided to formally adopt Diya under the HAMA.
>
> Since he was already married, he could not go ahead with the adoption unless Isha's mother, i.e., his wife agreed. He convinced Isha's mother to give her consent (convinced or coerced, we don't know). Today, Diya is also considered his biological daughter and has the same rights as Isha and her brother.
>
> You will be surprised to know that this is quite a common occurrence in India! I have heard of several instances where the husband has an affair and adopts the children born out of the affair to give them legal rights.

2. Can a single person (including divorced/widowed) adopt?

   Yes, of course! Here are the requirements to be fulfilled under HAMA and JJA:

   HAMA:
   i. If you are adopting a child of the opposite gender, there must be a minimum age gap of twenty-one years between the parent and the child.

JJA:
i. A single woman can adopt a child of any gender.
ii. A single man cannot adopt a daughter. He can only adopt a son.

Although the law says that every single person, including a single woman, is eligible to adopt, the ground reality is that agencies and institutions continue to discriminate based on gender and marital status. When Sushmita Sen wanted to adopt a daughter, she had a tough time convincing the judge that she was capable of being a good mother even if she was a young, single woman.[5]

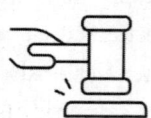

'If You Are a Single, Working Woman, How Will You Raise a Child?'[6]

In April 2023, a district court in Maharashtra rejected the adoption application of a forty-seven-year-old divorced woman who wanted to adopt her sister's child. The court's reason was: 'Being a working lady … she will not give personal attention to the child.'

This is despite the fact that the law allows single women to adopt. Nowhere does it say that she should be a stay-at-home mother. The judgment reflects the mindset of the judge, who seems to be stuck in a different era!

Later, the Bombay High Court reversed the district court's order and allowed the woman to adopt. It is noteworthy that the judge in this case, Justice Gauri Godse, was herself a working woman, which is likely to have made her more empathetic to the petitioner.

3. Can a same-sex couple adopt?
   The HAMA does not provide for adoption by a same-sex couple. The JJA, meanwhile, allows a couple to adopt only if they are in a stable marriage for two or more years. Since same-sex marriage is not legally recognized in India, the JJA, by association, does not permit adoption for a same-sex couple.
4. Can couples in a live-in relationship adopt?
   The same logic as above applies here as well. The HAMA does not provide for live-in relationships and the JJA requires a stable marriage of two years. Although the courts have held that a stable, long-term live-in relationship is considered like marriage, whether the courts apply this principle to adoption depends on a case-to-case basis.

Pro tip: If a same-sex couple, or a couple in a live-in relationship, wants to adopt a child, they will have to work around the law. One of the partners will have to adopt the child as a single person. The other partner can be the child's guardian. Both partners can raise the child as their own, but the child's legal relationship with each parent will be different.

Where Can You Adopt From?

Is adoption like walking into a plant nursery and selecting the plant that has the brightest roses? Or are there legal restrictions around who you can adopt and how?

First, we need to understand that not all adoptions happen from orphanages. Not all children who are adopted are orphans. Confused?

It is actually quite simple. Adoption is the process of taking in a child as your own. It does not mean that the child has to be an orphan.

There are mainly three sources from where one can adopt:
1. Adopting children of relatives: It is common practice in large Indian families that if one couple is not able to have a biological child, one of their relatives conceives on the couple's behalf and hands over the child to the couple for adoption.

Although this sounds like surrogacy, there is a difference. In surrogacy, we use either the eggs or the sperm (or both) of the parents and the pregnant woman is only the carrier. Here, the child is the biological child of the relatives who agree to give it up for adoption.

#ReelToReal

In 1995, at the age of twenty-one, actress Raveena Tandon adopted her cousin's daughters, Pooja and Chaya. In an interview, Tandon revealed that her cousin's children were not getting the life they deserved after both their parents passed away, which was why she decided to adopt them and give them a better life.[7]

---

2. Adoption by step-parents: Sometimes, a step-parent may adopt their partner's child from a previous marriage.

    For example, Saif Ali Khan already had two children, Sara and Ibrahim, before he married Kareena Kapoor. While Kareena is considered their stepmother, she does not have a legal relationship with them. Had Kareena chosen to legally adopt Sara and Ibrahim before they turned eighteen, then they would legally be considered Kareena's children and

would no longer be considered the children of Amrita Singh, their birth mother.
3. Adopting from an orphanage: This is the adoption method we most commonly know from and see in the movies. To adopt a child from an orphanage, you have to go through CARA (Central Adoption Resource Authority). For details, visit https://cara.wcd.gov.in/.

Under both laws (HAMA and JJA), you can adopt a child through any of the above methods.

Can You Choose the Child You Want to Adopt?

If you are adopting under the HAMA, or adopting within the family, the choice of the child is already made.

If you are adopting from an orphanage, you will be given three children to choose from. You cannot give any preference, such as 'I want options for three boys or three girls'. You will be matched with children based on factors such as your gender, marital status, your age, age of the child, etc.

You will also have to follow legal requirements regarding the child's age and your age. As per the HAMA, you can only adopt a child till they turn fifteen.

Under the JJA, you can adopt a child till they turn eighteen. The minimum age gap between the parent(s) and the adopted child should be at least twenty-five years. The age of the child you are eligible to adopt depends on the total age of the parents. You can find details on the CARA website.

What Is the Procedure for Adoption?

We will not get into the detailed step-by-step procedure for adoption here as it is an extremely lengthy process and the rules keep changing. The best place to find out the latest process for adoption is the CARA website (https://cara.wcd.gov.in/).

However, here is a bird's eye view of the process to give you a brief idea.

1. HAMA
    i. Adoption ceremony: Carry out an adoption ceremony, which consists of giving and receiving the child. The adoptive parents can also perform religious ceremonies, like a pooja, to complete the adoption.
    ii. Adoption deed: Get an adoption deed certified from the magistrate. This deed contains the basic information about the parents and the child, along with the statement that the custody of the child is being transferred from the biological parents to the adoptive parents under the HAMA. The deed needs to be signed by both adoptive parents along with the two witnesses.
2. JJA:
    i. Waiting list: Register with CARA and get yourself on the waiting list for adoption.
    ii. Assessment: A home study is conducted to assess your eligibility to adopt.
    iii. Choosing the child: If your application is accepted, you will be referred to three children. You have to choose one of them. If you don't select any, you will go to the bottom of the waiting list.
    iv. Compatibility test: The chosen child is placed in your foster care to test your compatibility. If all goes well, you can adopt the child permanently.

v. Adoption order: The court has to pass an adoption order in your favour, certifying the adoption.

vi. Monitoring: Post adoption, CARA will follow up with you for two years to make sure that the child is being taken care of well.

Which Law Should You Choose to Adopt Under?

If you are a non-Hindu, you do not have a choice; you have to go through the JJA. If you are a Hindu, you can either choose the JJA or the HAMA. As you must have noticed, the process under the HAMA is shorter and quicker, with very little involvement from CARA. Adoption under the JJA is a lengthy and time-consuming process. Therefore, if you have the option, you are better off adopting under the HAMA.

Note: Some international countries don't accept adoptions under the HAMA as legitimate. This can create issues for you if you wish to move abroad at some point. In such a situation, consult with a lawyer to discuss your specific situation and decide which law you should adopt under.

Pro tip: If you are considering adoption (from an orphanage), register with CARA at the earliest. Don't wait till the end, till you exhaust all other reproductive options, to get into the process. Adoption under the JJA can easily take two to three years. If you wait till the exhaustion of all other options, you lose out on precious time. If you change your mind about the adoption later, you can choose to drop out of the process. However, if you decide later that you want to adopt, you will have to wait for a couple of years to be able to bring a child home.

Let's sum up by outlining the differences between adoption under the HAMA and the JJA.

HAMA	JJA
Only Hindus (including Sikhs, Buddhists and Jains) can adopt under this law.	Anyone can adopt under this law. The religion does not matter.
Can only adopt a Hindu child.	Can adopt a child of any religion.
Can adopt a child only up to fifteen years.	Can adopt a child up to eighteen years.
If you already have a child, you cannot adopt a child of the same sex. E.g., if you have a daughter, you cannot adopt a girl. You will have to adopt a son.	No restrictions based on the child's sex.
No restriction on the number of children you can adopt.	If you already have three children, you cannot adopt.
No restrictions for a married couple to be eligible to adopt.	If married, you need to be in a stable marriage for at least two years to be eligible to adopt.
If single, you cannot adopt a child of the opposite gender, unless you have a twenty-one-year age gap between you and the child.	The age of the child depends on the total age of the adopting parents. A single woman can adopt a child of any gender. A single man can only adopt a male child.

HAMA	JJA
CARA has a minimal role to play, as long as you are qualified to adopt a child.	CARA governs every aspect of the adoption process.
Quicker process with less procedure.	Lengthier process with many steps.

POINTS TO REMEMBER

1. Two laws govern adoption in India, the Hindu Adoptions and Maintenance Act (HAMA) for Hindus and the Juvenile Justice Act (JJA) for all religions, including Hindus.
2. Once you adopt a child, s/he is treated like your biological child from the date of adoption. The adopted child has the same rights as a biological child.
3. Adoptions happen not only from orphanages but also from relatives or stepchildren.
4. The law allows married couples and single persons to adopt (based on certain rules). However, there is no clear law on the adoption rights of same-sex couples and live-in partners.
5. Adoption under the HAMA is simpler and faster, without much legal procedure. In comparison, adoption under the JJA must go through CARA (Central Adoption Resource Authority) and involves a longer waiting time and more paperwork.

EXERCISE TIME!

Guardians of the Heart

Solve the riddles below to decode terms related to adoption.

1. I am appointed with solemn trust,
   To protect those who rely on me, I must.
   In legal terms, I am a role defined,
   For minors or those who need support aligned.
   What am I?

2. I'm not born into, yet chosen with heart,
   From one's own kin, a different start.
   No blood binds us, yet love runs deep,
   In new arms, me forever keep.
   What am I?

3. A place of many, yet alone I stand,
   No family ties, just a helping hand.
   Children gather, hearts in search of care,
   A home where love becomes their air.
   What am I?

4. In Hindu law, I find my place,
   A legal act, with ancient grace.
   I ensure care and rights are sealed,
   In family bonds, my fate revealed.
   What am I?

Answer key:
1. Guardianship 2. Adoption 3. Orphanage
4. Hindu Adoption and Maintenance Act

Surrogacy

Actress Sushmita Sen once said that children come from the heart, not from the womb. This is a reality for many parents, who choose to have children through surrogacy, a method of assisted reproduction where a woman (the surrogate) carries and gives birth to a baby for another person or couple (the intended parents).

Surrogacy can be of two types, depending on the medical procedure:

1. Traditional: The surrogate's own egg is used for conception, often through artificial insemination. Hence, the surrogate is genetically related to the child.
2. Gestational: An embryo using the egg and sperm of the intended parents is implanted into the surrogate's uterus. In this case, the surrogate is not genetically related to the child.

#MovieTime

The 2001 Bollywood movie *Chori Chori Chupke Chupke* revolved around surrogacy. Raj (played by Salman Khan) and Priya (played by Rani Mukerji) face fertility issues after a miscarriage. Finally, they decide to seek the help of a surrogate. Enter Madhubala (played by Preity Zinta), a cheerful and independent woman who agrees to carry Raj and Priya's child.

Although the movie took a dramatic turn with Madhubala getting attached to Raj and refusing to hand over the baby, this movie was one of the earliest ones to introduce surrogacy in our society.

For the longest time, India did not have a law on surrogacy. It was neither legal nor illegal. This led to India becoming a commercial hub for couples from different countries, looking for cheap surrogacy options at the cost of underprivileged women. Therefore, in 2021, the Parliament passed the Surrogacy (Regulation) Act, 2021, which now governs surrogacy in India.

What Are the Rules for Surrogacy Under the Surrogacy (Regulation) Act?

1. No commercial surrogacy, only altruistic surrogacy. Commercial surrogacy is banned in India, i.e., you cannot 'hire' a woman to become your surrogate. You cannot give any payment, reward, monetary benefits, or fees to the surrogate or her dependants. You can only pay for her medical expenses, insurance and other expenses such as travel, clothes, medicines, etc.
2. NRIs and foreign couples cannot seek a surrogate in India. This has been provided to ensure that India doesn't remain a hub for 'baby-shopping'. It also stems from concerns about the welfare of the child. Once a child is taken out of India, it is difficult for our authorities to track his/her wellbeing.
3. Only gestational surrogacy is permitted. Intended parent(s) cannot use the surrogate's egg. They need to use their own egg, but can use a sperm donor, if needed. While this avoids complications regarding the biological parentage of the child, it makes it difficult for women who have medical issues to have a child through surrogacy.

4. Surrogacy is only permitted through registered clinics, which must comply with legal guidelines and obtain a licence to carry out surrogacy procedures. If they conduct any malpractice, their licence can be revoked.

So, does this mean that any individual/couple from India, who uses their own egg and does not pay the surrogate, can have a child through surrogacy? Unfortunately, no. The Surrogacy (Regulation) Act only allows certain categories of people to opt for surrogacy.

Who Can Opt for Surrogacy?

The list of people who are allowed surrogacy is tiny. It includes married couples who cannot conceive, or single women who are between thirty-five and forty-five years of age and are either divorced or widowed.

Since the law only permits the above two categories, the list for who *cannot* opt for surrogacy is much bigger!

1. A married couple who can conceive but want to choose surrogacy as an alternative method of reproduction.
2. A single woman who is neither divorced nor widowed, or is not within the thirty-five to forty-five years bracket.
3. Live-in couples: The law uses the term 'married couples'. It will be up to the courts to include live-in couples in the category of married couples.
4. Single men.
5. Same-sex couples.

>  **Food for thought**
>
> Do you think the law is fair for excluding the above categories? What do you think could be the logic (if any) behind this policy?
>
> For instance, what if a twenty-five-year-old woman wants to have a surrogate child? And what if a single woman wants to have a child through surrogacy without getting married? Why can't a serious live-in couple opt for surrogacy, even though the Supreme Court recognizes long-term live-in relationships to be as good as marriage?

Clearly, the Surrogacy (Regulation) Act leaves much to be desired. While the intention behind the law was to stop the exploitation of women, it denies the right to reproductive choice to several categories of people, many of them without any justification.

What Legal Documents Does a Couple Need to Opt for Surrogacy?

1. Certificate of eligibility from the District Medical Board concerned: To obtain this, they must satisfy the criteria below:
   i. Must be legally married.
   ii. Fall within the twenty-three to fifty years age bracket for women and twenty-six to fifty years for men.
   iii. Not have any children, whether biological, adopted or through surrogacy, unless their child suffers from

a life-threatening disease or is mentally or physically challenged.
2. Infertility certificate: The District Medical Board concerned needs to certify that the couple is infertile, i.e., they are unable to conceive naturally.
3. Custody order: The Magistrate Court concerned needs to pass an order stating that the couple will take custody of the child.
4. Insurance policy: The couple needs to take out an insurance policy for the surrogate woman to cover postpartum complications for thirty-six months after the delivery and guarantee it by signing an affidavit.

What Legal Documents Does a Single Woman Need to Opt for Surrogacy?

1. Certificate of eligibility from the District Medical Board: To obtain this, she must satisfy the criteria below:
   i. Must be divorced or widowed.
   ii. Fall within the age bracket of thirty-five to forty-five years.
   iii. Not have any children, whether biological, adopted or through surrogacy, unless the child suffers from a life-threatening disease or is mentally or physically challenged.
2. Infertility certificate: The District Medical Board needs to certify that she is infertile.
3. Custody order: The Magistrate Court needs to pass an order stating that she will take the custody of the child.

4. Insurance policy: She needs to take out an insurance policy for the surrogate woman to cover postpartum complications for thirty-six months after the delivery and guarantee it by signing an affidavit.

> **Quick checklist of documents**
> - ✓ Marriage certificate (for a couple)
> - ✓ Court order granting divorce (for a divorced woman)
> - ✓ Death certificate of spouse (for widowed woman)
> - ✓ Proof of age, such as Aadhaar card

Note: The above is an indicative checklist. The list may vary from jurisdiction to jurisdiction based on local procedures. Your gynaecologist will be able to help you out on this front.

Who Can Be a Surrogate?

A surrogate has to check these boxes below:
1. A woman who is already married.
2. Has a child of her own.
3. Consents to becoming a surrogate.
4. Is medically fit to carry out the surrogacy.

This means that a single or unmarried woman can no longer become a surrogate (like it was in *Chori Chori Chupke Chupke*).

When the new law was passed, there was confusion initially about whether the surrogate woman needed to be biologically related to the intending couple or woman. Later, the Union Ministry of Health clarified that she need not be related to them, which came as a big relief to hopeful parents, who would otherwise have to try to convince one of their female relatives to become a surrogate for them!

Now, you can either find a surrogate on your own or ask the surrogacy clinic to link you with one. Most people take the latter option as it is difficult to find a woman to be your surrogate.

What Are the Rights of the Surrogate Woman?

We now know that only a married woman with a child can become a surrogate. Also, a woman can become a surrogate only once in her life. Moreover, she cannot be paid for it. All this sounds like a huge sacrifice the surrogate makes for the intending parents(s). What rights and protection does she have under the law?

1. The surrogacy can happen only with her valid consent.
2. Only three surrogacy attempts are allowed on a surrogate.
3. The doctor is supposed to implant only one embryo at a time, unless it is an exceptional case.
4. The surrogate woman can change her mind till the embryo is planted in her womb.
5. No one can force the surrogate to have an abortion.
6. The intending parent(s) must obtain health insurance for the surrogate.
7. The intending parent(s) cannot abandon the child or change their minds once the surrogate conceives. They have to take custody of the child.

>  **Food for thought**
>
> Strangely, for a law that claims to be for the protection of surrogate women, there is no dedicated section for their rights. The above rights have to be inferred from other clauses in the Act. Do you think these rights are enough to protect the surrogate woman? What about provisions for taking care of her health, ensuring comfortable living conditions and access to a healthy lifestyle? These seem to be missing!

Legal Rules Applicable after the Surrogacy Process Begins

So you found a surrogate. Great! The embryo (fusion of your egg and sperm) has been planted in her uterus. The pregnancy is successful. Now what?

The law prescribes certain rules you need to follow:

1. You cannot change your mind during the pregnancy or after the child is born.
2. In the event of multiple births, such as twins or triplets, you will legally become the parents of all the children. You cannot choose to only accept one child and reject the others.
3. The pregnancy cannot be terminated, except as permitted under abortion laws. Moreover, it can only be done with the consent of the surrogate.
4. You cannot ask for the sex of the child to be determined.

All of the above is also in the contract you sign with your surrogacy clinic.

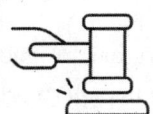 **Baby Manji: The Bizarre Case of an Abandoned Surrogate Child**

In this strange 2008 case, a Japanese surrogate baby was left parentless in India, till the Supreme Court stepped in and reunited the baby with its father. A Japanese couple had opted for surrogacy in India. During the pregnancy (of the surrogate), the couple got divorced. The mother refused to take custody of the child and the father was unable to obtain a visa to come to India.

For the longest time, Baby Manji was in India, without any legal status, citizenship or parents! Ultimately, the Supreme Court had to step in and direct the Japanese Embassy in India to facilitate the baby's travel to Japan. When Baby Manji finally flew to Japan, it not only made headlines in India but also brought to light the issue of surrogacy by foreign couples in India, which has now been banned under the Surrogacy (Regulation) Act of 2021.

What Is the Status of a Child Born through Surrogacy?

A surrogate child is treated the same as your biological child. Even though the child comes from the womb of a surrogate, legally the child has no connection with her. Surrogate children get the exact same rights from their parents as biological children.

Practically, as soon as the child is born, it is handed over to the intended parents. The surrogate does not nurse or feed the child.

Navigating Surrogacy Clinic Contracts

You have decided to take the plunge. You find the right surrogacy clinic. The next thing you know, you are drowning in paperwork. All surrogacy clinics make the intended parents sign multiple legal agreements. As with most legal matters, these contracts are lengthy and complicated, and most intended parents end up signing them without reading. We cannot blame them; most contracts are designed to keep the signee in the blind.

While most of the contract will be about the surrogacy procedure and legal requirements, beware of the below mentioned clauses.

It can sound technical or intimidating, but stay with me. Read it over and over again if you have to. This is not rocket science.

1. Hidden charges: Surrogacy has become a booming business in India, where clinics try to fleece hopeful parents. Ask the clinic to state very clearly the costs included and excluded from the total fee. E.g., they may charge extra for every medical procedure, scan or doctor's visit by the surrogate woman. You should also ensure that the clinic is actually carrying out all the procedures that it is supposed to, to ensure the wellbeing of the surrogate woman.
2. Indemnity clause: Beware! I have seen surrogacy contracts where the clinic tries to hold the intending parents responsible for any third-party claims about the surrogacy. This means that if a third-party raises any claim against the clinic (say, for procedural violations), the intended parents have to bear the costs of settling such a claim.

The thumb rule you should follow for indemnity is that their fault is their headache and your fault is your headache. This means that you will only indemnify them for a claim if it is your mistake (for example, a problem with your documentation). You will not indemnify them for a claim arising from their mistake (for example, they did not renew their licence on time).

Do not sign a blanket indemnification saying that no matter what (no matter whose fault it is), you will indemnify them.
3. Confidentiality: Ensure that your surrogacy clinic is responsible for maintaining confidentiality about the entire process, including keeping your identity and details private. This is not only to ensure that something so personal to you does not become the talk of the town but also to make sure that going forward there is no contact between the surrogate and your child.

Checklist for Choosing Your Surrogacy Clinic

When choosing a surrogacy clinic, make sure that it is compliant with the following:
1. Certificate for the clinic: The clinic should have a registration certificate authorizing it to carry out surrogacy procedures. This should be prominently displayed.
2. Certificate for the surrogate: Like the clinic, the surrogate also needs a legal certificate authorizing her to undertake surrogacy.
3. Medical qualifications: The clinic is required to satisfy the following medical requirements:

    i. Have at least one gynaecologist, anaesthetist, embryologist and counsellor.
    ii. The gynaecologist must hold a post-graduate degree in gynaecology and obstetrics, and have experience in alternative reproductive procedures.
4. Ethical surrogacy practices: Many clinics charge hopeful parents an arm and a leg as their fees for the surrogacy procedure. Of this, the surrogate woman may not even get a pittance. Make sure you ask your clinic all the right questions about how they take care of the surrogate. After all, you would want the woman who brings your child into the world to be treated with the same care and affection as the child, wouldn't you?

The law and rules on surrogacy are constantly evolving. As and when new, unforeseen issues come up, the government issues a clarification or carries out an amendment. Therefore, before you head down the surrogacy route, please check the latest status of the law.

Let's Conclude

I want to leave you with something to think about. In the 2021 Bollywood movie *Mimi*, which was about surrogacy, a small-town Indian girl decides to become a commercial surrogate for an American couple, for a sum of Rs 20 lakh. She agrees to do this to pursue her dream of becoming an actress.

A surrogate woman goes through immense physical, emotional and mental labour to carry out a pregnancy and deliver the baby, only to hand the infant over. While commercial surrogacy was banned in India to prevent exploitation of underprivileged women, the ground reality is that most women who become surrogates are from underprivileged backgrounds. They carry out the surrogacy to earn a livelihood and support their families. However, the current law expects them to do it for free—no compensation, only medical expenses. Why should we expect a woman, who is a stranger to the parents, to go through labour for free? Isn't this another form of exploitation?

Maybe it is time for the law to rethink the ban on commercial surrogacy. Of course, Rs 20 lakh as fees sounds good only in Bollywood movies, but how about a just compensation to the surrogate for her labour and sacrifice? Think about it.

> **POINTS TO REMEMBER**
>
> 1. Only altruistic surrogacy is permitted in India. Commercial surrogacy is banned.
> 2. The only categories of persons who can opt for surrogacy are heterosexual married couples who cannot conceive and single women between the ages thirty-five and forty-five, if they are divorced or widowed.
> 3. A woman can be a surrogate for someone only once in her life. She needs to be married and have a child of her own.
> 4. A child born through surrogacy is treated the same as a biological child and has the same rights as a biological child.
> 5. The surrogate woman has no rights over the child, and there is no legal link between them.

EXERCISE TIME!

Surrogacy Sparks: Match the Miracles

A. Commercial	1. A woman who carries a pregnancy for intended parents.
B. Altruistic	2. The inability to conceive or carry a pregnancy to term.
C. Infertility	3. Notable legal case involving international legal complexities in surrogacy arrangements.
D. Surrogate	4. A surrogacy arrangement involving financial compensation.
E. Baby Manji	5. Surrogacy where the surrogate volunteers without payment.

Answer key:
A-4; B-5; C-2; D-1; E-3

10

Legal Remedies: Knocking on the Doors of Justice

This chapter will help you understand how to file a police complaint, how courts function, and your rights for bail and arrest.

Introduction

What came first? The chicken or the egg? This is one of those impossible riddles. Let us, however, flip this riddle. When standing up for your legal rights, what comes first? Filing a court case or filing a police complaint, or both? Here, there is a clear answer.

> If it is a criminal offence, then you go to the police first.
> If it is a civil dispute, you can go to the court first.

A criminal offence, or crime, is an offence against society. Anything that can put the safety and security of society at risk is considered a crime, even if it is committed against one person. For example, murder, theft, sexual harassment, rape, cruelty by husband and in-laws, and some types of cyberbullying, among others. For a crime, the remedy is to punish the criminal with imprisonment and/or fine. A crime is prosecuted by the government.

A civil dispute is a private dispute between two or more parties, which violates the law. It does not put the safety and security of society at risk. For example, breach of contract, divorce, property disputes, landlord–tenant disputes, among others. For a civil dispute, the remedy is to compensate the wronged party. A civil offence is prosecuted by the wronged party.

Police Complaints

Most of the topics that we have covered in this book are related to criminal offences. Therefore, it is important for you to know all about taking action against a crime.

Fill in the blanks: When it comes to a crime, it all starts with a _____.

A dream? A coffee? Well, the right answer is PC (not Priyanka Chopra, but a police complaint).

What is a police complaint?
A police complaint is a first-hand account of any offence or crime, which describes in layman's words what happened. It is a narration of the facts of the incident. Remember, when you were small and someone tried to raid your lunch box or steal your pencil? You would go to your teacher and complain: 'Teacher, teacher, I had gone to the bathroom before eating my lunch. My lunch box was on the table. I had got roti and paneer curry for lunch. When I came back, so-and-so had eaten my lunch.'

A police complaint is a similar narration, except it is for a criminal offence and not a lunch box!

What is the difference between a police complaint and FIR?
A police complaint contains the narration of facts and the incident that a complainant gives to the police. An FIR (First Information Report) is the first report made by the police

about the offence after you lodge a complaint. In short, a police complaint is what you give to the police. An FIR is the report the police make after your complaint.

For serious crimes like murder, rape and kidnapping, the police will immediately register an FIR after you file a complaint. For less serious offences, the police will first do a background check and then register an FIR.

The 'Where, When, Who, How' of police complaints
Now that we have understood what exactly a police complaint is, let us get into the details.
1. Where to file a police complaint?
   i. At the police station
      You should file a police complaint in the jurisdiction where the crime is committed. For example, if the incident occurs in Connaught Place in Delhi, you should go to the Connaught Place police station. You can find out which police station has jurisdiction for the crime in question through a simple online search.
   ii. Online
      Nowadays, many police stations in metro cities let you file a complaint online, through email, WhatsApp, or their own app. You can do a simple online search to find out if this facility is available in your city. For example, the Delhi Police has the Himmat app and the Hyderabad Police has the Hawk Eye app. After you file the complaint online, check if there is an online follow-up

mechanism. If not, you may have to visit the police station of the jurisdiction concerned, with the complaint number, to follow up.

Zero FIR: A Special FIR without Jurisdiction

For certain serious offences like rape, kidnapping, murder, where it is important to start the police process quickly, you are allowed to file a complaint in any police station, regardless of the jurisdiction. This is called a Zero FIR.

You can file a Zero FIR in any police station within the city or anywhere in the country. For example, if the crime happened in Connaught Place in Delhi, you can file the complaint in a Gurgaon police station, or even in a police station in Hyderabad. You need to ask the police station to register a Zero FIR.

How does a Zero FIR work?

Every FIR (i.e., non-Zero FIR) has a serial number linked to the police station where it is registered. In a Zero FIR, the police station where you file a complaint assigns the serial number 'zero' to the FIR. This police station then transfers your complaint to the police station that has jurisdiction over the crime. Once the FIR is transferred to the investigating police station, they will give it a regular serial number. You will then have to track your complaint through the new serial number, with the investigating police station.

2. When to file a police complaint?
    i. Ideally, you should file a police complaint as soon as an incident takes place. This will help the police take fast action. It is also easier for the police to investigate and gather evidence when the crime is still fresh. As they say, strike while the iron is hot!
    ii. If you couldn't file the complaint early, don't worry. Technically, there is no time limit for reporting a crime. (For civil offences, however, the time limit is usually three years.) You can even file a complaint several years after the incident. In cases of domestic violence, sexual harassment, rape, etc., women usually take time to report due to mental trauma and the stigma attached. That is okay. Even if there is a delay, you can still file a police complaint. The police will write down the reason for the delay.

Pro tip: Remember when the #MeToo Movement surfaced in India in 2018? Many women came out about sexual harassment that they experienced years ago. Sadly, many of the complaints were closed without the accused being caught, because after so many years it was difficult to find concrete evidence and gather witnesses.

> ### What if I Don't Have Evidence?
>
> No worries! Many crimes against women, especially those related to domestic violence and sexual harassment, happen in private. Usually, there are no witnesses and the victim is unable to produce any evidence.
>
> Fear not, the courts understand this. Therefore, they have time and again ruled that the testimony of the victim is enough in such crimes, even if she is not able to support it with other evidence.
>
> This is especially true in sexual harassment cases, where the courts have emphasized that it is important to believe the victim. For domestic violence cases, the courts have unfortunately been more hesitant in taking a strong stand, as they consider 'matrimonial disputes' to be complex, involving complicated family dynamics.

3. Who can file a police complaint?

    Anyone can file a police complaint, irrespective of whether:
    - You are a victim, i.e. you are the affected person
    - You are a witness, i.e. you just saw something happening
    - You have information of the crime, i.e. you have heard about or seen a crime

Therefore, if you know someone who is a victim of any crime, you can file a police complaint on their behalf (make sure you have the victim's consent).

4. How to file a police complaint?
    i. Inform: You need to inform the police about the offence. You can either do this by physically going to the police station or filing a complaint online (if available). If you have filed a complaint online, the police may call you to the police station to take down your complaint.
    ii. Written form: If you provide information orally, the police will write it down for you. You can also choose to write down the complaint yourself (I recommend this so that you are in control of the narration). You can even write your complaint beforehand and take it to the police station. Make sure you mention all the details (that you know for sure) in the complaint. Don't skip anything! Ask for extra paper if you want.
    iii. Oral form: If you are giving an oral complaint that the police are writing down, the police will read all the information back to you for confirmation. This step is not necessary if you give a written complaint.
    iv. Verification and signature: The police will ask you to verify the facts and sign the complaint.
    v. Stamp and complaint number: The police will stamp the complaint carrying the daily diary number and give you a complaint number. Make sure you ask for this as the complaint number will

help you track the progress of your complaint. It is like an 'order number' that you use to track online shopping parcels.

vi. Your copy: The police will provide you with a free photocopy of your complaint, which should also be signed and stamped. Make sure you ask for this as this is proof of filing the complaint!

> **Filing a Police Complaint Is Not Scary**
>
> 1. You need not know the legal provisions applicable. You can just describe the incident, and the police will write down the laws and sections.
> 2. No documents are necessary to file a police complaint. However, if you do have any documents or evidence, attach it to the complaint to strengthen it.
> 3. The complaint can be typed or handwritten, based on your convenience. If handwritten, make sure you write clearly.
> 4. You can file the police complaint in any language (the regional language, Hindi or English). It need not necessarily be in English.
> 5. You don't need a lawyer to file a complaint. You can do so on your own. You've got this! Take someone with you for moral support if you want!
> 6. You need not know the accused persons or their details. Just give the police all the details you can remember. E.g., *'kitne aadmi the* (how many accused)', what clothes they wore, what they looked like (spectacles, scars, tattoos, etc.).

Pro tip: Remember, the devil is in the details. The more details you give, the easier it will be for the police to investigate. However, only mention details that you are absolutely sure about. If you have a doubt, give an approximate figure (e.g., say afternoon instead of 2.30 p.m.) or leave it out. Why so?

Well, a police complaint can be used as evidence in court. It can make or break your case. The defendant (accused) will try to find discrepancies in your complaint and testimony, to prove that you are lying. So, stick to the same information and details throughout the police and court process, to ensure that the defendant cannot break your case. Sometimes, even a minute detail like 'the accused was wearing an orange shirt, instead of a green shirt' can be used to cast a doubt on your testimony. Therefore, write only what you are sure about.

5. What happens after you file a police complaint?
    i. Investigation: The wheel of the criminal process is set in motion! If the offence is a serious one (called a cognizable offence), like murder, rape, molestation, stalking, dowry death, the police can directly file an FIR and begin investigation. If it is a less serious offence (a non-cognizable offence), like defamation or bigamy, the police have to first submit a report to the magistrate. Only after receiving the magistrate's go-ahead can the police file an FIR and start the investigation.

Note: Most crimes against women, including all types of sexual harassment, are cognizable offences. When in doubt, always Google the section number applicable.

ii. Charge sheet: After the police conduct their investigation, examine witnesses and gather evidence, if they believe that a crime was likely committed, they file a charge sheet and submit it to the magistrate. A charge sheet is a legal document that contains details of the charges filed against the accused (e.g., sexual harassment and outraging the modesty of a woman, along with attempt to disrobe a woman) with other details about the investigation.

On the other hand, if the police believe that it is smoke without fire (i.e., no crime was committed), they will close the case and submit a closure report to the magistrate.

> In the Aarushi Talwar murder case, which shook the country in 2008, the police had initially filed a closure report. However, the magistrate in this case questioned the report because there was enough evidence to carry out an investigation and asked the police to reopen the case. This was justice ensured by the magistrate behind the scenes.

iii. Criminal trial: Once the charge sheet is submitted, the court case, i.e. the criminal trial against the accused commences. This is the part that you usually see in the movies, with lawyers, evidence, witnesses (and some courtroom drama).

POINTS TO REMEMBER

1. A police complaint is a narration of facts of a crime to the police. An FIR is the first report made by the police after you file a complaint.
2. You should file a complaint with the police station that has jurisdiction over the area where the crime took place. Many cities also have the option to file a complaint online.
3. While there is no time bar for filing a police complaint, you should do it as soon as possible so that key evidence is not lost.
4. Anyone can file a police complaint, including the victim or anyone else on his/her behalf.
5. You should write all the facts and details you know in the police complaint. Make it as comprehensive as possible. However, if you are not sure about something, mention an approximation. E.g., if you can't remember the exact time, simply say afternoon or evening.

How Do I File a Court Case?

Before we get into the details of filing a case, let us understand the basic court structure in India, which follows a hierarchical system with three levels:

Supreme Court
This is the top court in the country. The Supreme Court's word is final; there is no appeal beyond this.

High Court
Each state has its own high court, which is the highest court of that state.

Lower Courts
This includes all the courts in every state, which are below the high court, such as the magistrate's court, sessions court, family courts, etc.

1. **Supreme Court:** The Supreme Court is the highest court of India. Its word is final and becomes the law of the country. It adjudicates on the following:
    i. Matters of constitutional importance (i.e., matters which affect the Constitution of India).
    ii. Disputes between two or more states.

iii. Appeals from high courts, which can either be private disputes between people or those in which the state is involved (e.g., Section 377 and the Sabarimala judgments were appeals from high courts).
2. **High courts:** The high court is the highest court of each state. The law laid down by a high court becomes applicable to that particular state. E.g., if the Bombay High Court states that plastic bags will be banned, the judgment will be applicable to the whole of Maharashtra but not to any other state in India.
3. **Lower courts:** Each state has an array of lower courts, which function below the high court. There are separate courts for civil and criminal matters. There are also special courts for important issues, like family courts, and fast-track courts for cases of rape and protection of children against sexual offences. Within the lower courts, too, there is a hierarchical system, but we won't get into that for now.

Where Should You File a Case?

Like a police complaint, you must file a case in the court that has jurisdiction over the matter. However, unlike a police complaint where jurisdiction is based only on geographical location, in a civil case, the jurisdiction of a court is determined based on the following factors:

   1. Subject matter of your case: All criminal cases go to criminal courts and all civil cases go to civil courts. Within civil courts, there are dedicated courts for

different subject matters. For instance, all family-law related cases (such as divorce, domestic violence, dowry) will go to family courts. Similarly, there are special company law courts for company-related cases.
2. Geographical location: This is the location of the matter in dispute and the parties who are fighting the case. For example, if you are fighting over a piece of land, the location of that land will determine the geographical jurisdiction.
3. Monetary value: The seniority of the court where you file the case depends on the monetary value of what you are fighting over. For example, if it is a property-related dispute, the value of the property will decide the seniority of the court. Monetary value will not apply to divorce and domestic violence cases since they already have a dedicated family law court.

What Happens after You File a Case?

Let us understand the process applicable through an example. After all, the basics remain the same; only the terminology changes. Say, Sheela is filing a divorce case against her husband, Vijay. Here is what will happen:
1. Filing a case: Sheela goes to the family law court, which has jurisdiction over where she is currently staying, or where she and Vijay stayed together. Sheela hires a lawyer and files a case. She pays the court fee (which is minimal for family law cases).
2. First hearing: The case will come up for admission before the court. The court will decide whether it

is a valid case or not. Once considered a valid case, the court will admit it and move to the next steps. If considered invalid, the court will dismiss the case.
3. Information and summons: The court will send a copy of the case to Vijay, informing him that a case has been filed against him. It will also summon (i.e., call) Vijay to appear before the court (in person or through a lawyer) on a fixed date, to defend himself.
4. Vijay's reply: Vijay now has to file his reply (basically his defence) to Sheela's allegations, either confirming or denying them.
5. Sheela's reply to Vijay's reply: Once Vijay places his reply on record, Sheela gets another chance to reply to his reply. Here, she can respond to the defence taken by Vijay and to any counter-allegations that he may have made.
6. Arguments: Once the parties complete the process of submitting their allegations, defence and replies in written form, the case moves to oral arguments, based on what the parties have submitted.

Note: This is a very broad view of what happens after you file a case, just to give you a basic idea. Within each stage, and during the lifetime of the case, there are several other smaller petitions that the parties file, for temporary and urgent reliefs. I will not go into that, as it will unnecessarily confuse you.

Also, I have purposely not used technical terms. It is more important for you to understand the concept than to get stuck in terminology.

Do I Need a Lawyer, or Can I Fight My Own Case in Court?

Every citizen in India has the right to fight his/her own case in court, with or without a lawyer. A person arguing their own case is called 'party in person'. However, I would recommend getting a good lawyer if you can. Indian laws and the legal system are complex; half the cases are won based on technicalities and procedural faults (rather than the actual case). A party in person will not know these technicalities and will find it difficult to fight a lawyer on the other side.

Note: Every woman in India has the right to free legal aid, *irrespective of her income or financial status*. This is provided in Section 12(c) of the Legal Services Authorities Act, 1987.

Free legal aid means you can get a state-appointed lawyer to fight your case, without any fees. You can opt for this if you cannot hire a lawyer and do not want to appear as party in person. I would recommend this option with a pinch of salt, as each person's experience with a state-appointed lawyer varies and may not always be the best. To understand where to approach for free legal aid, visit this website: https://nalsa.gov.in/

How Much Does It Cost to Fight a Case in Court?

You will incur two types of costs for fighting your case:
1. Court fees: These are the fees that you pay to the court at the time of filing your case. The amount varies from court to court and from case to case, and

depends on the monetary value of the dispute. For example, if it is a property-related dispute, the higher the value of the property, the higher the court fees. For most family law-related cases, you don't have to pay court fees. However, since court fees vary from state to state, always check what is applicable to your situation.
2. Lawyer fees: If you hire a lawyer to represent you in court, you will have to pay the lawyer's fees. Again, this can vary drastically based on whether you are in a city or town, the subject matter of the case, and the seniority, experience and reputation of the lawyer. Unfortunately, I cannot give you a standard figure because this is highly subjective. However, I can tell you the payment structure you can expect:
   i. Per case fees: This is a fixed fee for the entire case, including filing and all appearances and arguments.
   ii. Filing and per-appearance fees: Here, you pay an initial fixed fee for filing, and then you pay a fee for every appearance that the lawyer makes in court for your case. The appearance fee can vary based on whether the appearance is for administrative purposes (lesser fees) or for arguments (higher fees).
   iii. Revenue share: In this structure, you don't pay the lawyer anything, or maybe you pay a minimal initial fee. If you win the case, you split the wins

with the lawyer. If you lose the case, of course, there is nothing to split or pay.

The fee structure varies from lawyer to lawyer, but I hope this outline will ensure you are better prepared when you speak to a lawyer about the fees.

How Long Does a Case Take?

How I wish I could give you a positive and hopeful answer. Unfortunately, the sad truth is that the Indian court system is plagued with overload and massive delays. To add to it, the courts are not strict when it comes to delaying tactics used by parties, where they keep asking for date after date to drag the case and frustrate the other party.

To answer your question about how long a case takes. Well, it can be anywhere between two years to two generations! Yes, you read it right. Some cases, especially those related to property, go on for generations! The younger generation, along with inheriting their parents' money, also inherits case files and visits to lawyers.

Family law cases are usually resolved faster compared to property disputes. By faster, I mean two to three years.

But there is good news! Till the case takes its due course, you can get interim reliefs from the court. These are temporary reliefs given as remedies by the court till the final judgment is given. For example, in a domestic violence case, you can ask for the right to stay in your matrimonial home as interim relief, so that while the case proceeds you still have a roof to live under.

#ReelToReal

There is absolute truth in Sunny Deol's iconic line from the 1993 Bollywood movie *Damini*, where he played the lawyer of a rape victim.

'Tareekh par tareekh, tareekh par tareekh milti rahi hai, lekin insaaf nahi mila, my lord, insaaf nahi mila. Mili hai toh sirf yeh tareekh.' This roughly translates to: Date after date, date after date is all we have received, my lord. But we haven't received justice.

This line holds good even today, which is why, in several places in this book, we have suggested alternate remedies and recommended approaching the court as the last resort.

To give you an example, a case like Nirbhaya, which shook the entire country and made international headlines, took almost eight years to close. The crime took place in 2012, but the four death row convicts were hanged only in 2020. For the longest time, there was no judge for the case, causing delay! Can you imagine, if this was the situation for such a serious and high-profile case, what it must be like for other cases?

POINTS TO REMEMBER

1. India has a three-tier judicial system—the Supreme Court, high courts and lower courts. For most day-to-day matters like marriage, divorce and property disputes, you will need to file a case in the lower courts.
2. Every woman has the right to free legal aid, which is provided by the government. You can use this service if you can't afford to hire a lawyer.
3. Every citizen has the right to represent themselves in court, either through a lawyer or themselves. It is, however, recommended that you get a lawyer to help you navigate legal procedures.
4. Court cases in India are lengthy, involving financial and emotional drain. Do a cost–benefit analysis to decide whether a court case or an out-of-court settlement is better for you.
5. You can always ask the court for interim reliefs (temporary reliefs) during the pendency of your case, so that you don't have to wait for years to get basic and urgent relief.

As a Woman, What Are My Rights against Arrest?

When can the police arrest a person?

The police can arrest an accused person only after filing an FIR against them. Recall from above that, for cognizable offences, the police need not go to the magistrate. This means they can file an FIR and make an arrest. However, for a non-cognizable offence, the police will have to get permission from the magistrate's court.

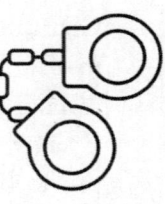

Here are some ground rules for an arrest:
1. The police can arrest the accused only if they need them for further investigation or questioning, and not 'simply because'.
2. The police can lock up an accused only for twenty-four hours without a magistrate's order. They need to produce the arrested person before the magistrate within twenty-four hours of arrest.
3. Beyond twenty-four hours, the magistrate will decide if the accused can be kept under arrest or will be released on bail. The order for arrest can only last for fifteen days and needs to be renewed every fifteen days.

Friday Evening Arrests

In some cases, where the police make political arrests, or arrest just for harassment, they usually do it on a Friday evening. Why? Because the magistrate's court is closed over the weekend and they can hold the accused person in custody till Monday.

Special Rules for Arrest of Women

Here are some important rules to be followed by the police before arresting a woman:

1. A woman cannot be arrested before sunrise or after sunset.
2. A male police officer cannot physically search a woman.
3. A woman can be arrested by a female police officer only.
4. A woman cannot be called to the police station for interrogation. The police should go to the woman's house, along with a female police officer, at a reasonable hour.
5. Women can have lawyers present during police interrogations.
6. The police cannot ask a woman, unaccompanied by a male, to get down from her car after sunset (unless a female police officer is present).

#MovieTime

In the Bollywood movie *Drishyam*, starring Ajay Devgn and Tabu, Devgn's family, including his wife and daughters, are arrested by the police and brought to the police station. During the interrogation, the police are shown to beat up the wife and daughters mercilessly. Needless to say, this is not allowed as per the law!

In the movie *Singham Returns*, when Avni (played by Kareena Kapoor) slaps politician Prakash Rao (played by Zakir Hussain), Rao asks police inspector Bajirao Singham (Ajay Devgn) to arrest her. Singham refuses and reminds him that, according to law, he being a male officer cannot arrest a woman.

Rights of an Arrested Woman

If you watch American movies, you know the drill the police repeat when they arrest someone. 'You have the right to remain silent. Anything you say can and will be used against you in a court of law. You have the right to an attorney. If you cannot afford an attorney, one will be provided for you.'

While these exact words don't apply in India, and Indian movies have not publicized our laws as much, every person arrested in India has certain legal rights. Women have a few extra rights, to ensure that there is no scope for abuse.

Here are the rights available to everyone:

1. You cannot be arrested without a warrant, unless you are suspected of having committed a cognizable offence.
2. You have the right to know the reason for your arrest.
3. You have the right to inform any member of your family or friend about your arrest.
4. You can remain silent in police custody. Surprised?
5. If you are arrested for a bailable offence, you can get bail at the police station itself.

In addition, here are the rights women have over and above the ones listed above:

1. Only a female officer can physically search you.
2. If you are being detained in police lock-up, you have to be put in a separate cell for women.
3. A female police officer has to be present in the police station 24×7.

> **Your Rights to a Lawyer**
>
> 1. Every person has the right to consult a lawyer after being arrested.
> 2. You can ask for your lawyer to be present at the time of interrogation.

What Should You Do in Case of an Arrest?

First, it is very rare that the police will arrest a woman, unless she is involved in a serious crime (or is an outspoken journalist!). Still, it is good to know the first steps to take in case of an arrest:

1. Inform your family or friends (anyone who can come to the police station and help you).
2. Get a criminal lawyer as soon as possible.
3. Ask for bail (explained in the next section).

Your focus should be to get out of the police station. You can deal with everything else once you go home and have a lawyer.

> **Activity time:** Play a quiz with your friends and family. Ask them how many of these rules they know? These are the very basics of our human rights and every citizen should know them.

How Do I Get Bail?

You must have heard the saying 'innocent until proven guilty'. This legal maxim has been made further popular by the media. It means that until a person is proven to be guilty, they are considered innocent. Under criminal law, a person will be considered guilty of a crime only if it is proved 'beyond reasonable doubt' that they have committed the crime. Even if there is a slight degree of doubt, the person will be considered innocent. And an innocent person cannot be kept in jail. They must be released on bail.

What is bail?
Bail is temporary release from jail for a person accused of a crime. To get bail, the accused person needs to deposit some money as security (called bail bond) and have a guarantor to assure that the accused will cooperate with the investigation.

There is another popular legal saying: 'The rule is bail not jail.' This is because, as per law, a person should be kept in jail only if it is absolutely necessary. Otherwise, they should be granted bail.

Bailable and non-bailable offences
Thanks to the media, you must have heard of the terms 'bailable' and 'non-bailable'. A common myth is that you can get bail for a bailable offence but not for a non-bailable offence. What do you think? What if I say that you can get bail for a non-bailable offence? Okay, let me explain.

A bailable offence means you have a right to bail. You can get bail from the police station itself.

A non-bailable offence means you do not have a right to bail, but you *can get* bail. This is granted by the magistrate's court.

Less serious offences are bailable (like occupying land, giving false information, etc.) and more serious offences are non-bailable (like rape, murder, etc.).

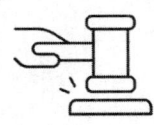

Sad but True

A senior lawyer I was working with was once arguing a case for a rape accused, a film producer. An actress had accused him of 'aggravated rape' over a period of six months. Internally, we all had a strong hunch that this producer was guilty.

My senior was arguing *for* the producer, to get him out on bail. He is such a skilled lawyer, that he convinced the court to grant bail despite the seriousness of the charges. He broke down the victim's testimony piece-by-piece to cast a doubt on her allegations, ensuring the accused walked out freely.

As a fresh law graduate, all dreamy-eyed and full of faith, I couldn't help but ask my senior, 'Didn't you feel guilty defending this man?' He just smiled and I felt utterly helpless.

Finally, justice prevailed at the apex level, as the Supreme Court reversed the high court's order. All is well that ends well!

> **EXERCISE TIME!**
>
> ### Law & Disorder: Unravel the Police Puzzles
>
> 1. I'm the first step when a crime is in play,
>   Reported to the police without delay.
>   What am I?
>
> 2. When you're not happy and need to vent,
>   To the police station, you will have it sent.
>   A formal statement to express your pain,
>   This document is called a _____.
>
> 3. Caught in a bind and locked away tight,
>   With a bit of cash, you'll be out by night.
>   Not quite freedom, just a legal sale,
>   It's the payment made for _____.
>
> 4. When the police catch you, they put you to the test,
>   With cuffs on your hands, you're under _____.
>
> 5. After investigation, the evidence they compile,
>   listing accusations, it might take a while.
>   It's a formal document, justice to greet,
>   This list of charges is called a _____.

Answer key:
1. FIR 2. Complaint 3. Bail 4. Arrest 5. Charge sheet

Conclusion

Tying It All Up and the Way Forward

Congratulations! If you have reached this section after going through the whole book, then you are now a legally well-informed and empowered woman. I hope you enjoyed the journey of educating yourself chapter by chapter, comprehending complex legal concepts in an understandable way, while having some fun with the quizzes and activities.

Through this book, I wanted you to know not just the law but to also be able to question what needs to be done to empower our women better. By now, I am sure you have understood that India has strong laws in favour of women, but rights on paper don't always translate to real life. The biggest problem that plagues the Indian legal system is poor implementation of laws and a sluggish court system.

Therefore, it is important for each one of us to stand up for our rights, demand their actualization, and question our lawmakers and legal institutions. The more we ask, the less they will be able to take us for granted. Remember the mass protest movement after the Nirbhaya gangrape? The movement led to more stringent rape laws. Similarly, the #MeToo movement created more awareness about sexual harassment at the workplace and made the POSH law a household name. Of course, a lot is yet to be done, but this is a start indeed. Dear reader, this is how revolutions start and the revolution of legal rights in India can start with you.

What can you do now?
Spread the word! Uplift the women around you by helping them understand their legal rights. Let us create a chain of empowerment that starts from each one of us. Here is a last fun activity before we say bye: Help educate any five women around you about their rights. Tell them about this book or even gift it to them.

To conclude, I would like to leave you with a few reminders, which you can hopefully apply in every aspect of your life:
1. Speak up. Stop suffering in silence.
2. Always document everything, so that you have evidence ready if you decide to take action.
3. Become financially and emotionally independent to be able to live your life the way you want to.
4. Build a support system around you, whether it is friends or family.
5. Don't be afraid to ask difficult questions.

Never stop shining just because someone is intimidated by your light!

Quiz Time!

Let's Play True or False!

Now that you have reached the end of this book, it is time to put on your thinking cap and test your knowledge. Gear up!

P.S. Resist the urge to peek at the answers! If you're stuck on a question, refer to the chapter concerned.

1. Kabir, a popular college senior, lays his eyes on Preeti, a fresher. The minute he sees her, he declares her his girlfriend and goes and kisses her without asking for consent. This amounts to sexual harassment. True or false?
2. Molestation is illegal only when it is done by a stranger. True or false?
3. If Khushi wants to tell Ravi that she does not agree to a sexual act, she has to explicitly say, 'No, I do not want to.' True or false?

4. If you willingly send explicit photos of yourself to your boyfriend, then the law will not protect you if he leaks them to his friends. True or false?
5. If a troll makes a deepfake video of actress Rashmika Mandanna, she can file a complaint with the cyber crime police. True or false?
6. If I am financially dependent on my husband, and he does not give me enough money to sustain myself, it will count as domestic abuse. True or false?
7. Domestic violence remedies are available not only against my husband but also against my in-laws. True or false?
8. If I am working from home, a Zoom call will count as my 'workplace' for the purpose of sexual harassment at the workplace. True or false?
9. If my boss is trying to set up late-night one-on-one meetings with me, and I am not comfortable, I can raise this issue under the POSH Act. True or false?
10. Every woman gets twenty-five weeks of paid maternity leave. True or false?
11. My employer can remove me from my job while I am on maternity leave, since I am not contributing to the organization. True or false?
12. Registration of marriages is not compulsory as long as I have wedding photos. True or false?
13. Pre-nuptial agreements are illegal in India. True or false?

Quiz Time!

14. I have to change my surname after marriage, as per the law. True or false?
15. My right to ask for a divorce from my husband depends on my religion. True or false?
16. Live-in relationships are illegal in India. True or false?
17. As a woman, I have no right to pass on my property to my loved ones. True or false?
18. I do not need to leave a will if I have a single child. True or false?
19. India allows no-questions-asked abortions up to twenty weeks of gestation. True or false?
20. The laws under which I can adopt a child vary depending on my religion. True or false?
21. Surrogacy is completely banned in India after the new Surrogacy (Regulation) Act, 2021. True or false?
22. A police complaint can be filed for both civil and criminal offences. True or false?
23. As a woman, I cannot be arrested after sunset and before sunrise. True or false?
24. I cannot fight my own court case. I need a lawyer to represent me. True or false?
25. As a woman, I have the right to free legal aid in any court in India. True or false?

Well done!
What's your score? ___/25

Quiz Time!

Answer key:

1. True. Any physical touch with a sexual intent, and without the consent of the person, is sexual harassment. 2. False. It does not matter who the molester is. 3. False. Consent, or lack of consent, can be expressed in any form (words, body language, or even gestures). 4. False. It does not matter if you sent those photos willingly or not. All that matters is that you did not consent to them being shared. 5. True. 6. True. This counts as financial abuse. 7. True. They are available against any relative you live with. 8. True. 9. True. You can try telling your boss that you are not comfortable. If he does not listen, you can file a complaint with the POSH committee or the HR of your office. 10. False. It is twenty-six weeks. 11. False. You cannot be fired or demoted during your maternity leave. 12. False. Registration of marriages is compulsory in India. 13. False. They fall in a grey area (see the relevant section for more details). 14. False. The law does not require you to change your surname. 15. True. 16. False. They are legal, but there is no codified law for them. 17. False. You are in charge of your property, but certain restrictions may apply based on your religion. 18. Neither true nor false. A will is completely voluntary, but it is highly recommended to leave behind one even if you have a single child. 19. True. 20. True. 21. False. Only commercial surrogacy is banned. Altruistic surrogacy is allowed. 22. False. It can only be filed for criminal offences. 23. True. 24. False. Everyone can fight their own case, but having a lawyer is recommended. 25. True.

Acknowledgements

To my parents, Shantanu and Dr Madhura Chaudhari, who encouraged me to fly with the biggest wings and gave me the widest runway for my flight. To my father, for being my calm in a storm and my mother for painstakingly driving me to all my classes. To my partner, my best friend, and steadfast support system, Abhishek Maharaju, my biggest cheerleader and critic—thank you for being happier about my every little accomplishment than I could ever be, and for always being there to catch me with open arms when I fall. Together, the three of you are the umbrella that shields me from the rain and the harsh sun. To my big, warm, extended family—thank you for being the family and siblings I never had!

To my editor at HarperCollins India, Ridhima Kumar—your phone call on that cold fall night in the UK turned my quiet dream of becoming an 'author' into a reality. Thank you for believing in me, for guiding me through this somewhat solitary journey and for your invaluable insights.

To my (late) great-grandfather, who passed down (genetically!) his flair for writing and my (late) Meena *ajji*, who instilled in me perfectionism since childhood. To my English teachers in school for honing my language skills and my mentor at law school, Prof. Dipika Jain, who pushed me to dream bigger for myself. A big part of who I am is shaped by what I've inherited and the influences that have guided me.

To my friends like family who add abundant joy, colour and laughter to my life—some of you were the first readers of my manuscript (talking to you, Ajju ☺) and have always been there to cheer me on!

To my work team, especially Yukti Gupta from Pink Legal, for stepping in when I had to push the accelerator in the final stretch, and for being someone I can count on. Also, the forever-growing Pink Legal community, for all the love that they have showered upon our work.

To my favourite coffee shops at Oxford (which I frequented with a passion) and the Oxford Union library, for providing a picture-perfect backdrop to write my book, all the while making me feel like I was in august company.

And finally, to myself—for embarking on this journey, for pushing through the hard work it demanded, and for not giving up during those exhausting weekends and late-night writing marathons. You did it, girl!

PS: The acknowledgements will be incomplete without thanking my puppy, Romeo, for bringing immeasurable joy to all our lives. ♥

Notes

Scan this QR code to access the detailed notes.

About the Author

Manasi Chaudhari is an award-winning lawyer and social entrepreneur. She graduated from the University of Oxford where she pursued her master's in law and finance. Manasi is the founder and CEO of Pink Legal, India's pioneering digital platform to educate women about their legal rights. She has been appointed by UN Women India as a Generation Equality Ally. Professionally, Manasi specializes in corporate and entertainment law and has experience spanning the Hyderabad High Court, the Supreme Court and lower courts.

A trusted voice on legal rights for women, Manasi is frequently invited as a speaker at events and workshops for women, including by the UN Women. She has collaborated with local police commissionerates and global brands like Meta, Puma and Tinder to create awareness on women's rights in a simplified and engaging manner. Manasi was named one of India's 'top law influencers' by ScoopWhoop, and has been featured in prestigious media publications such as *The Times of India*, *The Hindu*, *NDTV*, *Cosmopolitan Magazine*, NASDAQ and Lianhe Zaobao in Singapore, to name a few.

Manasi lives in Hyderabad, and frequents Mumbai and Delhi for work. You can reach her on Instagram @adv.manasi.

HarperCollins *Publishers* India

At HarperCollins India, we believe in telling the best stories and finding the widest readership for our books in every format possible. We started publishing in 1992; a great deal has changed since then, but what has remained constant is the passion with which our authors write their books, the love with which readers receive them, and the sheer joy and excitement that we as publishers feel in being a part of the publishing process.

Over the years, we've had the pleasure of publishing some of the finest writing from the subcontinent and around the world, including several award-winning titles and some of the biggest bestsellers in India's publishing history. But nothing has meant more to us than the fact that millions of people have read the books we published, and that somewhere, a book of ours might have made a difference.

As we look to the future, we go back to that one word— a word which has been a driving force for us all these years.

Read.